A Guide to Observation, Participation, and Reflection in the Classroom

FIFTH EDITION

Arthea J.S. Reed
University of North Carolina at Asheville

Verna E. Bergemann
University of North Carolina at Asheville

Boston   Burr Ridge, IL   Dubuque, IA   Madison, WI   New York   San Francisco   St. Louis
Bangkok   Bogotá   Caracas   Kuala Lumpur   Lisbon   London   Madrid   Mexico City
Milan   Montreal   New Delhi   Santiago   Seoul   Singapore   Sydney   Taipei   Toronto

Higher Education

A GUIDE TO OBSERVATION, PARTICIPATION, AND REFLECTION IN THE CLASSROOM, FIFTH EDITION

Published by McGraw-Hill, a business unit of The McGraw-Hill Companies, Inc., 1221 Avenue of the Americas, New York, NY, 10020. Copyright © 2005, 2001, 1998, 1995 by The McGraw-Hill Companies, Inc. All rights reserved. No part of this publication may be reproduced or distributed in any form or by any means, or stored in a database or retrieval system, without the prior written permission of The McGraw-Hill Companies, Inc., including, but not limited to, in any network or other electronic storage or transmission, or broadcast for distance learning.

Some ancillaries, including electronic and print components, may not be available to customers outside the United States.

This book is printed on recycled paper containing 10% postconsumer waste.

1 2 3 4 5 6 7 8 9 0 QPD/QPD 0 9 8 7 6 5 4

ISBN 0-07-287492-9

Publisher: *Emily Barosse*
Associate editor: *Allison McNamara*
Developmental editor: *Cara Harvey*
Senior marketing manager: *Pamela S. Cooper*
Media producer: *Shannon Gattens*
Project manager: *Richard H. Hecker*
Production Supervisor: *Janean A. Utley*
Designer: *Preston Thomas*
Media project manager: *Meghan Durko*
Cover image: *©2004 Punchstock*
Typeface: *10.5/12 Goudy*
Compositor: *Reuben Kantor, QEP Design*
Printer: *Quebecor World Dubuque Inc.*

www.mhhe.com

About the Authors

Verna E. Bergemann and Arthea J. S. Reed

Arthea J. S. Reed, called "Charlie" by her students, family, and friends, lives in Asheville, North Carolina. She taught at the University of North Carolina at Asheville for seventeen years, served as professor and chair of the Education Department, and then became Professor Emeritus at the liberal arts public university. Currently she is Director of Education and Development at Northwestern Mutual Life in Asheville. She received her Ph.D. from Florida State University, her M.S. from Southern Connecticut State University, and her B.S. from Bethany College in West Virginia. She has taught in grades two through twelve in the public schools of Connecticut, Ohio, and West Virginia. She is author of *Reaching Adolescents: The Young Adult Book and the School* (Merrill, 1993), *Comics to Classics: A Guide to Books for Teens and Preteens* (Penguin, 1994), *Presenting Harry Mazer* (Twayne, 1996), and numerous monographs, book chapters, and articles. For six years, she was editor of The ALAN Review, a highly regarded journal in the field of young-adult literature. She has been co-editor of the Penguin/Signet Classic teachers guide series since 1988, editing or writing guides to more than thirty classic books and CD-ROMs. She was the chair of the National Council of Teachers of English Promising Young Writers program from 1990–1995 and was co-director of the Mountain Area Writing Project, a site of the national Writing Project, for eight years. In 1996 she served as president of ALAN. She has served on numerous local, state, and national education committees, and in 1985 she was named the Ruth and Leon Feldman Professor by the UNC–A faculty for her service to education. In 2000 she wrote Norma Fox Mazer: *A Writer's World* (Scarecrow).

Verna E. Bergemann is Professor Emeritus and past chair of the Education Department at the University of North Carolina at Asheville, where she taught for twelve years. She currently lives in Marion, North Carolina. Prior to coming to UNC-A, she was a professor of education at the State University of New York at Oswego for thirteen years. She earned her Ed.D. at the University of Maryland, her M.A. at the State University of New York at Buffalo, and her B.A. at the State University of New York at Brockport. She taught elementary school in Niagara Falls, New York, and Los Alamos, New Mexico. She has worked with beginning teachers as a helping teacher, as a cooperating teacher in a university laboratory school, and as a consultant with the North Carolina Department of Public Instruction. She has been a professor of education at two universities and is the author of numerous articles and activity workbooks for teachers. For many years she has worked closely with volunteer organizations that attempt to improve adult literacy. In 1989, she was named Woman of Distinction and Woman of the Year by the city of Asheville for her outstanding contributions to literacy education. In 1992, she chaired a school-study committee for private schools in Asheville. In 1997, she was selected to appear in the 1997/1998 *Who's Who in the South and Southeast*. In 2004, she continues her work in teacher education, supervising student teachers.

Brief Contents

Contents

Resources for Observation CD-ROM

The *Resources for Observation* CD-ROM, packaged with your text*; includes the following resources.

PART I Forms

1 Anecdotal Record Form for Observing Teachers or Instructional Events—1
2 Anecdotal Teacher-Student Interaction Form
3 Anecdotal Record Form for Observing Teachers or Instructional Events—2
4 Anecdotal Record Form for Grouping Patterns
5 Observation Form for Rank Ordering
6 Coding System—Type and Tally of Student-Teacher Interaction
7 Observation Form for Examining Questions
8.1 Checklist for Determining Teaching Style
8.2 Checklist for Examining Teaching Practices Which Accommodate Diversity of Learning Styles
9 Observation Form for Structured Observation of a Lesson
10 Checklist of Interview Techniques
11 A Rating Scale for Observation of Standards for Teaching
12 A Rating Scale for Observation of Educational Technology Standards for Teachers
13 Reflective Observation of Teachers
14 Form for Anecdotal Record of Classroom Organization
15 Form for a Classroom Map
16 Form for Coding Scale of Classroom Social Environment
17 Checklist to Determine Student Assessments in the Classroom
18 Checklist of Competency Goals and Objectives Covered in a Seventh-Grade History Classroom
19 Examination of Curricular Strategies That Challenge Students' Multiple Intelligences
20 Form for Examining a Curriculum Guide
21 Checklist for Multicultural/Antibias Education Evaluation
22 Form for Types and Uses of Media/Technology in the Classroom or Lab
23 Software Evaluation Form
24 Checklist for School Personnel Interviews
25 Reflective Observation of Classrooms, Schools, and Curriculum
26 Anecdotal Record for Observing Students
27 Shadowing Form
28 Profile Card
29 Descriptive Profile Chart
30 Coding System to Observe Student Participation in Lessons

---

* If you purchased a used copy of the text, call McGraw-Hill customer service at 1-800-338-3987 to order the CD-ROM.

PART II Case Studies, Curricular Resources, and Guides for Parents Relationships

Chapter Two *Observing Teachers*

The Teacher-Parent Conference
Case Study: Observation of a 6th Grade Language Arts Teacher

Chapter Three *Observing Classrooms, Schools, and Curriculum*

Case Study: Organization of K, 1, 2 Classrooms
Computer/Technology Skills Curriculum
Science Curriculum

Chapter Four *Observing Students*

The Role of Parents in the Education of Exceptional Students
Assistive Technology for Special Needs Children

Chapter Five *Participation: Preteaching and Planning*

Book Talk Rubric

Chapter Six *Teaching*

Case Study: Learning from Doing: Initial Teaching in an 8th Grade Classroom

Preface

A Guide to Observation, Participation, and Reflection in the Classroom, fifth edition, is written for you, the student. However, it is designed to help you move beyond being a student. It provides you with sequenced school-based observation, teaching experiences, and reflection that not only will bridge the gap between the world of the student and the world of the teacher, but also help you connect the world of theory to the world of practice. In beginning the process of becoming an effective teacher, you must learn to view students, schools, and teachers as a teacher would. In addition, you must develop, practice, and reflect on the skills and techniques of effective teaching in order to perfect them.

Organization

The *Guide* is divided into five parts: Part I—Understanding Fieldwork, Part II—Observing in the Schools, Part III—Developing Successful Teaching Skills, Part IV—The Portfolio, and Part V—Forms.

Observation to gain knowledge and understanding must come first. Thus, Chapter 1 presents the importance of early fieldwork, based on the authors' experiences in elementary, secondary, and university classrooms and documented by recent research of teacher educators and by professional organizations that focus on teacher education.

The next three chapters of the guide provide examples and methods of anecdotal, structured, and reflective observations of teachers, as well as of classrooms, and students. The observation techniques have been designed to help you become a critical and objective observer.

Once you have had the opportunity to reflect on your observations, Chapters 5 and 6 provide you with guidance for developing a gradual and reflective approach to becoming a teacher and include many of the tools and techniques used by effective teachers. The first part of this section explains the importance of classroom participation during teacher training. The rest of Chapters 5 and 6 provides you with information for preteaching, planning, tutoring, teaching small groups, teaching large groups, and reflecting on your teaching. New topics in this edition include the "kidwatching" model, the use of a rubric for evaluation, classroom management and discipline, homework, and related case studies. Chapter 7 discusses the portfolio—what it is, why it is important, what goes into one, and how to create one.

The guide concludes with Part V, which contains forms.

The forms in the text are designed as a model for you. Each sample form in the text has a corresponding form in the back of the text for you to record your preservice teaching experiences. Each form/instrument has been extensively field-tested by college and university students over a period of two decades. Completing the forms on hard copy or electronic version will increase your understanding of students, schools, and teaching. They can also serve as useful artifacts for your teaching portfolio.

The authors of this guide hope that as you complete and reflect on each observation, participation, and teaching activity, you will strengthen your resolve to become an effective teacher.

New to the Fifth Edition

The fifth edition has been revised to include new coverage of:

- No Child Left Behind legislation
- Standards and their implications for teachers
- Learning styles
- Teacher–Parent relationships
- Educational technology
- The implications of brain research
- Inclusion
- How to start a portfolio
- Models for portfolios
- Templates for portfolios
- How to write your philosophy of teaching and learning

- Kidwatching
- RUBRIC
- Case studies
- Management and discipline
- Homework
- Teaching styles for diversity of learning styles

Also new to this edition is the *Resources for Observation* CD-ROM, which is packaged for free with new copies of the guide*. The CD-ROM contains blank copies of all of the forms and instruments of observation and participation discussed throughout this guide. Additionally, the CD-ROM includes Case Studies, Curricular Resources, and Guides for Teacher–Parent Relationships. See page xi for a listing of the resources on the CD-ROM.

Acknowledgments

Without the help and support of many individuals, this guide would never have been completed.

First and foremost, each of us wishes to thank the other for her contribution to all five editions of this book. Each recognizes not only the professional contribution of the other, but the friendship that has made a 25-year collaboration joyful and valuable. We have been each other's collaborator, colleague, co-author, confidant, mentor, and best friend. Neither of us could have achieved what we have without the other.

Next, we could not have written this book without the help of thousands of students from scores of classrooms during our more than 80 years of cumulative teaching. These students have provided us with laughter, tears, anecdotes, and, hopefully, wisdom. We learned from them, and they taught us most of what we know about teaching and learning.

Thanks, too, to our teaching colleagues—those professionals we observed, taught side by side with, shared experiences and ideas with, and learned to love—we appreciate the qualities of their teaching and humanity. Although they are too numerous to mention, we must name a few. Special thanks go to our UNC-Asheville colleagues Sandra Byrd and James E. McGlinn who contributed to this and previous editions. Also, great appreciation goes to Mary W. Olson, of UNC-Greensboro who helped us author the third edition of this work and has contributed to this edition. Also, thanks to our many good friends and research colleagues at UNC-Asheville's Ramsey Library. Without the help of the computer skills of Elizabeth E. Hunt, this book would have never been completed. Also, we cannot forget Don Reed, the best mentor we know, who kept us humble, but allowed us to believe in ourselves and each other.

---

* If you purchased a used copy of the text, call McGraw-Hill customer service at 1-800-338-3987 to order the CD-ROM.

We also want to thank the reviewers of this edition whose comments helped us make revisions in accord with current research, trends, and practice:

J. L. Fortson, Pepperdine University

J. Robert Hendricks, University of Arizona

Christy Gonzales, California State University, Stanislaus

Linda M. Holdman, University of North Carolina

David Gustavson, Louisiana State University

Gordon Castanza, City University

Linda Tabers-Kwak, University of Wisconsin, Green Bay

Finally, thanks to all of those who have made this fifth edition and the previous editions a reality. Marcuss Oslander, the original editor of this book, has our deepest gratitude. Thanks to Beth Kaufman, our first editor, and Cara Harvey, the editor of this edition. Much appreciation also goes to Jill Gordon, development editor for this edition, and members of the production team.

It goes without saying that without you, the professors who have chosen to utilize this book to help your students become better teachers, the book would not have an audience. Thanks to you and your students for bringing this work to life in the classroom.

Arthea J. S. (Charlie) Reed
Verna E. Bergemann
Asheville, N.C.

PART I

Understanding
Fieldwork

Chapter One
The Importance of Fieldwork

The amount of time you will spend in elementary and secondary school classrooms during your preservice training is about twice as much as students who completed their teacher education four years ago. In 1999, 38 states required field experiences before student teaching with a low of 40 clock hours and a high of 300 hours. In 2003, 42 states required from 90 to 500 clock hours of observation and participation in classrooms prior to student teaching. Why the significant increase in such a short period of time?

In part, the increase in preservice classroom-based observation and participation is because teachers have demanded it. In the fourth edition of this book, we cited a 1999 report, "Teacher Quality: A Report on the Preparation and Qualification of Public School Teachers" (U.S. Department of Education). The report concluded that preservice teachers did not spend enough time in elementary and secondary schools during their preservice training. The report emphasized that early field experiences play an important role in shaping and maintaining high-quality teachers. When Dalphia Raye Pierce, teacher educator at Utah State University, asked secondary teachers about the kinds of training experiences they had in teacher preparation, the most frequent complaint they voiced was they were not given the opportunity to work with students until reaching student-teaching status or on-the-job-training. Teachers thought that was too late and that they needed earlier field experiences during their first courses in their teacher-preparation program (Pierce, 1996, 223).

In 2001 the Center for the Study of Teaching and Policy (CTP), a national research consortium, synthesized the results of 57 research reports reiterating the value of fieldwork in teacher training programs. The study reported that experienced and beginning teachers found their classroom-based preservice teaching to be the single most powerful element of their preparations. According to these teachers, clinical experiences:

- Showed them what the job of teaching was like.
- Helped them learn about classroom management.
- Gave them practical opportunities to apply concepts encountered in university course work.
- Showed them that the conceptions of teaching and learning can be transformed through their observations and analysis of what goes on in the classroom (CTP, 2001, 1-3).

So, one of the answers to why you will have approximately twice as many hours in preservice fieldwork is that you and the teachers who have completed teacher education in the years immediately preceding have said over and over again that it was the single most important element in helping them succeed in the classroom.

However, are more hours in the classroom prior to your teaching guaranteed to make you a more effective teacher? Certainly, the number of hours you spend observing and working with children is important; however, what YOU do during those hours is even more critical. Education reforms of the early 21st century have addressed not only the issue of frequent but also well-designed field experiences for preservice teachers. In January 2002, President George W. Bush signed into law the most sweeping national education reform since the Elementary and

Secondary Education Act (ESEA) of 1965. The *No Child Left Behind* (NCLB) Act attempts to redefine the federal role in elementary and secondary public education and help close the gap between disadvantaged and minority students and their peers through increased accountability of results, local control and flexibility, expanded educational choices for parents, and an emphasis on effective teaching methods. This bill received bi-partisan support. Former North Carolina Governor James Hunt, a Democrat who is one of the leading voices advocating education reform, said of *No Child Left Behind*, "Its goal is to ensure that all children have an opportunity to learn—regardless of income, background or ethnic identity and it is a pledge that every child will have access to high quality teaching by 2005-2005" (Hunt, 2003, 4).

Title II, Part A of *No Child Left Behind* deals specifically with improving the professional development of classroom teachers by:

- Giving teachers knowledge and skills needed to help students meet challenging state academic content standards.
- Providing high quality, sustained intensive and classroom-focused field experiences in order to have a positive and lasting impact on classroom instructions. (U.S. Department of Education, NCLB, 2001, 1)

Today's reforms, including *No Child Left Behind*, lean heavily on the work of such groups as the National Board for Professional Standards (NBPTS). In 1989 that Board, under the leadership of Linda Darling Hammond, developed rigorous standards for what accomplished, experienced teachers should know and be able to do. These action-based standards have become the measure of successful teaching and have paved the way for increased accountability and evaluation of teaching activities and student learning. Inservice teachers can voluntarily seek certification by documenting how they meet the National Board's standards that are based on five propositions:

- Teachers are committed to students and their learning.
- Teachers know their subject and how to teach those subjects to their students.
- Teachers are responsible for managing and monitoring student learning.
- Teachers think systematically about their practice and learn from experience.
- Teachers are members of learning communities (Hammond, 1999, 6-9).

The connection between what elementary and secondary students learn and achieve and what teachers know and do has never been more closely aligned. Therefore, it is incumbent upon inservice teachers to be accountable for student achievement through documentation of their teaching practice coupled with their students' learning. This, then, has made it more important than ever for preservice teachers to not only learn how to teach through classroom-based field experiences, but also to reflect on, analyze, and document their own teaching and how it relates to their students' learning.

More than a decade ago, professional teaching organizations began weighing in on the growing significance of field experiences in preservice teacher education. The National Council for Accreditation of Teacher Education (NCATE), a national accrediting agency of teacher-education programs, sets aside clinical and field-based experiences as one of its major standards for accreditation of teacher-education programs. The NCATE also suggests that it is not only the quantity of experiences that is important, but that the experiences must be systematic and provide opportunities for preservice teachers to observe, plan, and practice their skills in a variety of settings and with culturally diverse and exceptional populations (NCATE, 2002, 20). These field experiences should encourage reflection and research by the preservice teacher, as well as feedback from university and public school faculty and the student's peers.

Today, these same organizations as well as others are modifying standards for preservice teaching field experiences to reflect the increasing diversity of the American classroom. *No Dream Denied: A Pledge to America's Children*, a 2003 report of the National Commission on Teaching and America's Future (NCTAF), confirmed that it takes both "a deep knowledge of the subjects to be taught" and "clinical practice in diverse settings under the supervision of faculty and accomplished teachers" to keep quality teachers in the classroom. According to the report, "The lack of clinical skills and experience feeds the high levels of burnout and attrition among new teachers throughout the country" (NCTAF, 2003, 77).

> Being a good teacher today means facing a class of students of unparalleled diversity and being accountable for helping each and every pupil reach unprecedented standards of achievement. He or she must know children's development, different learning styles, classroom management, curriculum, assessment, teach children who don't know English and those who have disabilities, and of course they must know the subject matter well (Carnegie Corporation of New York, *Teaching as a Clinical Profession: A New Challenge for Education*, 2002, 3).

What can you expect your preservice fieldwork to be like? Here is a summary of what teachers, professional education organizations, accrediting agencies, and the government have told us. Preservice teaching experiences should be:

- Frequent and sequential.
- Sustained, intensive, and classroom focused.
- Allow for data collection, reflection, and feedback.
- Diverse, allowing for experiences with culturally diverse and exceptional populations.

This *Guide* is designed to provide you with classroom-based experiences that meet all of the above criteria. This chapter provides you with guidelines for a gradual, reflective approach to beginning teaching. Chapters 2, 3, and 4 provide you with techniques for observing teachers, students, classrooms, schools, and curriculum. Chapters 5 and 6 give you tools to plan your teaching, organize what and how you will teach, and reflect upon your experience. Chapter 7 will help you develop a portfolio, the end product of your field experiences. The portfolio will be a compilation of all your completed work from Chapters 2 through 6, using the forms in Part V of this guide. It would be helpful to look ahead to Chapter 7 as you complete these forms.

Because the practical experiences our students have in the classroom prior to their student teaching are so critical to their development as teachers, we have spent more than two decades developing, adapting, revising, and field-testing these forms. If you use them carefully, we believe they will help you get the most from your preservice teaching experiences.

A Case Study: Initial Field Experience

By: Jennifer Davis

Date: November, 2003

During many of my initial field experiences, I experienced both fear and excitement. There was sudden fear at how differently the classroom looked from the position that I currently occupied. Up until this time I had entered the classroom as a student, but now I came into the classroom as an excited preservice teacher.

My first field experience was in a kindergarten classroom. At that time I was seeking high school certification in literature. This experience was far removed from where I thought I was going. What I discovered inside the kindergarten classroom changed my life. I observed the daily progress these five year olds made, as letters became words and words became sentences.

I observed the busy day the teacher and children had. They had reading, writing, math, social studies, science, computers, library, P.E. and lunch.

After observing, I read many stories to the children and helped individual children with writing letters and numbers.

Classroom management, I discovered, was absolutely necessary. If you could not control the students, you could not teach them. When the children became overly noisy, the classroom teacher clapped her hands and said, "crowd control." The children knew what that meant and went back to their tables. I'll never forget that and hope to use that in my classroom.

Later on, I truly valued my early field experiences because I learned so much about teaching in a kindergarten that it forced me to examine my choice to teach in high school.

Postscript: Jennifer changed her certification from high school literature to K-6 certification based, in part, on her initial observation in this kindergarten classroom.

How Teaching Standards Will Affect You

Think back to your own elementary, middle, and secondary school years. Were some years better than others? Of course, there were wonderful years, good years, and bad years. Why? What made the difference? You probably had something to do with it. Perhaps there were years when you were simply unhappy. Things outside of school may have affected your attitude toward school. And, there were probably years when activities, such as athletics or drama, made you look forward to going to school every day. Or, you may have had a good year because you had lots of friends or one special friend.

However, there is one element inside the school that you are likely to have cited. It is probably not the building, a laboratory or theater, or even the curriculum. The element that most people say is the most important in their success as a student and how they feel about school is a teacher. You probably have one or several teachers in mind. What made that teacher special? How did she or he contribute to your positive feelings about school? Not surprisingly, research has identified the quality of a child's teacher as the single most important influence on that child's achievement (Garvin, 2003, 6).

This is what standards are about. What are the attributes of the teacher who makes learning fun? How does the teacher make every student feel successful? How does the teacher contribute to each child's achievement? How can a teacher turn a bad year into a good year for a child? The goal of the 2001 *No Child Left Behind Act* is to have a highly qualified teacher in every public school classroom by 2005.

To this end, since the mid-1980s, professional teaching organizations have worked jointly to establish standards for what teachers should know (knowledge base) and be able to do (teaching competencies). One of these organizations, the Council of Chief State School Officers, sponsored the formation of the Interstate Teacher Assessment and Support Consortium (INTASC). INTASC has articulated a common core of teaching knowledge and skill that it contends should be required of all teachers. This includes preservice teachers, newly licensed teachers, as well as advanced certification teachers.

The INTASC Task Force concluded that preservice teachers must have at least an awareness of the kinds of knowledge and understanding needed, as well as the resources available to develop these skills, and must have some capacity to address the many facets of curriculum, classroom, and student life. Most states have adopted these standards (see Table 1.1) to guide their teacher education and licensure reform efforts.

Throughout this text each of the sample observation and participation forms will address one or more of these standards (ten principles) and key indicators. The key indicators are designed to assist the evaluator in assessing the teaching standards more easily. We have indicated on each form which of the standards are referenced. You will use the INTASC standards to develop your portfolio in Chapter 7 of this guide.

The best way to use these standards and key indicators is to observe professional teachers who exhibit them in their teaching and their relationship with students. These teachers can serve as models for the teacher you will become. Keep in mind that you will be held accountable to these standards. Of course, you will not achieve all of them at sophisticated levels in your first few years of teaching, but you will be expected to be making progress toward them. Some of the forms you will be using for your observations allude to differing levels of sophistication in achieving the standards. What is acceptable for a first-year teacher in terms of her/his success in reaching a standard may not be acceptable when she/he is a fifth-year teacher. So, it will become your responsibility to continuously, throughout your teaching career, evaluate yourself against these standards and grow in your sophistication in achieving them.

TABLE 1.1: INTASC Core Standards and Principles for Preservice and Inservice Teachers

Standard 1. Content Pedagogy

The teacher understands the central concepts, tools of inquiry, and structures of the discipline he or she teaches and can create learning experiences that make these aspects of subject matter meaningful for students.

KEY INDICATORS:

- Demonstrates an understanding of the central concepts of his or her discipline.
- Uses explanations and representations that link curriculum to prior learning.
- Evaluates resources and curriculum materials for appropriateness to the curriculum and instructional delivery.
- Engages students in interpreting ideas from a variety of perspectives.
- Uses interdisciplinary approaches to teaching and learning.
- Uses methods of inquiry that are central to the discipline.

Standard 2. Student Development

The teacher understands how children learn and develop, and can provide learning opportunities that support a child's intellectual, social, and personal development.

KEY INDICATORS:

- Evaluates student performance to design instruction appropriate for social, cognitive, and emotional development.
- Creates relevance for students by linking with their prior experiences.
- Provides opportunities for students to assume responsibility for and be actively engaged in their learning.
- Encourages student reflection on prior knowledge and its connection to new information.
- Accesses student thinking as a basis for instructional activities through group/individual interaction and written work (listening, encouraging discussion, eliciting samples of student thinking orally and in writing).

Standard 3. Diverse Learners

The teacher understands how students differ in their approaches to learning and creates instructional opportunities that are adapted to diverse learners.

KEY INDICATORS:

- Designs instruction appropriate to students' stages of development, learning styles, strengths and needs.
- Selects approaches that provide opportunities for different performance modes.
- Accesses appropriate services or resources to meet exceptional learning needs when needed.
- Adjusts instruction to accommodate the learning differences or needs of students (time and circumstance of work, tasks assigned, communication and response modes).

- Uses knowledge of different cultural contexts within the community (socio-economic, ethnic, cultural) and connects with the learner through types of interaction and assignments.
- Creates a learning community that respects individual differences.

Standard 4. Multiple Instructional Strategies

The teacher understands and uses a variety of instructional strategies to encourage student development of critical thinking, problem solving, and performance skills.

KEY INDICATORS:

- Selects and uses multiple teaching and learning strategies (a variety of presentations/explanations) to encourage student in critical thinking and problem solving.
- Encourages students to assume responsibility for identifying and using learning resources.
- Assumes different roles in the instructional process (instructor, facilitator, coach, audience) to accommodate content purpose, and learner needs.

Standard 5. Motivation and Management

The teacher uses an understanding of individual and group motivation and behavior to create a learning environment that encourages positive social interaction, active engagement in learning, and self motivation.

KEY INDICATORS:

- Encourages clear procedures and expectations that ensure students assume responsibility for themselves and others, working collaboratively and independently, and engages in purposeful learning activities.
- Engages students by relating lessons to students' personal interests, allowing students to have choices in their learning, and leading students to ask questions and solve problems that are meaningful to them.
- Organizes, allocates, and manages time, space and activities in a way that is conducive to learning.
- Organizes, prepares students for, and monitors independent and group work that allows for full and varied participation of all individuals.
- Analyzes classroom environment and interactions and makes adjustments to enhance social relationship, student motivation/engagement and productive work.

Standard 6. Communication and Technology

The teacher uses knowledge of effective verbal, nonverbal, and media communication techniques to foster active inquiry, collaboration, and supportive interaction in the classroom.

KEY INDICATORS:

- Models effective communication strategies in conveying ideas and information and when asking questions (e.g., monitoring the effects of messages, restating ideas and drawing connections, using visual, aural, and kinesthetic cures, being sensitive to nonverbal cues both given and received).
- Provides support for learner expression in speaking, writing, and other media.
- Demonstrates that communication is sensitive to gender and cultural differences (e.g., appropriate use of eye contact, interpretation of body language and verbal statement, acknowledgment of and responsiveness to different modes of communication and participation.
- Uses variety of media communication tools to enrich learning opportunities.

Standard 7. Planning

The teacher plans instruction based upon knowledge of subject matter, students, the community, and curriculum goals.

KEY INDICATORS:

- Plans lessons and activities to address variation in learning styles and performance modes, multiple development levels of diverse learners, and problem solving and exploration.
- Develops plans that are appropriate for curriculum goals and are based on effective instruction.
- Adjusts plans to respond to unanticipated sources of input and/or student needs.
- Develops short- and long-range plans.

Standard 8. **Assessment**

The teacher understands and uses formal and informal assessment strategies to evaluate and ensure the continuous intellectual, social, and physical development of the learner.

KEY INDICATORS:

- Selects, constructs, and uses assessment strategies appropriate to the learning outcomes.
- Uses a variety of informal and formal strategies to inform choices about student progress and to adjust instruction (e.g., standardized test data, peer and student self-assessment, informal assessments such as observation, surveys, interviews, student work, performance tasks, portfolio, and teacher made tests).
- Uses assessment strategies to involve learners in self-assessment activities to help them become aware of their strengths and needs, and to encourage them to set personal goals for learning.
- Evaluates the effects of class activities on individuals and on groups through observation of classroom interaction, questioning and analysis of student work.
- Solicits information about students' experiences, learning behavior, needs, and progress from parents, other colleagues, and students.

Standard 9. **Reflective Practice: Professional Growth**

The teacher is a reflective practitioner who continually evaluates the effects of his or her choices and actions on others (students, parents, and other professionals in the learning community) who actively seeks out opportunities to grow professionally.

KEY INDICATORS:

- Uses classroom observation, information about students and research as sources for evaluating the outcomes of teaching and learning and as a basis for experimenting with, reflecting on and revising practice.
- Uses professional literature, colleagues and other resources to support self-development as a learner and as a teacher.
- Consults with professional colleagues within the school and other professional arenas as support for reflection, problem-solving and new ideas, actively sharing and seeking and giving feedback.

Standard 10. **School and Community Involvement**

The teacher fosters relationships with school colleagues, parents, and agencies in the larger community to support students' learning and well being.

KEY INDICATORS:

- Participates in collegial activities designed to make the entire school a productive learning environment.
- Links with counselors, teachers of other classes and activities within the school, professionals in community agencies, and others in the community to support students' learning and well-being.
- Seeks to establish cooperative partnerships with parents/guardians to support student learning.
- Advocates for students.

Careful Observation: Your First Task

Observation is one effective means of learning how certain teaching methods are employed in the schools, how classrooms are organized, and how students respond to the classroom environment. This guide will provide you with information on the processes of observation and participation in general and with specific forms that can be used in specific classroom situations. It is helpful to keep a journal or log of the observations you make, even during field experiences in which you are primarily teaching. Here's an example of one such anecdotal log from a student teacher. You will notice that there is no attempt to record all of the events of the day. This log can then be used as the student teacher reflects on his observations and his teaching with his school-based cooperating teacher and college or university supervisor. It and other log entries like it can become a part of his portfolio.

Observation and Teaching Log

OBSERVER: Michael Kealohalan Anderson

GRADE: Fourth

January 3, 20—. first day of school

Oh, my goodness, so many unusual names to remember. The students seem to be excited to be back at the school. The schedule of the day is complicated (new to me). Students change classes at certain times during the day. Each teacher has a specialty that he or she teaches. Regardless of the specialty of the individual, each teacher must teach reading, spelling, and their specialty to their homeroom class. For example, my cooperating teacher (Ms. Owenbey) teaches reading, spelling, and computers to her homeroom. Then at 10:25 the students change classes. Then Ms. Owenbey teaches computers the remaining periods of the day.

January 4, 20—. Rain and rain. It's been raining for days now. Today I took the "roll." It is really helping me learn the students' names. After spelling and reading we had health. Oh, what a long day this has been. Health could surely be covered in the science class.

January 7, 20—. Nice weekend, no rain. However it is raining today. Yuk. The children seem to be getting back into the groove of school. Overall, I would say they seem to tolerate it without too much resistance.

January 8, 20—. Ms. Owenbey showed me how the students worked together on their "spelling kit." It is an interesting setup. The students are placed in pairs according to their ability to spell. They then go over lists of words out loud—taking turns, of course. Then, they each give one another a test by calling the words out while the other writes them down. This list is then checked by having the student call back the words they have spelled and checking for mistakes. The misspelled words are put on a separate piece of paper for further study. The students switch roles and go through the process again. After approximately 20 minutes, the teacher calls time and all the students go over their review sheets. I like the procedure, and it does seem successful in producing capable spellers.

January 14, 20—. Today I brought two of my pet mice to school. They are a hit! Most of the students are rather apprehensive about them. One boy (Erick) is quite knowledgeable about rodents in general. I now know all the kids by first name. Most of them know my name, too.

January 17, 20—. I followed my class around all day today. We began our day with reading and a handwriting exercise. Then at 9:45 we went to art. From there we went to math. The students went over some sample math exercises involving multiplication and division of small or single-digit numbers and some double-digit numbers. From there we went to social studies where the students were reviewing for a test the following day. After lunch the class went to science; here they were read to by the teacher about electrons and protons. After science the class moved to English. Here, the English teacher had the students write in their journals about "wintertime." Of all the lessons I observed this day, I enjoyed the English lesson best of all. At 1:45 the students went to computer lab, where they could freely choose which program they would like to work with.

Overall, I would say the day was sort of boring—with the exceptions of reading, art, computer, and English. It's no wonder the students go crazy when they get a free moment. They work in each class and have homework in all of them if they fail to complete their in-class assignments.

January 23–24, 20—. The days are running together now. My responsibilities are that of an observer and occasional participant. Most of my participation occurs in reading and computer lab. In reading, the students are all reading for a "Bookit Goal." This is a program done by Pizza Hut. Each month the students must read five books. The teacher verifies this by having the students retell the stories: main character, plot, etc. I listen to the students who have read short stories in their basal reader. They tell me the story. I grill them very thoroughly, demanding to know higher-level associations such as: Why do you think the character chose to respond the way he did?

In computer, the students do drills and exercises. They are then rewarded with some sort of game. They seem really content with this. Yet, am not so sure I really go along with all of it. I think there should be programs that "grade" the students' progress (for example, with multiplication and division). The days are flying fast now. I have been riding my bike to school every day it's not raining. The children are going crazy, wanting to know where I park it. I tell them I have been parking it in the "Bat Cave." I love it, and it's driving them crazy. The kids are great. I am still having a blast.

February 11, 20—. The mother mouse had babies. Tiquanna and I predicted the correct number. The children are jazzed up about the mice. I told the students I would be hanging with them for the next 12 weeks.

February 21, 20—. So much happens each day. Sometimes I am overwhelmed. It is no wonder teachers burn out. We hit the deck running about 8:00 and don't stop until 2:30. Then we plan and prepare for the next day until 3:30 or so. Tomorrow is a big day. Dr. Arnold is coming by to watch me teach my lesson. I am prepared, yet a little apprehensive. Cindy (Ms. Owenbey) has been letting me do lessons off and on, so the children are aware of my role as their teacher.

February 25, 20—. It worked great. I split the children into two groups and had them chorus read. They struggled with it, but I feel with a little time we will be moving along a lot more smoothly. I emphasized that we are to improve our reading skills by keeping up with the group. They struggled with the activity, but I think they did so because it was novel. Great day!

(The log continues in this manner, with Michael Kealohalan Anderson (called Lani) telling of his observations, his work with small groups and individuals, and his initial teaching experiences.)

Expanding Beyond Observation

School-based observation and teaching experiences are the bridge between the worlds of theory and practice. Throughout your education and psychology programs you will be examining theory: theories about how eight-year-olds learn, about the success of disabled youngsters in the regular classroom, about the best ways to group, about the most effective way to organize a lesson, about how to deal with disruptive students, etc. However, until you have had the opportunity to sit in a classroom and observe what occurs from the teacher's point of view, none of these theories will be real.

While surveying three teacher-preparation programs, Dorothy Sluss and Sam Minner of East Tennessee State University interviewed 26 classroom teachers. One teacher uttered a truism we often apply to teaching children, but frequently forget when teaching adults: "Children learn what they live. So do people who want to be teachers. If you want to learn about children, go where the children are. Don't just read about it in some book" (1999, 283).

Learning to "observe carefully and listen astutely will be your vehicle for becoming a reflective teacher" (Grant and Sleeter, 1998, 12). Therefore, observation—gaining knowledge and understanding—should come first. Once you have had the opportunity to reflect on the teachers, students, classrooms, and schools that you will observe, as will be discussed in Chapters 2 through 4, you will begin using what you have learned in your own planning and teaching. Pierce calls this kind of learning, "authentic learning" (1996, 217). For many of you, this will begin as early as your first class in education. For others, authentic learning will not occur until much later in your teacher-education program.

Observing a teacher can show you a great deal about how to teach, but it will not tell you how *you* will teach. Educator Philip Jackson at the University of Chicago relates a time when he was a principal and visited several nursery-school classrooms. He noted how teachers bent down to the eye level of children, how they held books on their laps, reading upside down so the children could see. He thought he could probably teach nursery school. But as he talked to the teachers, he realized that it was more than holding the book, bandaging the knee, and eyeballing the child. It was "seeing/reacting in a certain spirit or manner to a special portion of the world—rooms full of three- and four-year-olds" (1986, 88). According to Jackson, specific skills such as how to make play dough are important, but feeling and acting at home in a particular instructional milieu is essential for a true teacher. Until you have had the experience of teaching, you will not know whether you feel at home with particular students in a particular educational setting.

A good analogy for the importance of early school-based teaching experiences is that of learning to fly an airplane. Initially, student pilots might use flight simulators to experience flying a plane, but very early in their training they take command of the real plane as the instructor watches and critiques. This does not mean the simulator stops serving a function for them. In fact, they will use it many times to simulate uncommon occurrences. However, nothing substitutes for the experience of actually flying the plane. Simulated teaching experiences—role-playing classroom experiences with peers—will continue to be a helpful tool throughout your teacher training. But nothing will substitute for the teacher serving as your evaluator and mentor. As one preservice teacher reported at the end of her observation and participation experience, "We have all heard that experience is the best teacher. I can assure you that is the case with me. I know that I will refer to this experience for many years to come as a constant reminder to learn by doing. I admit I dreaded this experience at first. I would do it again and again, but this time, not for a grade, but for the experience!" (Chance, Morris, and Rakes, 1996, 388).

Experience Alone Is Not Always a Good Teacher

Throughout your time observing and participating in the classroom, you will need to make meaning of the events you see and experience. You will gain deeper understanding of student behaviors, teaching styles, and curriculum if you learn to make them meaningful. Researcher Selma Wasserman of Simon Fraser University in British Columbia concludes that making meaning from your field experiences can be more complicated than it appears. Your developmental history, your beliefs, and your values have formed your perceptions. Most likely they will play a part in the way you observe and what you take away from those observations. Also, factors such as the time of day, your physical and emotional state, personal biases, and your classroom mentor and professor can influence the meaning you derive from your experiences (Wasserman, 1999, 466–67).

It is your responsibility to make your observation and participation as meaningful and helpful as possible by collecting data, analyzing it, and reflecting upon it. Throughout your preservice time in the classroom, you will be using techniques such as checklists, anecdotal records, coding, and interviewing. Following the collection of data from these instruments, you will be involved in the process of reflection. Objective data collection and reflective thinking will enable you to gain meaningful information and knowledge about teaching and learning.

For the preservice teacher, teaching and learning should go hand in hand. For example, those who first experience teaching in student-centered classrooms might think the students are off task and out of control if they are not familiar with the student-centered approach. They may come away from this experience saying, "This kind of classroom is not for me." However, if they had first studied the student-centered classroom, observed in one, and examined teaching techniques common in such environments, the experience might have been different. Their conclusions would be based on knowledge rather than on misinterpretations of what they had experienced.

Frequently, novice teachers make incorrect assumptions about the success of lessons they have taught. For example, Hank believed a lesson was successful because the students were well behaved and responsive to his jokes and questions. His conclusion may be misleading. Assume that Hank has spent little or no time preparing the lesson. However, because he is glib and funny, the students are well behaved and appear to respond. Their behavior may have little or nothing to do with the lesson or with Hank. Perhaps the students are exceptionally well behaved. Perhaps the classroom teacher has prepared them for Hank's teaching by telling them they must be on their best behavior, or by rewarding them for good behavior. Hank, like the cat who jumps on the cold stove and assumes it will always be cold, assumes that students will always behave and respond positively to his teaching and that he doesn't need to change anything in his preparation or approach.

This example is also mis-educative in that Hank assumes that the only role of the teacher is to deliver lessons. He neglects to see the teacher setting realistic objectives and evaluating students on those objectives. If he continually fails to plan, how will he know what his teaching objectives are? If he has no objectives, how will he know if the students have learned what he's taught?

The Importance of Feedback in Early Teaching Experiences

Nothing is more important than good feedback about initial teaching experiences. Good does not necessarily mean positive. Good feedback for Hank might include a preteaching conference with the classroom teacher, Mr. Thornberg, to discuss the lesson. This conference could lead Hank to develop plans. Mr. Thornberg might ask: What will you be teaching today? What are your objectives for the lesson? How will you ensure the students are progressing toward the objectives? How will you determine if they learned what you taught?

If the preteaching conference does not lead to plan development, the after-teaching conference between Hank and Mr. Thornberg might. Mr. Thornberg tells Hank that he has good rapport with the students. Then he asks these questions: What did you expect the students to learn from your lesson? What methods did you employ to ensure they learned it? How did you involve the students in their own learning? How will you evaluate what they have learned? How will you grade them on what occurred today? If Karen's mother comes in and asks what Karen missed while she was absent, what will you tell her? Hank may now understand that he must do more than perform.

The belief that all genuine education comes through experiences does not mean that all experiences are genuinely or equally educative. Experience and education cannot be directly equated to each other. For some experiences are mis-educative. Any experience is mis-educative that has the effect of arresting or distorting the growth of future experience (Dewey, 1938, 25).

Unfortunately, the feedback that preservice teachers receive can also be mis-educative. Most of us want to give positive feedback to our students, and, unlike the situation in an airplane cockpit, positive feedback about teaching is not immediately dangerous. In fact, most teachers have discovered that positive feedback increases motivation and improves results. However, if preservice teachers accept positive feedback as the final truth, they may miss opportunities to gain valuable insight. To avoid this problem, you should always ask teachers who evaluate your classroom performance, "What would you have done differently?"

Overly negative feedback can be just as misleading. Sometimes classroom teachers expect preservice teachers to perform beyond their capabilities. This usually occurs because the classroom teacher is unfamiliar with the preservice teacher's education program. The classroom teacher may not understand that it is the preservice teacher's first class in education, or she may not know that the student is expected to be working only with an individual child. To avoid this problem, the preservice teacher should acquaint the classroom teacher with the role he or she is expected to play. Communication and feedback between preservice teacher, classroom teacher, and university supervisor is essential if the early field experience is to be beneficial. Other suggestions later in this book will help students avoid misunderstandings about roles.

The Importance of Reflective Observation

John J. Loughran, who teaches preservice teachers at Monash University, suggests that one common element seen in reflective individuals in a variety of professions is the notion of a problem. Reflective people see a problem as a puzzling, curious, or perplexing situation (2002, 33).

What is reflection? Why is it so important? And what's the big deal anyway? Although using reflection as a tool to improve learning about teaching is a relatively recent phenomenon, the process of reflection is one that scholars have touted for generations. Philosopher and educator John Dewey wrote in 1921, "Reflection is aimed at the discovery of facts that will serve a purpose." The guiding factor in the process of reflection, according to Dewey, is the "demand for the solution of a perplexity" (Dewey, 1921). So, if we want to solve a problem, we must reflect on it. Educational theorist Jerome Bruner went even further. "Reflection," he said, "is central to all learning" (Bruner, 1960, 13). There is hardly a self-help book on the market today that does not mention the importance of reflection. Books that claim to document the attributes of successful people always stress the reflective process that leads an individual to success. Sometime watch the face of an accomplished athlete after he has missed the ball in the end zone or she has fallen from the balance beam; you will see in the athlete's eyes a rapid analysis of what occurred. There may be only a few seconds to reflect on what went wrong, but reflection is necessary so that the same mistake will not occur again. This, of course, is why teams watch videos of the game and performers tape performances. This is what makes greatness. Many people who are "naturals" never become accomplished. Why? They have not learned the skill of reflection. So, too, with teachers. Those who reflect on their actions and performance are more successful than those who merely react.

Is reflection a skill that can be taught and learned? Of course it is. And, once you learn it, like riding a bike, you never lose it. Reflective individuals simply think about what they have seen and done. They gather information and analyze it. Frequently they write down what they have observed, as a way of processing their thoughts. Sometimes they video or audiotape their "performances." Sometimes they talk to themselves and even tape their thoughts. Often they clarify their thinking by talking to others and testing their thoughts. Reflection is at first introspective, but later it becomes active and interactive. Of course, true reflective thinkers choose carefully whom they share their thoughts with—selecting those people who can help them grow in their understanding. At the same time, reflective people continue the introspective process while they are actively pursing information and clarification. Reflection is not difficult. Often it merely requires answering simple questions: What did I do? How do I feel? Why do I feel that way? What was the best thing that happened? Were there any things I could have done better? What would I do differently if I could do it again? Sometime these questions are processed in a matter of seconds, such as with the gymnast who must immediately return to the balance beam. Other times the process is deliberate and slow. These simple questions, whether processed quickly or with deliberance, will lead you to become a reflective thinker.

The Reflection Process

Becoming a reflective practitioner requires time, practice, and an environment supportive to the development and organization of the reflection process. This is a highly individualized process, and each individual should find the structure and method of reflection that best suits him or her.

FIGURE 1.1   The Reflection Cycle

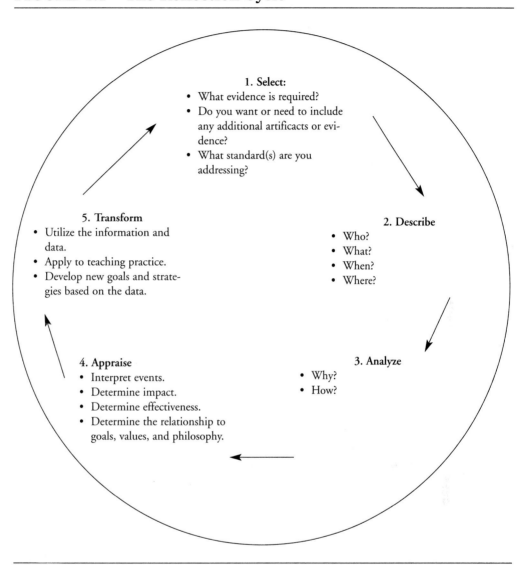

1. Select:
- What evidence is required?
- Do you want or need to include any additional artificacts or evidence?
- What standard(s) are you addressing?

5. Transform
- Utilize the information and data.
- Apply to teaching practice.
- Develop new goals and strategies based on the data.

2. Describe
- Who?
- What?
- When?
- Where?

4. Appraise
- Interpret events.
- Determine impact.
- Determine effectiveness.
- Determine the relationship to goals, values, and philosophy.

3. Analyze
- Why?
- How?

Source: Adapted from the Administrator Appraisal System Institute, North Carolina Department of Public Instruction, *Performance-Based Licensure,* 1998–1999.

This includes answering these questions: When is the best time for me to reflect on what I have learned and experienced? Where will I be most comfortable reflecting? Do I need any tools to help me in the process, such as a computer, a journal, copies of lessons, etc.? However, it is a reflective process (Holm and Horn, 2003, 30).

The reflective process itself can be seen as a series of steps known as the reflection cycle (see Figure 1.1). Although at first this cycle may seem complex, when you learn to utilize it you can reach a solution to a problem on the spot. It can also be used at a quiet time when you have the luxury to really think through a complex set of circumstances. The goal of this cycle is not to dictate how you will reflect on what you observe or experience in the classroom, but rather as a beginning place in the development of your own reflective process. One of the best ways to learn to become a reflective practitioner is by observing people who are. Truly reflective teachers are "powerful models because they question, observe, record, reflect and try out new ideas, as they work toward meeting the varied needs of a diverse student population" (Holm and Horn, 2003, 30).

Writing a Reflection

To help you become a reflective practitioner, it is necessary to practice the process of reflection. As with most people, it may be a good idea for you to begin by writing your reflections in a journal, a notebook, or in a special file in your computer documents. Figure 1.2 shows a series of suggested steps for writing a reflection related to your classroom observation or experience.

The power of the reflective cycle seems to rest in its ability first to slow down teachers' thinking so that they can attend to what is, rather than what they wish were so, and then to shift the weight of that thinking from their own thinking to their student's thinking (Rodgers, 2002, 231).

Initially when you use this cycle you will probably find yourself simply relating what you did and how you did it. Later, as you become more comfortable with the process, your thinking will begin to shift from your own to your student's. You should find this both enlightening and enjoyable. Examples of the development of reflective thinking are found throughout this guide.

FIGURE 1.2   **Writing a Reflection**

Select:	What evidence/artifacts have you included?
Describe:	This step involves a description of the circumstances, situations, or issues related to the evidence or artifact. Four "W" questions are usually addressed:

- Who was involved?
- What were the circumstances, concerns, or issues?
- When did the event occur?
- Where did the event occur?

Analyze:	This step involves "digging deeper." The "Why" of the evidence or artifact and the "How" of its relationship to your teaching practice should be addressed.
Appraise:	In the previous three steps, you have described and analyzed an experience, a piece of evidence, or an activity. The actual self-assessment occurs at this stage as you interpret the activity or evidence and evaluate its appropriateness and impact.
Transform:	This step holds the greatest opportunity for growth as you use the insights gained from reflection in improving and transforming your practice.

Source: Adapted from the Administrator Appraisal System Institute, North Carolina Department of Public Instruction, *Performance-Based Licensure*, 1998–1999.

PART II

Observing in the Schools

Chapter Two
Observing Teachers

Effective observation is a process of "selective watching." This means the observation should have both an objective and a procedure of what to look for (Duckett, 1980, 1). We all know the story of several people watching the same fender bender and each seeing a totally different accident. Why does this occur? The answer is simple. What we see is based on our experiences, values, and beliefs. Hence, if observation is to be effective in the learning process, it must be objective. To be objective, observation requires structure. You must have a plan, an objective, and a guide to follow. In addition, you must plan ahead. You need to be aware of exactly what you are looking for so you can see it even when dozens of other things have the potential of distracting you. Think for a minute about the typical classroom. How many things are occurring at any given time? Dozens. Hundreds. Julio is shifting around in his seat. Sara is sharpening her pencil. A poster falls off the wall. Kenya is asking a question. Ten students are raising their hands. Marquette is at the teacher's desk listing the names of those students who have paid for the field trip. Mr. Lazaro is putting the assignment on the board. You get the idea. Unless you know what you are looking for, how can you find it?

Becoming a professional requires observing others and incorporating what is learned into your behavior (Borich and Martin, 1999, 2). The carefully developed and field-tested observation instruments in this guide will assist you in completing objective observations that are effective in helping you learn about teaching. By utilizing the observation instruments, you will maximize the usefulness of the hours you spend in classroom observation and participation.

Observing in Classrooms

One important technique for learning about effective teaching is observing capable teachers at work in their classrooms. Observing is a skill that needs to be developed in order to yield the best results. As education professors and authors Michael Morehead and David Cropp suggest, "Observation which is conducted by the preservice teacher without the benefit of a prescribed structure . . . may not assist in the development of a future teacher" (1994, 2). A review of fifty-seven research studies revealed that in "field experiences with focus, well structured activities, significant learning occurs" (Wilson, Floden, and Ferrin-Munday, 2001, 3). One needs to know what to look for, how to look for it, and how to be objective in one's analysis.

In the following excerpts, two university students observe the same teacher in a second-grade classroom. You should note how, in their analyses, they come to different conclusions.

Sarah's Observation Log

As soon as the bell rang the children moved quietly to their seats. They seemed to know exactly what to do, exactly what was expected of them. They put their books in their desks and folded their hands on top of the desks as Mrs. Menotti instructed the two class monitors to collect the lunch and the picture money. She reminded them to have the students check off their names on the list when the money was turned in. As the students did this, Mrs. Menotti read the morning announcements. All the time she read, she was monitoring the students collecting the money. There were no disruptions, and the students seemed to collect the money in an orderly fashion. She did not call the roll, but I saw her put the attendance slip on the outside of the classroom door. Because the children have assigned seats, she could simply look to see who was not present. All of this was accomplished in less than ten minutes.

Mrs. Menotti told the children she would meet first with the red reading group in the reading circle. The other children would find their assignments on the board written in the color of their reading group. What a great idea! I'll have to remember this one. The children quietly took out their books, and all but two began to work while Mrs. Menotti was telling the reading group what to do. When she looked up and saw one child not working and another talking to the child next to him, she went to the board and wrote their names on it. The children immediately got to work.

Although I couldn't really hear the reading group, I could see the flip chart on which Mrs. Menotti had written letter combinations that would be used in the story. I could tell that each child was reading round-robin fashion, and that Mrs. Menotti interrupted only when a child needed help sounding out a word.

Since the rest of the class was working quietly in their workbooks, I took this time to look at the classroom. I was impressed with how neat and organized it was. All the desks were in neat rows. In the right front of the room was the reading circle. Mrs. Menotti sat so that she could see the children in the circle as well as the rest of the room. On the walls were colorful posters. The bookshelves were very carefully organized. On the bulletin board behind Mrs. Menotti's desk was a neat display of student work, which was very nicely done. There was an overhead projector in the front of the room. Also there were maps and a globe. There were lots of dictionaries and books in the book cabinets. There were no papers on the floor, and the children kept their books in their desks. Mrs. Menotti kept the shades drawn most of the way down so the children were not distracted.

Only once during the reading group did Mrs. Menotti have to stop to reprimand a student. It was one of the same students as earlier, and she went to the board to put a check next to his name and reminded him that it was not art time and he shouldn't be drawing and should be working in his workbook. He put his drawing in his desk, and I noticed that he did not concentrate on his workbook, but instead doodled around the edge of the page. At one point, I noticed that he was doing his drawing inside his desk. Mrs. Menotti did not seem to notice, and I wondered if I should have told her.

After about twenty minutes, the reading groups changed in an orderly fashion. The blue group went to the reading circle, and the red group took out their books and began doing the assignments written in red on the board.

I was really impressed with the order and organization in this classroom. Almost all of the students were quiet and actively involved in their work. Mrs. Menotti was able to work with the few students in the reading group. I hope I can have such an orderly classroom some day.

Steve's Observation Log

That same morning, Steve observed in Mrs. Menotti's classroom. Here are some excerpts from his observation log:

I got to the classroom about ten minutes before the bell rang. I introduced myself to Mrs. Menotti. Although she seemed friendly and told me to make myself at home, I had the feeling that she was distracted and rather cool. The children were having a wonderful time talking and giggling in small groups. The boys in the group nearest to me were talking about the soccer game. They were really excited that they had won. I already knew that I'd like these children. They were enthusiastic, bright-eyed, and bushy-tailed.

When the bell rang, everything changed. The atmosphere became rigid. Mrs. Menotti stood in the front of the room, staring at the class. She didn't say anything, but her message was clear: "It's time to get to work." The students stopped talking and moved to their desks, which were in rigid rows. Mrs. Menotti never smiled or said "Good morning." She just told the two monitors to collect lunch and picture money as she read the announcements. I noticed that the students selected as monitors appeared to be upper-class students in expensive-looking clothes. While they were taking the money, one of them seemed to be giving some of the less-well-dressed children a hard time, but Mrs. Menotti had not seemed to notice. Since the children's seats seemed to be assigned, she took attendance without calling roll. Although the class was orderly, it seemed as if the children might as well not have been there. The only ones Mrs. Menotti called by name were the monitors. I think my first impression was right: Mrs. Menotti is a very cold woman.

I couldn't help but notice how cold the classroom was. The only work of the children that was displayed was behind Mrs. M.'s desk, where the children can't go easily. It looked like perfect penmanship papers to me. The only other decorations in the room were mass-marketed posters that looked like they'd been here since Mrs. M. started teaching twenty years ago. The shades were down, and the only light in the room was artificial. I would hate to be a student here, and my sense was that the children didn't much like it either. I hadn't seen one smile since the bell rang.

When it was time to go to reading group, Mrs. Menotti called the red group to the circle. Is this class ability-grouped? I think so. It looked like all the children in the red group were wearing designer clothes. The two monitors were in that group. When they got in the group, Mrs. M. noticed two boys who had not yet started to work in their workbooks. It seemed that one boy couldn't read the assignment on the board, and I can understand why. He was in the yellow group, so the assignment was written in yellow and hard to see from where he sat. However, Mrs. M. didn't ask why he was talking; she just put his name on the board. I noticed a tear in his eye. I was beginning to dislike Mrs. Menotti. Another boy was fussing in his desk. He didn't seem to be able to find his book, so his name went on the board, too.

I watched the reading group for about ten minutes, and it looked deadly. Mrs. Menotti had letter combinations on the flip chart. As the children read in order she pointed to the letters and asked them to make the sound. It seemed to me that the children read very well and did not need this kind of instruction. Since I was bored I decided to walk around to see what kind of seatwork the kids were doing. Each group seemed to be working on a different page in the same workbook. I can tell who the "smart" kids are. They can tell, too. At one point, Mrs. Menotti stopped the reading group to yell at the same boy who could not see the board earlier. He was still not doing his work. I noticed earlier that he was drawing, and he is a really good artist. But, she does not acknowledge his ability. Instead his name got a check, and she told him he could come in after school to do his seatwork. So much for the value of art in this classroom!

It's no wonder so many kids drop out of school before they graduate. Mrs. Menotti has already decided that Shane, the artist, will be one of them. What hopes are there for Shane?

Conclusion. Both Sarah and Steve observed the same class during the same period of time; each saw a totally different Mrs. Menotti from a radically different perspective. Sarah's Mrs. Menotti was well organized, and the classroom environment was conducive to work and study. Steve's Mrs. Menotti distanced herself from the students, and the environment was controlled and nonproductive. How could two students from the same university class see such different things in the identical classroom?

Effective Observation

Most simply, observation is the act or practice of paying attention to people, events, and/or the environment. The difficulty with observation is that every individual brings to an event his or her perception of it.

However, not all observation is subjective. It also can occur systematically and be conducted fairly objectively. The fact that Sarah and Steve were required to observe in Mrs. Menotti's classroom means that the observation was deliberate, and, therefore, more formalized than everyday observation. However, it was not systematic. Systematic observation is long-term observation involving visiting a classroom many times and observing many different situations. It is planned, objective, and goal or question oriented. The observers identify beforehand what they are looking for and how they will carry it out. This is known as "targeted observation" (Yapp and Young, 1999, 27). Sarah and Steve's observations were not targeted. Thus, their observations may simply have reinforced their existing prejudices, thereby "arresting or distorting the growth from further experiences" (Evertson and Green, 1986, 95). One of the values of your teacher education program is that it helps you identify your targets. "Without some outside direction it is possible that classroom observations may serve to validate much of what (you) already 'expect' to see—allowing (you) to over-emphasize some things and overlook others. As a result, observations need to be focused if they are to be helpful in (your) professional life" (Borich and Martin, 1999, 3).

Objectivity in Observation.   Because teachers and classrooms are so different, observation can be difficult. If the observer tries to do more than record exactly what he or she sees, the conclusions will be filtered through his or her prejudices and biases.

The goal of the systematic observer, then, is to gather as much data as possible over a period of several observations about the classroom, the students, the teacher, and the curriculum. Pierce states that in order for observations to be of practical use, "they must be structured and focused on specific events that (you) have been well prepared to identify and analyze" (1996, 218). The more data that are identified and analyzed, the easier it will be to get a complete picture. The methods of obtaining as objective a point of view as possible involve anecdotal observation, structured observation, and interview. The goal of this chapter is to help you develop as a teacher by providing you with objective, systematic observation tools and techniques as the beginning step to learning how effective teachers teach. In subsequent chapters, you will find tools for objective observations of classrooms, schools, students, and curriculum.

Techniques of Observation.   Anecdotal observations focus on the situation and specifically on who says or does what rather than on personalities or interpretations of events. Structured observations are formal and require that you look for and record specified information that is called for on such things as checklists, sociograms, and profiles. The interview is a technique that seeks to find information through direct questioning. This method can be extremely valuable in understanding a procedure you have observed or the rationale behind it. The interview must be planned for and conducted as objectively as possible.

Anecdotal Observation

Anecdotal observations focus on exactly what occurs in a classroom or on what a child does or says in a specific situation over a limited period of time. Anecdotal observations are informally recorded narrative in an observation log. As much as possible, they are an exact description of a classroom event or incident. Anecdotal observations are simple to do. You need no training, but must follow the rules of all objective observation: (1) observe the entire sequence or event, (2) set goals, limits, or guidelines, (3) record completely and carefully, and (4) be as objective as possible.

Observing the Entire Event or Sequence

Typically, anecdotal observations deal with what might be called minimal situations. The observer watches one child or one teaching or management technique for a specified period of time over several observations. This observation allows you to make dated notes while focusing attention on a single element or individual in the classroom or school. The minimal situation technique narrows your focus to one event. Trying to follow too many elements of the classroom at one time usually leads to incomplete observation of all of them. Focusing on too much caused Sarah and Steve to make inaccurate judgments.

SAMPLE FORM 1   Anecdotal Record Form for Observing Teachers or Instructional Events—1

NAME OF OBSERVER: Karen Susan Richie

DATE AND TIME OF OBSERVATION: December 2, 20—, 10:30 a.m.

LENGTH OF OBSERVATION: Approximately 35 minutes

PERSON AND/OR EVENT OBSERVED: Mrs. Menotti teaching a reading lesson

GRADE LEVEL AND/OR SUBJECT: Second grade; reading

OBJECTIVE OF OBSERVATION: To determine how Mrs. Menotti works with individuals within the reading group

Instructions to the Observer: As completely and accurately as possible, describe the person or the event. If appropriate, include direct quotes and descriptions of the location or individual. Try to avoid making judgments.

Mrs. Menotti called the red group, the Space Invaders, to the reading corner at the right rear of the classroom. "Be sure to bring your free reading books with you, Space Invaders," said Mrs. M.

I moved over to the reading corner so I could better observe the group. The reading corner was next to the window and the students' chairs were arranged in a circle. Mrs. M.'s chair was a large, wooden-slat rocking chair next to the bookcase. Her chair was in the circle of chairs.

The students got their books from their desks. Miguel said, "Mrs. M., I finished my book, and I need to see if I can find it in the library." "Is it in the classroom library, Miguel?" Mrs. M. asked. "Yes." "O.K., you can look for it, Miguel. Just don't disturb the rest of us while you're looking."

Once all the students (except Miguel) were seated in the circle, Mrs. M. took out her own book. She said to Miguel, "Have you found it?" "Not yet," Miguel replied. "Well, join us while I read, and you can go back to the library and look afterward."

Mrs. M. asked Melody if she could remember what happened last in the story. (I couldn't see the title of the book Mrs. M. was reading from. I must remember to ask her.) Melody began to tell the story. She talked so quietly that it was difficult to hear her. Mrs. M. asked the other students some questions. "Sandy, can you remember what happened to the rabbit when the boy got sick?" "They took him from the nursery," Sandy said. "They were afraid the rabbit was comintated [sic]," said Maggie. "Do you mean 'contaminated'?"

(continued)

asked Mrs. M. Maggie looking at her hands. "Yes," said Maggie very quietly. "Very good, Maggie. That's right," said Mrs. M. Maggie looked up and smiled. "Why do you think they were afraid the rabbit might be contaminated, Sean?" Sean replied, "Well, he was stuffed and the boy is real sick, so the rabbit might have germs." "Very good, Sean," said Mrs. M.

She began to read. All the students were listening. After each page she showed the children the illustration on the page. She read one page and turned to the next and Sean said, "Hey, Mrs. M., you forgot to show us the picture." "There isn't one on that page, Sean."

She read for about ten minutes and asked, "Do you like the story, Abbie?" Abbie nodded her head. "Why do you like it?" she asked. "I like the boy and I want him to get well and get his rabbit back. It's sad," said Abbie. "Do you like sad stories, Mark?" "Yes, sometimes," said Mark. "Is the story you've been reading sad?" "No," Mark said. "Would you tell us about your book, Mark, please?" Mark did. It's the story of a space trip to Mars taken by a little boy. Melody said, "Did he really take that trip, Mark? I think it was all a dream." "No," said Mark. "It was real." "How do you know, Mark?" asked Sean. Mark said back very loudly, "Because the book doesn't say it's a dream." "Yeah," said Melody, "but in the beginning of the book he's in bed, and in the end he's back in his bed." Mark was quiet. Mrs. M. smiled, "When you read a story you can decide for yourself what it means. If Melody thinks it was a dream, that's O.K., even if Mark doesn't think it's a dream. Why don't you read it, Melody, and see if you still think it's a dream." Melody did not answer. Mrs. M. turned to Miguel and said, "Miguel, do you want to get your book so that you can tell us about it after Abbie tells us about hers?"

(Karen's observation continues until the reading group is over.)

Referenced to INTACS Standards 1 and 2

Setting Goals, Limits, or Guidelines

As with all observation, the observer must know the objective of the observation. What is it you hope to see in the classroom or school? You may simply want to explore how the teacher communicates with individual students, as Karen observed in this sample anecdotal record form for observing teachers. Another way is to keep a simple anecdotal record of student-teacher communication. Write as accurately as possible all the communication that occurs between the teacher and one student during a specified period of time. Since one important element of an effective school is good communication, examining how the teacher communicates with individual students can reveal a great deal about whether or not the classroom is effective. Of course, several observations of this student and other students would be required before a judgment could be made.

SAMPLE FORM 2   Anecdotal Teacher-Student Interaction Form

NAME OF OBSERVER: Karen Susan Richie

DATE AND TIME OF OBSERVATION: December 2, 20—, 10:30 a.m.

LENGTH OF OBSERVATION: Approximately 35 minutes

TEACHER: Mrs. Menotti

STUDENT: Miguel

GRADE LEVEL AND/OR SUBJECT: Second grade

OBJECTIVE OF OBSERVATION: How does Mrs. Menotti interact with an individual student?

Instructions to the Observer: As completely and accurately as possible, describe the interactions between the teacher and one selected student. Include direct quotes and descriptions of the teacher and the student, including facial expressions, gestures, and voice quality. However, be careful to avoid making judgments.

Time	Teacher	Student
10:36	Mrs. Menotti Mrs. M. smiled at Joey and made a "sh" sign. She looked him directly in the eye, "Is it in the classroom library, Joey?" "OK, you can look for it, Joey. Just don't disturb the rest of us while you're looking."	JOEY "Mrs. M., I finished my book, and I need to see if I can find it in the library." Joey called out very loudly across the room to Mrs. M. "Yes." Joey answered much more quietly and smiled back at Mrs. M. Joey moved quietly to the classroom library behind Mrs. M's rocking chair and began to search.

Perhaps you might want to examine another element of an effective school: rewarding student achievement. Use the anecdotal recording technique to determine how the teacher and the school reward the students for academic achievement. To do this, simply examine the classroom and the school building for signs that student achievement has been rewarded and list them in the observation log.

Referenced to INTASC Standards 1 and 2

SAMPLE FORM 3   Anecdotal Record Form for Observing Teachers or Instructional Events—2

NAME OF OBSERVER: James McClure

DATE AND TIME OF OBSERVATION: January 6, 20—, 9:35 a.m.

LENGTH OF OBSERVATION: 30 minutes

PERSON AND/OR EVENT OBSERVED: Mr. Penski's classroom

GRADE LEVEL AND/OR SUBJECT: Eighth grade; language arts and social studies

OBJECTIVE OF OBSERVATION: To determine how school/classroom environment promotes student achievement

Instructions to the Observer: As completely and accurately as possible, describe the person or the event. If appropriate, include direct quotes and descriptions of the location or the individual. Try to avoid making judgments.

1. Student work displayed on bulletin boards in hallways.

2. Students who won speech contest mentioned over intercom during morning announcements.

3. Teacher mentioned a student who won a Boy Scout honor.

4. Classroom bulletin board displayed students' writing from last week.

5. Students were working on putting together a desktop computer publication of their writing.

6. Books children have written and illustrated were on check-out shelf at the rear of the room.

7. Student artwork related to social studies unit was displayed on the wall above the windows.

8. Students' use of computer graphics to highlight work received a sticker of a computer as a reward. These graphics were prominently displayed on the bulletin boards.

Referenced to INTASC Standards 1–4

Recording Completely and Carefully

Anecdotal records require carefully recording events over a specified period of time. It might be useful to do two or more recordings, since it is impossible to write down everything that occurs in just one observation. For example, in observing one child, you might record the child's activities every five minutes for an hour. Later you can record her activities every five minutes for another hour. It is important for you to write down exactly what the child is doing, avoiding any judgments of her behavior. A schedule is also important if your goal is to examine classroom organization. For example, if you are watching grouping techniques in a classroom, record the formal and informal grouping patterns every thirty minutes. An anecdotal observation like this reveals an interesting grouping pattern in Mr. Hanks's classroom that observation of everything in the classroom might not.

SAMPLE FORM 4   Anecdotal Record Form for Grouping Patterns

Name of Observer: Sylvia Rodriguez

Date and Time of Observation: October 29, 20—, 8:45 a.m.

Length of Observation: All day

Person and/or Event Observed: Mr. Hanks

Grade Level and/or Subject: Fifth grade

Objective of Observation: To examine grouping patterns

Instructions to the Observer: As completely and accurately as possible, describe the different groups in the classroom. If appropriate, include direct quotes and descriptions of locations or individuals. Try to avoid making judgments.

8:45   Reading groups met with teacher; all of the children in each group read in turn from the same-level basal reader; three different level readers were used by the five groups. The teacher reinforced skills by calling the children's attention to words on a flip chart.

9:15   Math groups in which all the children were working on different kinds of math problems; two groups were doing long division, another multiplication, another fractions (population of the math groups differs from population of the reading groups—i.e., Sarah Jane is in the fraction math group, but was reading from the lowest-level reader).

9:45   Children continued in math groups; three larger groups divided into pairs; the pairs were helping each other complete the homework assignments listed for each group on the chalkboard. Mr. Hanks spent all his time working with the multiplication group—the only group not working in pairs—except for a few minutes to answer the questions of the other groups.

10:15   Recess—children formed their own groups: a group of ten boys was playing soccer, a group of seven girls was skipping rope, two girls were reading, a group of four boys was playing chase, two girls were walking, one girl was sitting with Mr. Hanks.

10:45   Social studies groups—students were investigating different aspects of the community. The children seemed to know their assignments; each student had a folder which was picked up at the front of the room when Mr. Hanks announced it was time for social studies; the students went to the supply cabinet or the bookshelves when they needed materials; they went up to Mr. Hanks's desk with questions. (Mr. Hanks did not work with these groups, but observed their activities from his desk.)

11:45   Lunch (did not observe).

12:00   All students participated in a class meeting with Mr. Hanks about the Halloween party (the class president presided over this large group); students sat in a large circle; they raised their hands when they wanted to make a point; Mr. Hanks recorded each point made on a flip chart; he only spoke to redirect the discussion to other students.

12:30   Students lined up by row, as called by Mr. Hanks, to go to music; one row of mostly boys was not allowed to leave until they quieted down; they did not have their materials put away and were busy talking; it took about three minutes for them to get organized and quiet; then Mr. Hanks let them leave.

2:15   Small groups participated in a variety of classroom management chores (i.e., one group picked up papers and cleaned desks, tables, and floor; another group rearranged the chairs and adjusted the blinds; a third group put papers in students' folders; a fourth group collected books and placed them on the bookshelves).

Referenced to INTASC Standards 1–5.

Structured Observations

Structured observations follow a specific format. As in anecdotal observations, you should follow the rules of objective observation. Unlike anecdotal observations, structured observations are formal and require that specific information be recorded. Structured observations include rank ordering, coding, checklists, interviews (discussed in this chapter), profiles, and sociograms (discussed in Chapter 4). Instruction is dynamic and much too complex to be evaluated by only one measurement method. That is why it is necessary to examine teaching from a variety of perspectives using multiple techniques of data collection (Duckett, 1999, 64).

Rank Ordering

One easy, nonjudgmental way to examine what has been observed in the classroom is to organize the observations in order of frequency. Many things can be rank ordered. For example, it is possible to rank order the following techniques employed by the teacher: instructional techniques (lecturing, discussion, small group work, individual work, etc.), grouping patterns, management approaches, methods of discipline, types of questions, and types of assignments.

Rank-ordered information is helpful not only in knowing the frequency of behaviors, but also in giving information about which behaviors occurred most or least often (McNeely, 1997, 27). If Karen — the observer from the sample anecdotal record form for observing teachers or instructional events — had been observing grouping patterns in Mrs. Menotti's classroom over the period of a *week,* she could have rank ordered the grouping patterns by frequency of occurrence. To do this, of course, she would first have to know what types of groups she had seen.

SAMPLE FORM 5   Observation Form for Rank Ordering

NAME OF OBSERVER: Karen Susan Richie

DATE AND TIME OF OBSERVATION: Week of November 4, 20—

LENGTH OF OBSERVATION: One week

TECHNIQUES OR TYPES OBSERVED: Mrs. Menotti—Grouping Patterns

GRADE LEVEL AND/OR SUBJECT: Second grade

OBJECTIVE OF OBSERVATION: To examine grouping patterns

Instructions to the Observer: Over a period of one week list a variety of possible techniques or types of grouping patterns. Keep a tally of those you observe. At the end of the observation period, count the number of occurrences of each technique or type.

Techniques or Types of Grouping Patterns	Number of Occurrences
Homogeneous grouping for skills	10
Interest grouping	7
Management grouping	5
Groups based on book read	3
Groups for completing project	2
Total Number of Groups (Date: Week of November 4, 20—)	27

To gain additional insight into the grouping patterns used in Mrs. Menotti's classroom, the percentage of times particular types of grouping patterns were used might be interesting. For example, 37 percent of the groups in Mrs. Menotti's classroom were homogeneous skill groups, and 26 percent were based on interest.

Referenced to INTASC Standards 1–5.

Coding Systems

A coding system is another simple, structured tool for observing in the classroom. A coding system looks for specific elements of teacher and/or student behavior. The observer usually records these elements at a specific interval, or simply tallies the number of times the particular behavior occurs. To complete a coding observation, you need a list of specified behaviors. In this chapter we will provide two types of coding systems: one based on Ned Flanders's student and teacher interactions system, the second based on Norris Sanders's system of questioning. In the first type of coding, the observer records the interaction during a specific interval.

Observing Student-Teacher Interaction. In each of the teacher-student interaction examples, tally the number of times the following nine categories of interaction between the teacher and students occur.

The first four types of interaction, according to Flanders, show an **indirect teacher influence:**

1. **Accepts feelings**—The teacher accepts or acknowledges student-expressed feelings/concerns in a non-threatening manner. (For example, *Student:* "I don't understand the assignment." *Teacher:* "It is a difficult concept to grasp, isn't it?")

2. **Praises and encourages**—The teacher gives positive evaluation of a student contribution. (For example, *Teacher:* "That's an especially good paper, Sammy.")

3. **Accepts or uses ideas of student**—The teacher clarifies, develops, or refers to a student contribution, usually without evaluation. (For example, *Student:* "The electoral college decides which presidential candidate is elected." *Teacher:* "And, the electoral college awards its votes based on the popular vote in each state.")

4. **Asks questions**—The teacher solicits information or asks opinions with the intent that a student answers. (For example, *Teacher:* "What is one fact about the electoral college?")

The next three types of student-teacher interaction are considered to be **direct teacher influences:**

5. **Lectures**—The teacher presents ideas, information, or orientation. Lecturing includes rhetorical questions.

6. **Gives directions**—The teacher directs or suggests in a way which indicates that the student is expected to comply. (For example, *Teacher:* "Turn to page 72 and complete exercise B.")

7. **Criticizes or justifies authority**—The teacher evaluates a student's contribution negatively or refers to the teacher's authoritative position. (For example, *Teacher:* "No, George, the electoral college is not a college for engineers. Where are the notes you took yesterday on this? You know it is your responsibility to take notes in class every day.")

The following two responses fall under the heading of **student talk:**

8. **Student talk-response**—The student directly answers the teacher's question. The answer is usually responsive to the question. (For example, *Teacher:* "What is one fact about the electoral college?" *Student:* "The electoral college decides which presidential candidate is elected.")

9. **Student talk-initiation**—The student initiates a comment or question that is unpredictable and/or creative in content. (For example, *Student:* "We didn't discuss this yesterday, but I know that eleven presidents won the election by winning the electoral college votes even though they lost the popular vote.")

Referenced to INTASC Standards 1–5.

SAMPLE FORM 6 Coding System—Type and Tally of Student-Teacher Interaction

NAME OF OBSERVER: Eric Dreibholz

DATE AND TIME OF OBSERVATION: December 16, 20—, 2:15 p.m.

LENGTH OF OBSERVATION: 1 hour

ELEMENT OBSERVED: Teacher-student interaction

TEACHER AND/OR STUDENT: Mrs. Rodriguez

GRADE LEVEL AND/OR SUBJECT: Sixth grade; social studies (Civil War)

OBJECTIVE OF OBSERVATION: To examine types of indirect and direct teacher interaction with students and type of student talk in one lesson

Instructions to the Observer: Tally the number of times each interactive behavior occurs during your observation period. Try to record at least one example of each type of interaction. At the end of the observation period, total the number of all teacher-student interactions, and calculate the percentage of the total for each interaction.

Type of Interactive Behavior	Tally of Times Observed	Percentage
INDIRECT		
Accepts Feelings **Example:** "I know some of you don't feel well. You may be discouraged, but let's keep trying."	////	8%
Praises/Encourages **Example:** "I like what you're saying." "Good." "Can you tell us more?"	//// ///	12%
Accepts or Uses Student Ideas **Example:** "Nick said General Lee was an outstanding leader—let's talk about that."	////	7%

(continued)

Type of Interactive Behavior	Tally of Times Observed	Percentage
Asks Questions **Example:** "Why do you think General Lee surrendered at that time?" "What was the turning point of the war?"	//// //// ///	21%
DIRECT		
Lectures **Example:** Gave background of Gettysburg Address	///	5%
Gives Directions **Example:** "Think about this question." "Answer questions 1–6 on page 97."	//// //	11%
Criticizes or Justifies Authority **Example:** "I don't like the way you crumbled your paper."	///	5%
STUDENT TALK		
Student Talk-Response **Example:** Students answered all directed questions in one or two words or with deeper explanations.	//// //// ///	21%
Student Talk-Initiation **Example:** "I agree with Tom, but I think Lee should have waited longer before he surrendered."	//// /	10%
TOTALS	62	100%
MOST FREQUENTLY USED TYPE OF INTERACTION	Accepts or uses student ideas and student talk-response.	

Source: Adapted from Ned Flanders, 1985. *Analyzing Teacher Behavior.* Reading, MA: Addison-Wesley.

Referenced to INTASC Standards 2, 3, 4, and 6

Observing Questioning Techniques

There are many approaches for examining questions asked by teachers. A coding system can help you examine the types of questions asked. We will focus on a technique developed by Norris Sanders (see Table 2.1), based on the cognitive taxonomy of Benjamin Bloom. Bloom's cognitive taxonomy assumes that development of cognitive ability is hierarchical. In other words, understanding of concepts progresses from simple understanding, what Bloom calls knowledge or recall (Sanders calls this memory), and comprehension (Sanders calls this translation and interpretation) to more complex knowledge. Bloom labels these higher levels of cognition as analysis, synthesis, and evaluation. In between the less and more complex levels of understanding is the ability to apply (application) one's knowledge to problems and new situations. Bloom's cognitive taxonomy is diagrammed in Figure 2.1. As the chart shows, knowledge is cyclical. Once high levels of knowledge of a concept are achieved, an individual must begin to add to this knowledge by developing new concepts.

Sanders, using Bloom's taxonomy, identifies seven levels of questions, from least to most complex.

1. **Memory:** The student recalls or recognizes information.

2. **Translation:** The student changes information into a different symbolic form or language.

3. **Interpretation:** The student discovers relationships among facts, generalizations, definitions, values, and skills.

4. **Application:** The student solves a real-life problem that requires identification of the issue and the selection and use of appropriate generalizations and skills.

5. **Analysis:** The student solves a problem in the light of conscious knowledge of the parts and forms of thinking.

6. **Synthesis:** The student solves a problem that requires original, creative thinking.

7. **Evaluation:** The student makes a judgment of good or bad, right or wrong, according to standards he designates (Sanders, 1966, 3).

If you compare Sanders' levels of questions to Bloom's taxonomy, you will note a few minor differences. Sanders calls the lowest level of questioning *memory* rather than *recall,* as it is designated by Bloom. And Sanders divides the second level of the domain, *comprehension,* into two levels of questions: *translation* and *interpretation.*

To recognize the level of question asked, you must be able to examine the question and place it at the appropriate level. The best way to do this is to list all questions asked by the teacher, oral and written, and examine them based on examples of each level provided in Table 2.1. You can also use the verbs provided in the central circle of Bloom's cognitive domain in Figure 2.1 to identify the level of a question. The use of a cassette recorder is very helpful in this process. Caution: simply list or record the questions without attempting the examination process until each question asked can be carefully compared with sample questions. It is important to note that if two observers listen to the same lesson, it is likely that even if the questions are identically recorded, the observers' placement of them within levels will differ to some extent.

Since most educators, including Bloom and Sanders, agree that too many lower-level questions (memory, translation, interpretation) and not enough higher-level questions (application, analysis, synthesis, evaluation) are asked, it is helpful to note the frequency of the type of question asked. Keep in mind, however, that in a well-planned lesson, the level of questions asked will directly relate to the teacher's objective for the students. For example, if the teacher's objective is, "The students will examine the feud in *Romeo and Juliet,*" it is likely that the questions will be at the lower levels. If, however, the objective is, "The students will compare and contrast the feud in *Romeo and Juliet* with other literary and nonliterary feuds," the questions will move from memory to analysis.

FIGURE 2.1   Cognitive Behaviors and Verbs*
Based on Bloom's Cognitive Domain

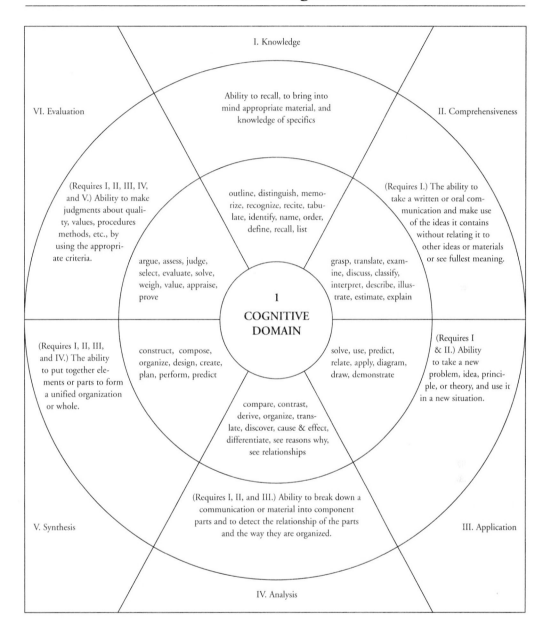

This diagram identifies and explains the six levels of cognitive behaviors; it also gives a sample list of verbs that may be used in relating behavioral evaluation to the proper level of cognitive behavior.

*Adapted by Sanchon S. Funk, Jeffrey L. Hoffman, Anne Keithley, and Bruce E. Long of the Florida State University Office of Field Experiences from Benjamin Bloom et al. (ed.), *Taxonomy of Education Objectives: Cognitive Domain,* Longman S. Green and Company, Inc., 1985.

TABLE 2.1   Examples of Levels of Questions Based on Sanders and Bloom

1. Memory	How much is . . . ? Who is . . .? When was . . . ? Outline the chapter.
2. Translation	What does the definition say? What is the English translation of that passage? Look on page 27; what does your text say about . . . ? Draw a picture of the character in the story as we read.
3. Interpretation	In your own words, what does that passage mean? Without looking at your text, what is meant by . . . ? Write a sentence using the vocabulary word . . . Explain the meaning of the graph. What is the word problem asking you to do? Estimate the number of votes needed to win.
4. Application	What would happen if . . . ? What would you do in a similar situation? How would you solve that problem? Using this play as a model, write your own play based on the story we read. Solve the word problem. Diagram the . . . Demonstrate . . .
5. Analysis	Compare this story to that story. Contrast this battle to that battle. What was the effect of his decision? What caused the problem? Is this story based on fact or opinion? What is the major theme of the novel? What conclusion would you derive from the following . . . ?
6. Synthesis	Write an essay about . . . Write an original short story. Design your own experiment. Using all you have learned about oil painting and portraiture, paint a portrait in oils. Develop solutions for the problem of . . . Write a computer program.
7. Evaluation	Write a critique of the novel . . . Evaluate the quality of . . . Argue the following point . . . Debate . . . Write a point-counterpoint paper on . . . Based on all you have learned, evaluate your own work. Whose solution proved the most effective?

SAMPLE FORM 7   Observation Form for Examining Questions

NAME OF OBSERVER: Ramon Auenida

DATE AND TIME OF OBSERVATION: December 11, 20—, 1:15 p.m.

TEACHER: Mr. Cortines

GRADE LEVEL AND/OR SUBJECT: Tenth grade; science—"The Characteristics of Life"

OBJECTIVE OF OBSERVATION: To examine the level of questions asked by Mr. Cortines

Instructions to the Observer: On a separate piece of paper or on a cassette, record all questions asked by the teacher, orally and in writing, for one lesson. Then place each question below at the appropriate level. Next, tally the number of questions at each level. Count the total number of questions asked, and compute a percentage for each level.

Type of Question	Total Number of Questions
1. Memory: —What is another name for a living thing? —What are the characteristics common to all living things? —How do living things obtain food? —What kind of energy do plants need in order to carry out photosynthesis? —Who discovered the existence of microorganisms?	5
2. Translation: —Tell me in your own words what photosynthesis means. —Explain the meaning of spontaneous generation. —What is the derivation of metabolism?	3
3. Interpretation: —How does movement in plants differ from movement in animals? —What happens to energy taken into an organism?	2
4. Application: —What would happen to the plants in this room if they didn't get sun and water? —Diagram the concept of phytosynthesis.	2
5. Analysis: —What are the similarities and differences between living and nonliving things? —Which of the scientist's experiments supported abiogenesis and which supported biogenesis? —How does the movement of an animal differ from the movement of a wind-up toy?	3
6. Synthesis: —Write a paper on pasteurization. Discuss what the process is, how it is done, and why it is done. —Do an oral report on how people do home canning from things that grow in their gardens. Explain how these procedures relate to the experiments on spontaneous generation in this chapter.	2

(continued)

Type of Question	Total Number of Questions
7. **Evaluation:** —Whose experiments do you think were most effective: Spallanzani's, Needham's, or Pasteur's? Why?	1
TOTAL Number of Questions, All Levels:	18

Percentage of Memory *27%;* Translation *17%;* Interpretation *11%;* Application *11%;* Analysis *17%;* Synthesis *11%;* Evaluation *6%*

Referenced to INTASC Standards 1–5 and 8

Checklists

A checklist is a simple structured tool to use while observing in a classroom. It serves the function of limiting the observation to the items on the list and allows the observer simply to mark when a task has been completed. Checklists are most useful when you are observing behaviors that are difficult to evaluate in degree, but that can be identified as either occurring or non-occurring (Grant and Sleeter, 1998, 49). The checklist does not evaluate; it documents.

Although many commercial checklists are available, the best are specifically designed for the observation at hand. As with all observational tools, it is essential to limit the items on the checklist to the objectives set for the specific observation. The keys to developing a good checklist are: (1) knowing the purpose for the checklist and (2) developing items that help determine whether the items looked for are found. Checklists can be designed to look for many things in the classroom, such as the classroom environment, classroom management techniques, elements of the curriculum, teaching styles, competencies taught, and teaching practices that accommodate different learning styles. We have provided one specific checklist for observing teaching styles (Sample Form 8.1) and another for observing teaching practices that accommodate different learning styles (Sample Form 8.2). Teaching styles are the unique ways that teachers organize instruction based on their philosophy of teaching and learning, and learning styles are the ways each learner processes and remembers new information (NC Teaching Academy, 4).

As stated in Chapter 1, preservice teachers must have experiences with culturally diverse and exceptional populations and recognize different learning styles. Form 8.2 is included to assist you in observing teaching practices that accommodate diversity in learning styles.

SAMPLE FORM 8.1   Checklist for Determining Teaching Style

NAME OF OBSERVER: *José Perez*

DATE AND TIME OF OBSERVATION: *October 17, 20—, 9:50 a.m.*

TEACHER: *Nisha Mendez*

GRADE LEVEL AND/OR SUBJECT: *Eighth grade; mathematics*

OBJECTIVE OF OBSERVATION: *To determine the teaching style of a particular teacher*

Instructions to the Observer: Prior to the observation, read over the items below. These items represent various teaching styles used by teachers. During and after the observation, place an "X" next to those items you have observed.

__X__ prefers teaching situations that allow interaction and discussion with students	____ has students work in small groups
__X__ uses questions to check on student learning following instruction	____ prefers impersonal teaching situations
____ viewed by students as teaching facts	__X__ uses questions to introduce topics and probe student answers
____ provides feedback, avoids negative evaluation	____ uses teacher-organized learning situations
__X__ strong in establishing a warm and personal learning environment	__X__ viewed by students as encouraging to apply principles
____ tells students the objectives of the lesson	____ gives feedback, uses negative evaluation
__X__ uses a variety of media and technological resources	__X__ strong in organizing and guiding student learning

Adapted from: [online] Internet path: http://www.aismissstate.edu.\ALS/Unit9modulers.num and Dean Boyd, computer system coordinator, Mississippi State University of Starkville, MS, College of Agriculture and Life Sciences, September 22, 1999.

Referenced to INTASC Standards 1–9

SAMPLE FORM 8.2   Checklist for Examining Teaching Practices Which Accommodate Diversity of Learning Styles

NAME OF OBSERVER: Ricardo Diaz

DATE AND TIME OF OBSERVATION: October 30, 20—, 10:30 a.m.

TEACHER: Nanette Joyce

GRADE LEVEL AND/OR SUBJECT: Fourth grade

OBJECTIVE OF OBSERVATION: To determine which teaching practices accommodate different learning styles in the classrooms.

Instructions to the Observer: Prior to the observation, read over the items below. These items represent various teaching practices used to accommodate different learning styles of students in the classrooms. During and after the observation put an "X" next to those items you observe(d).

VISUAL

____ writes directions on board as well as giving them orally.

____ uses flash cards, printed in bold letters

____ uses resources that require reading and seeing

____ uses transparencies

____ uses models, graphs, charts

____ assigns written reports

____ has students write/draw comic strips related to lessons/projects

____ has students take notes on important words, concepts

____ gives a written copy of boardwork if student has difficulty copying

____ uses videos

TACTILE

____ uses manipulative objects especially when teaching abstract concepts (measurement, geometry)

____ allows students to build models, draw/paint pictures, make a display instead of written reports

---

AUDITORY

____ gives oral rather than written tests

____ uses lectures

____ uses audiotapes

____ uses music related to themes/holidays

____ allows students to use tape recorder to recite then play back

____ substitutes oral reports for written assignments

____ uses CD's

____ uses books on discs

KINESTHETIC

____ allows students to make multimedia production (PowerPoint)

____ allows students to use computers and calculators

____ uses role playing and simulations

____ provides opportunities for movement, games, activities

Adapted from the North Carolina Teacher Academy, North Carolina Department of Public Instruction, Raleigh, NC 2001

Referenced to INTASC Standards 1–8 and 10

Structured Observation of a Lesson

One way to observe the structure of a lesson is to use a lesson-planning form on which elements of a lesson are outlined. The observer can watch a lesson being taught and outline the lesson using specific examples on the lesson-planning form. Of course, it is important to note that not all lessons have all the elements of a particular structure. And each element may be included in more than one lesson. Sometimes lessons include elements in a variety of orders. At times, only a few of the elements occur. We have chosen to provide an example based on the work of Madeline Hunter and developed by Lois Sprinthall. However, any lesson-planning form can be used.

SAMPLE FORM 9   Observation Form for Structured Observation of a Lesson

NAME OF OBSERVER: Angie Carl

DATE AND TIME OF OBSERVATION: November 11, 20—, 12:40 p.m.

TEACHER: Olivia Smith

GRADE LEVEL AND/OR SUBJECT: Seventh grade; social studies (Civil War)

OBJECTIVE OF OBSERVATION: To identify how the elements of a lesson are implemented by the teacher

Instructions to the Observer: As you observe in the classroom, write the elements of the lesson which fit under the categories below. A description of each category appears in italics.

1. **Anticipatory Set**—*In every lesson, the teacher provides initial motivation and focus for the lesson. Sometimes this focus takes the form of a review of previous knowledge important to this lesson; at other times it is designed to "grab" the students' attention. Key words: alerting, relevance, relationship (to previous lesson), meaningfulness, etc.*

   Teacher read from letters by two brothers, one fighting for the North, the other for the South. Students were attentive and appeared to be listening.

2. **Objective**—*In almost every lesson, the teacher specifies the behaviors the students will be expected to perform. In other words, the students know what is expected of them and what they are expected to learn.*

   Objective on board was pointed out to the students—"The student will compose a letter from the perspective of a soldier from the North or the South during the Civil War."

3. **Teacher Input**—*In most lessons, the teacher will provide the students with the information needed to reach the objective successfully. Sometimes the teacher will show the students how to accomplish the task by modeling appropriate performance.*

   Using a variety of questioning techniques, the students and the teacher reviewed two battles discussed in previous lesson. Teacher listed key information on overhead projector.

   The students were reminded to be sure they had all this information in their notebooks since they will need it to complete their assignment.

(continued)

4. **Checking for Understanding**—*Throughout the lesson, the teacher checks to ensure that the students understand the concepts or skills being taught. This can be accomplished through random questioning or individual tutoring.*

The teacher asked the students if they understood the importance of the two battles. She then discussed with them how the perspective of the Northern and Southern soldiers would have differed in each battle.

As the students worked together, the teacher circulated to be sure they were on task and understood what they were doing.

5. **Guided Practice**—*In every lesson, students practice the expected performance. This may include exercises completed with the teacher, examples done by students on the board, students reading aloud, students working together to complete assignments, games that allow the students to exhibit understanding, etc.*

The teacher brainstormed with the students about a Southern soldier's impression of one of the two battles. The brainstorming was listed on the board—the information about the battle was still projected on the screen above the board.

The teacher told the students to do the same in small groups from the perspective of a Northern soldier in the same battle.

The teacher and the students composed on the overhead one letter from a Northern soldier to his sweetheart.

6. **Independent Practice**—*Student independently exhibit the behaviors set forth in the objective. To accomplish this, students might complete problems, write a paper, do an experiment, give a report, complete a project, do research, etc.*

The students were instructed to begin a letter from either a Northern or Southern soldier to a member of his family or friend from the other battle. They were told to use the same process—first brainstorming by themselves about what that soldier was feeling, and then writing the letter.

7. **Closure**—*The teacher helps students review what they have learned in the lesson. This may include a summary of the lesson, questions about what happened during the students' independent practice, the students' report of their progress, an evaluation by the teacher, a discussion of the relationship of this lesson to the next lesson or the unit, or an assignment of additional independent practice.*

The teacher asked for a Northern and Southern volunteer to tell the class what he or she had written or brainstormed thus far.

Source: Lois Sprinthall, *A Strategy Guide for Teachers: Guide Book for Supervisors of Novice Teachers.* Unpublished manuscript. Based on the work of Madeline Hunter.

Referenced to INTASC Standards 1–9

Interview Methods

Frequently, observations do not yield enough data for complete understanding of the situation. For example, it is not always possible to observe all the grouping patterns employed in a single classroom over a period of weeks. University students are unlikely to be able to return two weeks after an initial classroom observation to observe other classes of the same teacher. Therefore, you may be unable to see how the grouping patterns change and develop based on the students and the content. An interview with the teacher, when conducted objectively, can help you determine this sequence. The interview should be designed to reveal data that cannot be observed in one observation, or even in a series.

The interview is a fact-finding technique in which you attempt to obtain information from the respondent through direct questioning. Of course, a good interview requires planning and nonjudgmental questions that reveal important data.

Following is a checklist of important interview techniques to use prior to and during an interview.

SAMPLE FORM 10   Checklist of Interview Techniques

NAME OF OBSERVER: Maria Ortiz

DATE, TIME, AND PLACE OF OBSERVATION: November 6, 20—, 3:30 p.m., Teacher's classroom

PERSON TO BE INTERVIEWED: Mr. Maldonado

GRADE LEVEL AND/OR SUBJECT: Fifth grade

OBJECTIVE OF OBSERVATION: To find out about grouping patterns different from those observed on November 4, 20—

Instructions to the Observer: Review this checklist prior to and after your interview. Check off those items you have completed.

1. Prior to the Interview

✓ Establish the purpose for the interview.

✓ Request an appointment (time and place), giving sufficient lead time for you and the person to be interviewed.

✓ Plan objective, specific questions related to the purpose of the interview.

✓ Prioritize questions, asking the most important first.

✓ Remind the person to be interviewd of the time, place, and purpose of the interview.

2. The Interview

✓ Arrive at the pre-established place several minutes before the scheduled time for the interview.

✓ Start the interview by reminding the person to be interviewed of its purpose.

(continued)

✓ Request permission to tape the interview (if appropriate).

✓ If taping is unfeasible, take careful, objective notes, trying to list direct quotes as often as possible.

✓ Avoid inserting impressions or judgments.

✓ Limit the interview to no more than 15-30 minutes.

3. After the Interview

✓ Review with the respondent what has been said or heard.

✓ Express your appreciation for the interview.

✓ Offer to share the interview report with the respondent.

Referenced to INTASC Standards 1, 2, 6, and 9

Observing Teaching Standards

You were introduced to INTACS (Interstate New Teacher Assessment and Support Consortium) standards, principles, and key indicators in Chapter 1. In this Chapter you will learn how to observe these in action.

On the rating scale for observing teaching standards (Form 11) you will be asked to assess the level at which each principle is met. The distinction between 1 and 5 on the scale is the level of sophistication exhibited. For example, a preservice student teacher of high school English should know the rules of English grammar (Content Pedagogy), but may not be able to totally integrate the teaching of grammar and writing for many years. Therefore, if you were assessing a thorough grammar lesson on prepositional phrases using a grammar textbook and examples from literature currently being read in the classroom, this beginning teacher might receive a 2 to 3 on the rating scale. In this lesson the teacher demonstrated "an understanding of the central concepts of (the) discipline," linked the current lesson to prior learning, and used appropriate resources and delivery. However, the students did not examine differing perspectives on the use of prepositional phrases. Nor did they see how the use of prepositional phrases might affect historical documents. Likewise, they did not examine prepositional phrases from their own writing and attempt to evaluate and improve their usage.

The rating scale appears in this text to assist preservice teachers in recognizing the common core teaching standards and learning how to assess their presence based on classroom performance. You should not use it to judge whether or not the teacher is effective. Only knowledgeable supervisors who understand how the lesson you are observing fits into the entire curricular sequence and are aware of the teacher's education and experience can make this type of judgment. It is also important to note that you are observing one lesson. This rating scale must be utilized many times over a long period by sophisticated, advanced-certification teacher observers to provide an accurate picture of the teacher's level of sophistication in each of the core teaching standards. Therefore, the best use of this rating scale may be as a self-evaluation instrument.

SAMPLE FORM 11   A Rating Scale for Observation of Standards for Teaching

NAME OF OBSERVER: Amy Anderson

DATE AND TIME OF OBSERVATION: May 16, 20—

LENGTH OF OBSERVATION: Approximately 45 minutes

TEACHER: Charles Arrowood

GRADE LEVEL OBSERVED: Ninth grade

OBJECTIVE OF OBSERVATION: To examine the level of teaching standards exhibited by a particular teacher

Instructions to the Observer: Prior to your observation, read carefully over each principle and key indicators. During and after your observation, put a mark (✓) on the rating scale that best describes what you observed. The check may be either on one number or between two numbers. NOTE: This rating is based on one observation and does not constitute a complete evaluation of the teacher's sophistication or effectiveness.

Content Pedagogy

Principle 1

The teacher understands the central concepts, tools of inquiry, and structures of the discipline he or she teaches and can create learning experiences that make these aspects of subject matter meaningful for students.

KEY INDICATORS:

- Demonstrates an understanding of the central concepts of his or her discipline.
- Uses explanations and representations that link curriculum to prior learning.
- Evaluated resources and curriculum materials for appropriateness to the curriculum and instructional delivery.
- Engages students in interpreting ideas from a variety of perspectives.
- Uses interdisciplinary approaches to teaching and learning.
- Uses methods of inquiry that are central to the discipline.

1	2	3	✓ 4	5
Limited Sophistication		Moderate Sophistication		High Sophistication

Student Development

Principle 2

The teacher understands how children learn and develop, and can provide learning opportunities that support a child's intellectual, social, and personal development.

KEY INDICATORS:

- Evaluates student performance to design instruction appropriate for social, cognitive, and emotional development.
- Creates relevance for students by linking with their prior experiences.
- Provides opportunities for students to assume responsibility for and be actively engaged in their learning.

(continued)

- Encourages student reflection on prior knowledge and its connection to new information.
- Accesses student thinking as a basis for instructional activities through group/individual interaction and written work (listening, encouraging discussion, eliciting samples of student thinking orally and in writing).

1	2	3 ✓	4	5
Limited Sophistication		Moderate Sophistication		High Sophistication

Diverse Learners

Principle 3

The teacher understands how students differ in their approaches to learning and creates instructional opportunities that are adapted to diverse learners.

KEY INDICATORS:

- Designs instruction appropriate to students' stages of development, learning styles, strengths and needs.
- Selects approaches that provide opportunities for different performance modes.
- Accesses appropriate services or resources to meet exceptional learning needs when needed.
- Adjusts instruction to accommodate the learning differences or needs of students (time and circumstance of work, tasks assigned, communication and response modes).
- Uses knowledge of different cultural contexts within the community (socio-economic, ethnic, cultural) and connects with the learner through types of interaction and assignments.
- Creates a learning community that respects individual differences.

1	2 ✓	3	4	5
Limited Sophistication		Moderate Sophistication		High Sophistication

Multiple Instructional Strategies

Principle 4

The teacher understands and uses a variety of instructional strategies to encourage student development of critical thinking, problem solving, and performance skills.

KEY INDICATORS:

- Selects and uses multiple teaching and learning strategies (a variety of presentations/explanations) to encourage student in critical thinking and problem solving.
- Encourages students to assume responsibility for identifying and using learning resources.
- Assures different roles in the instructional process (instructor, facilitator, coach, audience) to accommodate content purpose, and learner needs.

1	2	3 ✓	4	5
Limited Sophistication		Moderate Sophistication		High Sophistication

(continued)

Motivation and Management

Principle 5

The teacher uses an understanding of individual and group motivation and behavior to create a learning environment that encourages positive social interaction, active engagement in learning, and self-motivation.

- Encourages clear procedures and expectations that ensure students assume responsibility for themselves and others, working collaboratively and independently and engages in purposeful learning activities.

- Engages students by relating lessons to students' personal interests, allowing students to have choices in their learning, and leading students to ask questions and solve problems that are meaningful to them.

- Organizes, allocates, and manages time, space and activities in a way that is conducive to learning.

- Organizes, prepares students for, and monitors independent and group work that allows for full and varied participation of all individuals.

- Analyzes classroom environment and interactions and makes adjustments to enhance social relationships, student motivation/engagement and productive work.

1	2	3 ✓	4	5
Limited Sophistication		Moderate Sophistication		High Sophistication

Communication and Technology

Principle 6

The teacher uses knowledge of effective verbal, nonverbal, and media communication techniques to foster active inquiry, collaboration, and supportive interaction in the classroom.

KEY INDICATORS:

- Models effective communication strategies in conveying ideas and information when asking questions (e.g., monitoring the effects of messages, restating ideas and drawing connection, using visual, aural, and kinesthetic cues, being sensitive to nonverbal cues both given and received).

- Provides support for learner expression in speaking, writing, and other media.

- Demonstrates that communication is sensitive to gender and cultural differences (e.g., appropriate use of eye contact, interpretation of body language and verbal statement, acknowledgement of and responsiveness to different modes of communication and participation.

- Uses variety of media communication tools to enrich learning opportunities.

1	2	3	4	✓ 5
Limited Sophistication		Moderate Sophistication		High Sophistication

Planning

Principle 7

The teacher plans instruction based upon knowledge of subject matter, students, the community, and curriculum goals.

KEY INDICATORS:

- Plans lessons and activities to address variation in learning styles and performance modes, multiple development levels of diverse learners, and problem solving and exploration.

- Develops plans that are appropriate for curriculum goals and are based on effective instruction.

(continued)

- Adjusts plans to respond to unanticipated sources of input and/or student needs.
- Develops short- and long-range plans.

1	2	3 ✓	4	5
Limited Sophistication		Moderate Sophistication		High Sophistication

Assessment

Principle 8

The teacher understands and uses formal and informal assessment strategies to evaluate and ensure the continuous intellectual, social, and physical development of the learner.

KEY INDICATORS:

- Selects, constructs, and uses assessment strategies appropriate to the learning outcomes.
- Uses a variety of informal and formal strategies to inform choices about student progress and to adjust instruction (e.g., standardized test data, peer and student self-assessment, informal assessments such as observation, surveys, interviews, student work, performance tasks, portfolio, and teacher made tests).
- Uses assessment strategies to involve learners in self-assessment activities to help them become aware of their strengths and needs, and to encourage them to set personal goals for learning.
- Evaluates the effects of class activities on individuals and on groups through observation of classroom interaction, questioning and analysis of student work.
- Maintains useful records of student work and performance and can communicate student progress knowledgeably and responsibly.
- Solicits information about students' experiences, learning behavior, needs, and progress from parents, other colleagues, and students.

1	2	3 ✓	4	5
Limited Sophistication		Moderate Sophistication		High Sophistication

Reflective Practice

Principle 9

The teacher is a reflective practitioner who continually evaluates the effects of his or her choices and actions on others (student, parents, and other professionals in the learning community) who actively seeks out opportunities to grow professionally.

KEY INDICATORS:

- Uses classroom observation, information about students and research as sources for evaluating the outcomes of teaching and learning and as a basis for experimenting with, reflection on and revising practice.
- Uses professional literature, colleagues and other resources to support self-development as a learner and as a teacher.
- Consults with professional colleagues within the school and other professional arenas as support for reflection, problem solving and new ideas, actively sharing and seeking and giving feedback.

1	2	3	✓ 4	5
Limited Sophistication		Moderate Sophistication		High Sophistication

(continued)

School and Community Development

Principle 10

The teacher fosters relationships with school colleagues, parents, and agencies in the larger community to support student' learning and well being.

KEY INDICATORS:

- Participates in collegial activities designed to make the entire school a productive learning environment.
- Links with counselors, teachers of other classes and activities within the school, professionals in community agencies, and others in the community to support students' learning and well-being.
- Seeks to establish cooperative partnerships with parents/guardians to support student learning.
- Advocates for students.

1	2	3	4	✓	5
Limited		Moderate			High
Sophistication		Sophistication			Sophistication

Source: Robert F. Yinger. 1999. "The Role of Standards in Teaching and Teacher Education" in *The Education of Teachers.* National Society for the Study of Education (NSSE), pp. 100-101.

....

Referenced to INTASC Standards 1–10

....

For today's students to compete successfully in a global economy, they must become proficient with the use of technology. The *No Child Left Behind Act* established a new standard for all teachers "to demonstrate and integrate modern technology into curricula to support student learning" (National Commission on Teaching and America's Future, 2003, 7). The National Educational Technology Standards (NETS) were developed following enactment of this law (http://www.iste.org/standards/ March 2003).

Use the rating scale in Sample Form 12 to examine the educational technology standards of a teacher you are observing. Before completing this observation review the narrative found under the heading "Observing Teaching Standards" (p. 42). This scale, like Form 11, is most useful as a self-evaluation instrument.

SAMPLE FORM 12 A Rating Scale for Observation of Education Technology Standards for Teachers

NAME OF OBSERVER: James McKinney

DATE AND TIME OF OBSERVATION: October 21, 20—

LENGTH OF OBSERVATION: 30 minutes

TEACHER: Martha Matteu

GRADE LEVEL OBSERVED: Eleventh grade

OBJECTIVE OF OBSERVATION: To examine the level of educational technology standards exhibited by a particular teacher.

Instructions to the Observer: Prior to your observation, read over each standard carefully. During and after your observation, put a check on the rating scale that best describes what you observed. The check may be either on, or between, the numbers 1–5.

(continued)

Note: This observation is based on one limited observation.

1. Technology operations and concepts

Teacher demonstrates a sound understanding of technology operations and concepts.

1	2	3	4 ✓	5
Limited Sophistication		Moderate Sophistication		High Sophistication

2. Planning and designing learning environments and experiences

Teachers plan and design effective learning environments and experiences supported by technology.

1	2	3	4 ✓	5
Limited Sophistication		Moderate Sophistication		High Sophistication

3. Teaching, learning, and the curriculum

Teachers implement curriculum plans that include methods and strategies for applying technology to maximize student learning.

1	2	✓ 3	4	5
Limited Sophistication		Moderate Sophistication		High Sophistication

4. Assessment and evaluation

Teachers apply technology to facilitate a variety of effective assessment and evaluation strategies.

1	2	✓ 3	4	5
Limited Sophistication		Moderate Sophistication		High Sophistication

5. Productivity and professional practice

Teachers use technology to enhance their productivity and professional practices.

1	2 ✓	3	4	5
Limited Sophistication		Moderate Sophistication		High Sophistication

6. Social ethical, legal, and human issues

Teachers understand the social, ethical, legal and human issues surrounding the use of technology in PK-12 schools and apply that understanding in practice.

1	2	3	✓ 4	5
Limited Sophistication		Moderate Sophistication		High Sophistication

Source: National Educational Technology Project (NETS) http://www.iste.org/standards/. March 2003.

Referenced to INTASC Standards 1–10

The Importance of Teacher-Parent Relationships

Educators have always known that parents or guardians make a huge difference in each student's school experience. It is parents or guardians who provide their children with what they need to begin school and it is parents or guardians who support the learning process by helping their children with their homework, being present at school events and conferences, and making it clear to their children that it is the child's job to go to school and to do well. However, it is teachers who make the supportive role of the parents or guardians easy or difficult. Now, you must begin to build relationships with your students' parents or guardians. These relationships are key to your students' success and required of effective teachers.

The last two INTASC standards relate to teacher/parent or guardian relationships. Principle 9 states that "the teacher is a reflective practitioner who continually evaluates the effects of his/her choices and actions on others (students, parents, other professionals in the learning community) and who actively seeks out opportunities to grow professionally."

Principle 10 states that "the teacher fosters relationships with school colleagues, parents and agencies in the larger community to support students' learning and well-being" (Council of Chief State Officers, 1992, 1).

The National Coalition for Parent Involvement in Education (NCPIE) has been working to create meaningful family-school partnerships in every school in America. Recent research from NCPIE has found that when parents and teachers work together:

- Parents are more able to exchange information with their child's teacher.
- Parent can have a more active role in decision making (discipline, assessment, learning styles, etc.).
- Students gain higher grades and test scores.
- Students attend school more regularly.
- Students have a more positive attitude toward school.
- Teacher morale improves.

One of the principles of the National Commission on Teaching and America's Future states that "schools must forge close ties with parents." The report asserts that each student in middle and high schools should have the same advisor for more than one year, with multiple conferences scheduled throughout the year, rather than just the frenzied back-to-school nights when parents dash from class to class (2003, 57). This, according to the report, will encourage better student-teacher-parent relationships.

Dr. Sara Lawrence-Lightfoot, a sociologist and Professor of Education at Harvard University, believes that children, beginning in the early years, should be present and given a voice at parent-teacher conferences. She states that children are the best interpreters and authorities of their own experiences and their presence helps the parent and teacher stay focused on the purpose of the conference. She is aware, however, there are times when parents and teachers need to speak privately, but believes these conversations should be the exception not the rule (The Essential Conversation, 2003, pp. 224, 225).

In September, 2003, New York City employed 1,200 parent coordinators who were charged with being other "parents first stop in their search for information." "The New York City school system hopes this will make it easier for parents to be involved in school affairs, to find the information they need, and to voice concerns when they have them" (Jacobson, L. September 17, 2003, 5).

What can you do to foster teacher-parent relationships during your preservice observation and teaching?

You can:

- Observe how your classroom teacher works with parents.
- Sit in on teacher–parent conferences.
- Involve parent, grandparent, and guardian volunteers whenever possible.
- Consider using parents, grandparents, and guardians to mentor children other than their own.
- Read letters and notes your classroom teacher sends to parents.
- Ask if you can communicate with the parents about particular students and projects, as you begin tutoring and teaching.
- Let parents know their time and involvement are appreciated.
- Ask parents when they are available to visit the classroom for a special project.
- Have a family night where parents and students play math games, conduct science experiments, and do research on the Internet together.
- Suggest that you have various times for parents and guardians to visit the classroom or attend conferences.
- Share quality multicultural children and young adult books with parents.
- Avoid having the attitude: "We're the experts—we expect you to accept this."
- Be courteous, make parents feel welcome and listen to them, especially when you receive complaints from parents about your practices.
- Do not hesitate to call parents when you need their help resolving a problem or issue with their child; make them partners in the resolution of the problem.
- Encourage parents to be involved in learning activities at home. (See Mrs. Bragg's letter to parents on the CD.)
- Suggest that your cooperating school and cooperating teacher experiment including children in some of the teacher–parent conference. (See comment on CD about an excellent reference on teacher–parent conferences.)

Using the Reflection Process

Have you ever found yourself in the midst of an argument and not know how to defend your point of view? Later you reflect on the discussion and say, "Why didn't I think of that then?" This is a common experience for all of us. Why is it that we know exactly what to say or do upon reflection? Many people refer to this as "20-20 hindsight." No doubt this is somewhat true; however, it is also true that we can improve our ability to react on the spot when we reflect on our words and actions and modify our behavior based on this reflection.

We discussed the process of reflection in Chapter 1. In this and subsequent chapters you will complete reflections after your observation and teaching. Reflection, according to a recent study, assists preservice teachers in examining their educational beliefs and perceptions and changing ill-founded beliefs to promote self-evaluation and change. This process is critical if teachers are to become the sophisticated professionals required by the INTASC standards (Minor, Onwuegbuzie, Witcher, and James, 2002, 5). Form 13 is the first of these Reflective Observation forms.

SAMPLE FORM 13   Reflective Observation of Teachers

NAME OF OBSERVER: Angela Alexander

DATE AND TIME OF REFLECTIVE OBSERVATION: March 30, 20—, 12:45 p.m.

TEACHER: Raymond Davenport

GRADE LEVEL AND/OR SUBJECT: Eighth grade; mathematics

OBJECTIVE OF OBSERVATION: To think carefully and reflect about your observation of teachers. Below are some guiding questions/statements related to each of the five steps in the reflection cycle (Chapter 1, p. 15). The questions/statements are directly related to the ten principles from the INTASC Standards (Chapter 2, pp. 43–47).

Instructions to the Observer: Use Form 12 to respond to the following questions after you have completed your observations of teachers.

1. **Select**
    a. What two types of observation did you complete?
    b. What principles from INTASC standards did you address?

2. **Describe**
    a. What grade level(s) did you observe?
    b. Briefly describe your anecdotal observations.
    c. Briefly describe your structured observations.
    d. Briefly describe the type of assessments you used.

3. **Analyze**
    a. How did your prior experience with observation of teachers influence this experience?
    b. How will your observation of different teaching styles affect your future teaching?
    c. How will your observation of educational technology standards affect your future teaching?

4. **Appraise**
    a. Describe the teacher-student interaction you observed. Was it appropriate?
    b. Did the ten principles based on the common core of standards (INTASC) influence your decision to become a teacher? Explain.

5. **Transform**
    a. What did you learn about teaching through your observation?
    b. What did you learn about types of assessment?
    c. How do you think this observation will help you in your future teaching?

Source: Adapted from North Carolina State Department of Public Instruction. *Performance Based Licensure,* Raleigh, NC, 1998–1999.

Referenced to INTASC Standards 8 and 9

Chapter Three
Observing Classrooms, Schools, and Curriculum

Anecdotal Observation of Classrooms, Schools, and Curriculum

Anecdotal observations can be completed while observing the classroom, the school, and the curriculum. These observations can reveal many interesting aspects of the operation of the school and its instructional program and how individual teachers adapt the instructional program to their students. In addition, these observations can show how teachers and schools deal with such things as brain research, as well as physical constraints such as overcrowding, lack of equipment, and poor facilities.

Anecdotal Observations of Classrooms

An anecdotal observation of classroom organization includes a description of the physical environment and its layout. It is important to include information about the lighting source and whatever classroom decoration is displayed.

SAMPLE FORM 14   Form for Anecdotal Record of Classroom Organization

NAME OF OBSERVER: Marvin Anderson

DATE AND TIME OF OBSERVATION: September 19, 20—, 8:15 a.m.

LENGTH OF OBSERVATION: 30 minutes

PERSON AND/OR EVENT OBSERVED: Mr. Schroeder's classroom

GRADE LEVEL AND/OR SUBJECT: Fourth grade; all subjects

OBJECTIVE OF OBSERVATION: To see how Mr. Schroeder's classroom is organized

Instructions to the Observer: As completely and accurately as possible, describe the organization of the classroom. Be sure to include as much detail as possible. Try to avoid making judgments.

The classroom is quite small for the 29 students. The students' desks are arranged in five rows of five or six desks each, with the chalkboard in the front. The desks have small cubbies in them

(continued)

and separate chairs. In the front of the room to the students' right is a stool and a small podium. To the students' left are windows that run the length of the room. The shades are pulled down against the morning sun. On the students' right are high windows that face the hallway; beneath these windows are bulletin boards. Mr. Schroeder's desk is at the rear of the classroom next to the exterior windows. Next to the window is a four-drawer file cabinet. On the other side of the teacher's desk is a student desk and chair. At the right rear is a student worktable and eight chairs. Behind the worktable, along most of the rear wall, are student cubbies and bookshelves. On the floor, there is a royal blue carpet that has many stains on it.

Light in the classroom is good. There is a lot of exterior light from outside and additional light from the hallway. The classroom is additionally lit by long fluorescent fixtures. Mr. Schroeder has a lamp on his desk, which is also lit. Under the exterior windows is a ledge. Under about one-quarter of the length of the ledge is the heating and cooling unit. The classroom is air-conditioned. Under the rest (of the ledge) there are bookcases and cabinets.

Above the front chalkboard is a bulletin board. On this board is a large poster with the classroom rules. Also on this bulletin board there are some mass-produced posters about the writing process and reading books. Near the center of this bulletin board, there is a group of a dozen or so hanging maps. On the bulletin boards to the students' right, there is an opening school display with all the students' photographs. Under each photo is a paper that each student wrote on the first day of school, introducing himself or herself to Mr. Schroeder. The next bulletin board is empty. Nearest the door to the hallway at the rear right are school announcements and the weekly list of classroom jobs. The jobs include plants, attendance, lunch monitor, hallway monitor, bus monitor, playground monitors, classroom monitors, and care of pets. The names of one or more students are listed next to each job. Along the top of the cubbies at the rear of the room there are plants. Next to the cubbies there is a watering can with a long spout. On top of one of the bookshelves there is an aquarium; nearby is a cage with two gerbils (I think).

Along the ledge, under the exterior windows, are what appear to be learning centers. Most seem to be related to the Revolutionary War. One deals with the battles of the revolution; another with the personalities of the war. I can't read the headings on the other two. Nearest the front of the room, on the ledge, there is a globe.

When the students enter the room it is very crowded. There is not much room between their desks, and they are continuously bumping into one another. It gets noisy very quickly. Mr. Schroeder is in the front of the room with the attendance monitor for the week, taking attendance and collecting lunch money. Several students are milling around the podium, trying to ask the teacher questions. Three boys are sitting at the table at the rear of the room. Mr. Schroeder walks up to them to tell them that they will have new desks by the end of the week, though he's not quite sure where they'll put them. The students on the left side of the room are so close to the ledge that it would not be possible to use the learning centers without moving their desks. (I'll watch to see how Mr. Schroeder handles this later.) A girl raises her hand and asks if she can go to the restroom to get water for the gerbils. Mr. Schroeder says, "Take the restroom pass and the watering can, and also get enough water for the plants." She leaves.

The intercom clicks on and Mr. Schroeder attempts to "shush" the talking students. They get quieter but continue to talk. He walks to the rear of the room and flicks the lights; most of the students quiet down. However, the boys at the rear table are still talking. He walks over to them, and points to the classroom rules, one of which is "Respect others when they are speaking." They quiet down.

When the announcements are over, Mr. Schroeder has each of the three boys go to a chart under the class rules and put a check next to his name. If the students get five checks during the week, they cannot participate in Fun Friday, which is an event that occurs each Friday afternoon.

Another method of classroom observation is to draw a simple diagram of the classroom, illustrating the seating arrangement and the placement of furniture and equipment. Since a diagram cannot show what is on the bulletin boards or walls, the observer should discuss these elements after mapping the classroom.

....

Referenced to INTASC Standards 1–3 and 5

....

SAMPLE FORM 15   Form for a Classroom Map

NAME OF **O**BSERVER: Kim Philbeck

DATE AND **T**IME OF **O**BSERVATION: September 16, 20—, 9:15 a.m.

PERSON AND/OR **E**VENT **O**BSERVED: Mrs. Romano

GRADE **L**EVEL AND/OR **S**UBJECT: Eleventh grade; American history

OBJECTIVE OF **O**BSERVATION: To determine how the organization of the classroom relates to instruction, management, and motivation of students

Instructions to the Observer: First, draw a map of the classroom you are observing, including seating arrangements, placement of furniture, computers, telephone, and other equipment. Then, give a brief anecodotal description of these classroom elements: use of technology, lighting, traffic patterns, instructional displays, management, and motivational elements.

1. Draw classroom map:

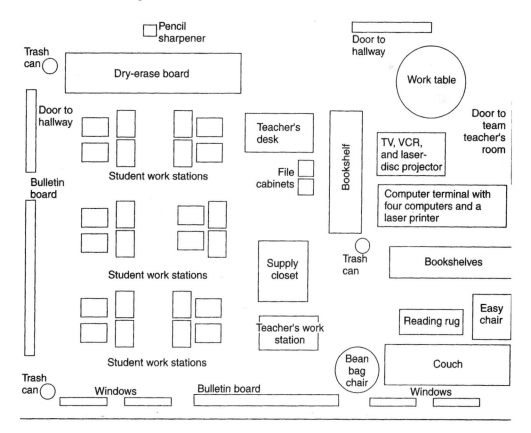

Courtesy of Kim Philbeck and Stephanie Price, Preservice teachers, UNC Ashville.

(continued)

2. Anecdotal description of classroom elements:

The students' desks are arranged in clusters because group work is one of the main instructional strategies used by Mrs. Romano. However, the students also have enough space in between the desks to work independently. Some of the students have to twist their heads around or move their seats to be facing the dry-erase board and the main instructional area of the classroom. Mrs. Romano is very flexible, however, and allows students to move their desks to face the front of the room during instructional time. When the time comes to work in small groups, the students move their desks back into clusters. The clusters of desks are spread out so the teacher can easily move around the room to reach each student. A reading corner with comfortable seating and many books is in the corner of the classroom. Supplies are centrally located with plenty of floor space surrounding the supply closet and the teacher's work station (where homework and assignments are turned in), since those are high-traffic areas. They also have storage space under their desktops.

(a) Use of Technology:

The classroom contains four computer terminals and is equipped with a laser printer. There is also one laptop, usually used by the teacher, but can be checked out by the students. Students are assigned computer time each week to draft papers (students are learning how to use desktop publishing to publish their work) or use other educational software. A TV, VCR, DVD and laserdisc projector are located on a rolling cart beside the computer terminals. The cart can be rolled to the main instructional area when the equipment is used in presentations. Mrs. Romano's computer is facing away from students' desks to deter wandering eyes. The file cabinet is located in the corner behind her desk and is not accessible to the students.

(b) Lighting and Traffic Patterns:

The students' desks are facing the board rather than facing the door or windows. This is to prevent students' preoccupation with events outside of the classroom. It also makes it easier for them to see the board since the light is not in their eyes. In the corner of the room, Mrs. Romano has a designated private area. The computer terminals are separated from the student workstations and the reading corner by bookcases, which ensures as little disruption as possible for students in all spaces in the classroom. The overhead projector is permanently located so it remains safe and does not block the students' view of the board. Students can enter and exit by either side or center aisles.

(c) Instructional Displays, Management, and Motivational Elements:

There are two long bulletin boards. The side bulletin board contains things pertinent to what is to be covered. There are numerous displays on the bulletin boards across the wall and opposite the window wall. Rules and consequences are posted on the front wall so students will be reminded of them daily. Resources are located in the back of the room and out of students' way until they are needed. There is also a table in the back corner for peer tutoring. There are computers in the room for students to use if they finish early with classwork. Mrs. Romano models procedures on one of the classroom computers; then students can go to the library or computer lab to carry out individual work. Classroom computers are used only for word processing and Internet research. Students must sign up to use computers. Their usage is limited to 30 minutes. Parents have to sign a form before students can use the Internet.

Referenced to INTASC Standards 1, 2, and 4–7

Many other anecdotal observations of the classroom can be useful. For example, you can focus on the instructional elements of the classroom or on how the students move throughout the classroom for certain purposes. Marvin notes in his anecdotal discussion of Mr. Schroeder's classroom that it is crowded, and that three of the students do not yet have their own desks. Marvin may want to spend part of a day observing how Mr. Schroeder deals with this problem. If the students are using the learning centers during social studies, what happens to the student desks nearest the ledge? Does Mr. Schroeder use the rear table for reading or other groups? What happens to the three children if they are not a part of the group using the table? When students leave the classroom for special classes, how do they do so without disturbing the other students?

Classroom Organization: Implications of Brain Research

Brain-related research influences not only how we teach, but also how classrooms are organized (Lackney, 1998). You can see many of the following in the classroom map above. Look around the classroom in which you are observing. Which of these important brain research-related elements do you find?

- Rich stimulating environment—color, texture, "teaching architecture," displays created by students to connect students with and provide ownership of the product.
- Places for group learning—breakout spaces, alcoves, "living rooms" for conversation, table groupings to facilitate social learning and the social brain.
- Linking indoor and outdoor spaces—facilitation of movement from inside to outside.
- Safe places—a feeling of security and safety especially in urban environments.
- Variety—different shapes, colors, lighting, nooks and crannies.
- Changing displays—a changing environment that encourages interaction and stimulates brain development; stage set type construction.
- Availability of resources—wet areas for science, computer-rich workspaces, multiple functions of workspaces to provide educational and physical variety and close proximity of necessary resources to encourage creativity and the rapid development of ideas.
- Active and passive spaces—areas for reflection to encourage intrapersonal intelligence as well as active work areas to encourage interpersonal intelligence.
- Personalized space—homeyness and uniqueness of the space, allowing learners to express their self-identity and personalize their own workspace.

Anecdotal Observations of Schools

Similar anecdotal observations can be done on various aspects of an entire school. Observing students in hallways during a change of class periods can reveal a great deal about the organization of the school. It is also interesting to examine the "decorations" in the hallways. Are there bulletin boards displaying student work? Do the bulletin boards have locked glass doors? Are there display cabinets in the hallways? What is in these cabinets? Are the hallways well lit? Do the students have individual lockers? Where are the various school administrative offices? Are they easily accessible to students, teachers, and visitors? How are the offices furnished? What are the "decorations" in the offices, such as the guidance office, that cater to students? What are the school's grounds like? How about the lunchroom, auditorium, and gym? Are there public areas in which students gather? Where are they, and what are they like? What is the playground like? Is there playground equipment? Examining all of these elements helps you become more familiar with the school.

Anecdotal Observations of Curriculum

Anecdotal observations can also be used to examine the curriculum. The observer in Mr. Schroeder's classroom might want to know more about the social studies curriculum. He might write an anecdotal observation that includes information about the text and other classroom materials. Or, he might discuss more detailed information about the learning centers. The observer might seek out the school, district, or state curriculum guide to learn the competencies, goals, and objectives for fourth-grade social studies. How does what Mr. Schroeder is teaching relate to the required standards of the school, district, or state? The observer might compare Mr. Schroeder's interpretation of the curriculum in his lessons with the interpretation of another fourth-grade teacher. All of these elements tell a great deal about the school, its curriculum, and its instructional policies.

Structured Observation of Classrooms, Schools, and Curriculum

Structured observations of classrooms, schools, and curriculum can be conducted by using the techniques of coding, checklists, interviews, and surveys. Structured observations allow you look for very specific elements. Instruments may be developed by you, adapted from other sources, or copied from this text.

Observing the Social Environment in a Classroom

There are numerous ways to look at the social environment in a classroom. We will discuss one way that is based on the research of Talcott Parsons and Edward A. Shills (1951) and Herbert J. Walberg and Gary J. Anderson (1968). Their research has led to the development of fifteen dimensions of a classroom social environment. Those dimensions, with brief descriptions developed by Gary D. Borich (1990), are as follows:

1. **Cohesiveness**—When a group of individuals interacts for a period of time, a feeling of intimacy or togetherness develops. Too much cohesiveness within a classroom may separate members of the group from nonmembers, and reduce the motivation and willingness of some students to become engaged in the learning process. Too little cohesiveness may discourage students from an allegiance to group norms and encourage them to focus exclusively on their own personal interests and desires.

2. **Diversity**—The extent to which the class provides for different student interests and activities is important to school learning. Too much diversity in a classroom can make teaching to the average student difficult, while too little may fail to respond to individual learning needs.

3. **Formality**—The extent to which behavior within a class is guided by formal rules can influence the flexibility both teacher and students may need to achieve stated goals. A classroom with an extensive or inflexible system of rules and procedures may be less productive than a classroom with fewer rules that are phased in and out or changed periodically to accommodate changing goals and conditions.

4. **Speed**—Student commitment to the goals of the class is best achieved when students feel they are learning at the same rate as other students. Too fast a pace will discourage a commitment to group goals for less able learners, while too slow a pace will discourage a commitment from more able learners.

5. **Environment**—The classroom physical environment, including the amount of space and type of equipment, can influence the structure of the group and relationships among its members. Generally the more the classroom reflects the world outside, the more opportunity there is to learn from its environment.

6. **Friction**—This refers to the extent to which certain students are responsible for class tension and hostility among members of the class. The greater the friction, the more time spent on classroom management, leaving the students less task-oriented.

7. **Goal direction**—Clearly stated goals and their acceptance by the group orient the class and provide expected roles for class members. Students in highly goal-directed classes are expected to reach instructional goals more quickly than those in classes where the goals are unspecified.

8. **Favoritism**—This indicates the extent to which some students and the teacher behave in ways that benefit some at the expense of others. A classroom in which there are many "favorites" lessens the self-concepts of those who are not and disengages them from a commitment to class goals.

9. **Cliquishness**—Cliques within a class can lead to hostility among class members and alternate norms, causing less optimal group productivity. A high degree of cliquishness can distract and cause them to move off-task, especially during group work when students may be loyal to the clique and not obedient to the teacher.

10. **Satisfaction**—Student's learning abilities are affected when they gain a sense of accomplishment from completing the events and activities that are assigned. Low satisfaction or low sense of accomplishment leads to greater frustration and less interest in the class, eventually reducing a student's need to achieve.

11. **Disorganization**—Class disorganization is believed to be related to reduced instructional time and, therefore, reduced opportunity to learn. Extreme disorganization can result in classroom management problems and large increases in the time needed to achieve instructional goals.

12. **Difficulty**—Generally, students who perceive the content as easy tend to perform more poorly on measures of achievement than those who do not. A high degree of perceived difficulty, however, will make some students give up and disengage from the learning task.

13. **Apathy**—Students who fail to see the purpose or relevance of class activities to themselves perform more poorly than those who do. Those students fail to behave according to the accepted group norms, which increases both the rate of misbehavior and the time spent on classroom management.

14. **Democratic**—This indicates where the class perceives itself on the authoritarian-democratic continuum. Optimal learning may occur under both extremes, depending on the degree of warmth perceived by students. An authoritarian climate in which the teacher is warm and nurturing may be as productive for learning as a democratic climate in which students have greater control over their learning environment.

15. **Competitiveness**—The effect of competitiveness has been shown to differ widely both within and across classrooms. Too little or too much competitiveness is believed to be detrimental to learning, with repetitive cycles of competition and cooperation being optimal.

Based on these dimensions, Borich developed a coding scale on which the observer indicates the level to which three elements of each dimension are observed in the classroom. An average score for each dimension on this scale, particularly when it is employed several times in the same classroom, can help you become aware of various elements of a classroom's social environment. Borich points out that the scale is not appropriate for research purposes, but is particularly useful if you complete several administrations of it while observing a variety of grouping patterns, across subject areas, over a long period of time.

SAMPLE FORM 16   Form for Coding Scale of Classroom Social Environment

NAME OF OBSERVER: Enrique Valdez

DATE AND TIME OF OBSERVATION: January 15, 20—, 10:40 a.m.

LENGTH OF OBSERVATION: 50 minutes

PERSON AND/OR EVENT OBSERVED: Sara Schmidtson's classroom

GRADE LEVEL AND/OR SUBJECT: First grade; mathematics

OBJECTIVE OF OBSERVATION: To observe the classroom social environment

Instructions to the Observer: Before using the coding scale, become familiar with each of the fifteen dimensions that describe the classroom social environment found on pages 58–59.

Each dimension is divided into three elements (or statements). Each of these three elements appears in the same order, once per set, in the three sets that comprise the coding scale.

To use the coding scale effectively, you should circle the appropriate rating and average the scores *for all three statements* in any given dimension(s) you want to examine. For example, to study classroom diversity, you would compare the scores for numbers 2, 17, and 32.

The scale may also be used to determine what you might want to examine further. Thus, after one or more classroom observations, you may want to average the scores for all three sets, and then pick out those that stand out in some way.

When scoring, you should note the following: (1) some statements are phrased negatively and, thus, their ratings have been reversed, and (2) in several of the dimensions being measured (diversity, speed, difficulty, democracy, and competitiveness), a higher score is not necessarily more desirable.

Dimension Elements	Strongly Disagree	Disagree	Agree	Strongly Agree	No Information
Set 1					
1. A student in this class has the chance to get to know all the students (cohesiveness).	1	2	3	(4)	N/I
2. The class has students with many different interests (diversity).	1	2	3	(4)	N/I
3. There is a set of rules for the students to follow (formality).	1	2	3	(4)	N/I
4. Most of the class has difficulty keeping up with the assigned work (speed).	1	(2)	3	4	N/I
5. The books and equipment students need or want are easily available in the classroom (environment).	1	2	3	(4)	N/I
6. There are tensions among certain students that tend to infere with class activities (friction).	1	(2)	3	4	N/I

(continued)

Dimension Elements	Strongly Disagree	Disagree	Agree	Strongly Agree	No Information
7. Most students have little idea of what the class is attempting to accomplish (goal direction).	(4)	3	2	1	N/I
8. The better students' questions are answered more sympathetically than those of the average students (favoritism).	1	2	(3)	4	N/I
9. Some students refuse to mix with the rest of the class (cliquishness).	1	2	(3)	4	N/I
10. The students seem to enjoy their classwork (satisfaction).	1	2	(3)	4	N/I
11. There are long periods during which the class does nothing (disorganization).	(1)	2	3	4	N/I
12. Some students in the class consider the work difficult (difficulty).	1	2	(3)	4	N/I
13. Few students seem to have a concern for the progress of the class (apathy).	4	(3)	2	1	N/I
14. When group discussions occur, all students tend to contribute (democracy).	1	(2)	3	4	N/I
15. Most students cooperate rather than compete with one another in this class (cooperativeness).	4	3	(2)	1	N/I
Set 2					
16. Students in this class are in close enough contact to develop likes and dislikes one another (cohesiveness).	4	(3)	2	1	N/I
17. The class is working toward many different goals (diversity).	1	(2)	3	4	N/I
18. Students who break the rules are penalized (formality).	1	2	3	(4)	N/I
19. Most of the class covers the prescribed amount of work in the time given (speed).	4	3	(2)	1	N/I
20. A comprehensive collection of reference materials is available in the classroom for students to use (environment).	1	(2)	3	4	N/I

(continued)

Dimension Elements	Strongly Disagree	Disagree	Agree	Strongly Agree	No Information
21. Certain students seem to have no respect for other students (friction).	1	2	③	4	N/I
22. The objectives of the class are not clearly recognized (goal direction).	④	3	2	1	N/I
23. Not every member of the class is given the same privileges (favoritism).	4	3	②	1	N/I
24. Certain students work only with their close friends (cliquishness).	1	2	③	4	N/I
25. There is considerable student dissatisfaction with the classwork (satisfaction).	④	3	2	1	N/I
26. Classwork is frequently interrupted by some students with nothing to do (disorganization).	4	③	2	1	N/I
27. Most students in this class are constantly challenged (difficulty).	1	②	3	4	N/I
28. Some members of the class don't care what the class does (apathy).	1	2	③	4	N/I
29. Certain students have more influence on the class than others (democracy).	4	3	2	①	N/I
30. Most students in the class want their work to be better than their friends' work (competitiveness).	1	2	③	4	N/I

Set 3

Dimension Elements	Strongly Disagree	Disagree	Agree	Strongly Agree	No Information
31. This class is made up of individuals who do not know each other well (cohesiveness).	4	③	2	1	N/I
32. Different students are interested in different aspects of the class (diversity).	4	3	②	1	N/I
33. There is a right and wrong way of going about class activities (formality).	④	3	2	1	N/I
34. There is little time in this class for daydreaming (speed).	4	3	②	1	N/I
35. There are bulletin board displays and pictutes around the room (environment).	4	3	2	①	N/I
36. Certain students in this class are uncooperative (friction).	1	2	3	④	N/I

(continued)

Dimension Elements	Strongly Disagree	Disagree	Agree	Strongly Agree	No Information
37. Most of the class realizes exactly how much work is required (goal direction).	1	2	3	(4)	N/I
38. Certain students in the class are favored over others (favoritism).	(1)	2	3	4	N/I
39. Most students cooperate equally well with all class members (cliquishness).	4	3	2	(1)	N/I
40. After an assignment, most students have a sense of satisfaction (satisfaction).	1	2	3	(4)	N/I
41. The class is well-organized and efficient (disorganization).	4	3	2	(1)	N/I
42. Most students consider the subject matter easy (difficulty).	4	3	(2)	1	N/I
43. Students show a common concern for the success of the class (apathy).	4	3	2	(1)	N/I
44. Each member of the class has as much influence as does any other member (democracy).	4	3	2	(1)	N/I
45. Students compete to see who can do the best work (competitiveness).	(4)	3	2	1	N/I

Source: Gary Borich. *Observation Skills for Effective Teaching,* pp.113–115, 1990.

Referenced to INTASC Standards 1–8

Student Assessments Used in the Classroom

Because students learn in different ways, it is important that teachers develop diverse techniques for assessing student skills and progress. Following is a checklist to help you indicate the evaluation tools used in the classroom to assess student work.

SAMPLE FORM 17   Checklist to Determine Student Assessments in the Classroom

NAME OF OBSERVER: Loyda Chacon

DATE AND TIME OF OBSERVATION: December 12, 20—, 8:45 a.m.

PERSON AND/OR EVENT OBSERVED: Mr. Ramos

GRADE LEVEL AND/OR SUBJECT: Fourth grade

SCHOOL: Riverside Elementary

OBJECTIVE OF OBSERVATION: To determine various assessment techniques

Instructions to the Observer: After structured observation or an interview with the classroom teacher, put a check in the appropriate column. List additional assessments where required next to items marked with an asterisk.

Type of Assessment	Observed	From Interview
1. Commercial Workbooks in Curricular Areas Reading Mathematics Science Social Studies Language Arts Others* (*handwriting*)	/ / / /	
2. Duplicated Sheets	/	/
3. Homework Assignments		/
4. Oral Presentation/Report		/
5. Hands-On Performance Computers Science Experiment Construction Project Dramatic Performances/Skits Chalkboard Work Art Project Musical Production Classroom Displays/Bulletin Board School Displays Others*	/ / / / / / /	/ / /

(continued)

Type of Assessment	Observed	From Interview
6. Written Work Reports Research Projects Creative Writing Others*	/ /	/
7. Teacher-Made Tests		/
8. Prepared Tests from Students' Texts		/
9. Standardized Tests		/
10. State Competency Tests		/
11. State End-of-Year Tests		/
12. Anecdotal Records Writing Journals/Folders Art Folders Cumulative Record Folders Portfolios Others*	/ /	/ /
13. Others*		

Referenced to INTASC Standards 1–9

Examining the Teaching of Required Material

Most schools have a guide describing the required curriculum for each subject and the skills or competencies that the students are expected to learn. The guide may be produced at the school or school district level and is usually based on state requirements. A checklist for examining which competency is actually performed in the classroom can be designed based on the objectives or content outline of any curriculum guide. For example, if you are observing in a seventh-grade history class as in the sample below, you can design a checklist based on what the students are required to learn in history, according to the curriculum guide. As you observe, you can check off those activities that are actually performed. Sample Form 18, a checklist based on 2003 goals and performance indicators set by the North Carolina State Department of Public Instruction for eleventh-grade history, is partially listed below and is not filled in because the method is relatively simple, and each state will have its own curricular requirements. Form 18 can be found at the end of the book on page 194. You should design your own checklist based on the curricular requirements in the school in which you are observing.

SAMPLE FORM 18   Checklist of Goals and Objectives Covered in a Seventh-Grade History Classroom

NAME OF OBSERVER: Julie Lo

DATE AND TIME OF OBSERVATION: October 14, 20—, 11:00 a.m.

TEACHER: Mr. Siskell

SCHOOL: Freedom Middle School

OBJECTIVE OF OBSERVATION: To acquaint the observer with a curriculum guide, then list the competency goals and objectives for a subject being taught in the school observed

Instructions to the Observer: Use the list of goals and objectives from a curriculum guide to develop your own checklist. For an example of a checklist of goals and performance indicators in a seventh-grade history classroom, see below. If the competency, goal, objective and/or performance indicator is observed, place an "X" in the right-hand column.

(continued)

Competency Goals	Objectives	Observed
1. The learner will use the five theses of geography and geographic tools to answer geographic questions and analyze geographic concepts.	1.01 Create maps, chards, graphs, databases, and models as tools to illustrate information about different people, places and regions in Africa, Asia, and Australia.	X
	1.02 Generate, interpret, and manipulate information from tools such as maps, globes, charts, graphs, databases, and models to pose and answer questions about space and place, environment and society, and spatial dynamics and connections.	X
	1.03 Use tools such as maps, globes, charts, databases, models, and artifacts to compare date on different countries of Africa, Asia, and Australia and to identify patterns as well as similarities and differences.	X
2. The learner will assess the relationship between physical environment and cultural characteristics of selected societies and regions of Africa, Asia, and Australia	2.01 Identify key physical characteristics such as landforms, water forms, and climate and evaluate their influence on the development of cultures in selected African, Asian and Australian regions.	X
	2.02 Describe factors that influence changes in distribution patterns of population, resources, and climate in selected regions of Africa, Asia, and Australia and evaluate their impact on the environment.	X
3. The learner will analyze the impact of interactions between humans and their physical environments in Africa, Asia, and Australia.	3.01 Identify ways in which people of selected areas in Africa, Asia, and Australia have used, altered, and adapted to their environments in order to meet their needs and evaluate the impact of their actions on the development of cultures and regions.	X
	3.02 Describe the environmental impact of regional activities such as deforestation, urbanization, and industrialization and evaluate their significance to the global community	X
	3.03 Examine the development and use of tools and technologies and assess their influence on the human ability to use, modify, or adapt to their environment.	X
	3.04 Describe how physical processes such as erosion, earthquakes, and volcanoes have resulted in physical patterns on the earth's surface and analyze the effects on human activities.	X
4. The learner will identify significant patterns in the movement of people, goods, and ideas over time and place in Africa, Asia, and Australia.	4.01 Describe the patterns of and motives for migrations of people, and evaluate the impact on the political, economic, and social development of selected societies and regions.	X
	4.02 Identify the main commodities of trade over time in selected areas of Africa, Asia, and Australia and evaluate their significance for the economic, political, and social development of cultures and regions.	X

(continued)

Competency Goals	Objectives	Observed
	4.03 Examine key et+hical ideas anad values deriving from religious, artistic, political, economic, and educational traditions, as well as their diffusion over time, and assess their influence on the development of selected societies and regions in Africa, Asia, and Australia.	X
5. The learner will evaluate the varied ways people of Africa, Asia, and Australia make decisions about the allocation and use of economic resources.	5.01 Describe the relationship between the location of natural resources and economic development, and analyze the impact on selected cultures, countries, and regions in Africa, Asia, and Australia.	X
	5.02 Examine the different economic systems (traditional, command, and market) developed in selected societies in Africa, Asia, and Australia, and assess their effectiveness in meeting basic needs.	X

Source: Adapted from North Carolina Department of Public Instruction, *North Carolina Social Studies Standard Course of Study.* Raleigh, NC, 2003, 45-49.

....
Referenced to INTASC Standards 1–9
....

Examining Curriculum Strategies That Address Multiple Intelligences

You have probably already studied Howard Gardner's theory of multiple intelligences. The first seven intelligences were documented by Gardner in 1983. In 1996, he added the eighth. According to Gardner, the following eight intelligences are not fixed or static, can be taught and learned, and are multi-dimensional, occurring at multiple levels in the brain and body. Gardner's studies at Harvard University identified the following types of intelligence:

1. **Verbal/Linguistic**—The use of words.

2. **Logical/Mathematical**—The use of numbers and reasoning strategies.

3. **Spatial**—Involving pictures and images.

4. **Bodily**—Using the hands and body.

5. **Musical**—The use of tones, rhymes, and rhythms.

6. **Interpersonal**—Social understanding.

7. **Intrapersonal**—Self-knowledge.

8. **Naturalist**—Nature knowledge.

While some research seems to suggest that certain parts of the brain are more active during particular types of learning experiences, there is no evidence to show a direct correspondence between parts of the brain and particular intelligences. Until research reveals more about the neurological basis for multiple intelligence theory, the best strategy for educators is giving children the opportunity to engage in all modes of intelligence (Bergen and Coscia, 2001, 60).

Sample Form 19 is a checklist of possible teaching strategies for multiple intelligences that can be utilized and observed in the classroom. Form 19 (page 196) is the form you will use as you observe teaching, the classroom environment, and learning.

SAMPLE FORM 19 Examination of Curricular Strategies That Challenge Students' Multiple Intelligences

NAME OF OBSERVER: Oscar Miller

DATE AND TIME OF OBSERVATION: February 18, 20—, 9:00 a.m.

TEACHER: Mrs. Hewitt

SCHOOL: Hayden Elementary School

OBJECTIVE OF OBSERVATION: To observe curricular strategies that challenge students' multiple intelligences

Instructions to the Observer: A list of curricular descriptors that challenge students' multiple intelligences is given below. Place a check before each descriptor observed.

Visual/Spatial	Logical/Mathematical	Verbal/Linguistic	Bodily/Kinesthetic
✔ charts	✔ problem solving	✔ stories	✔ field trips
— graphs	— tangrams	✔ retelling	— activities
— photography	✔ geometry	✔ journals	✔ creative movement
— visual awareness	— measuring	— process writing	✔ hands-on experiments
— organizers	✔ classifying	— reader's theatre	✔ body language
✔ visual metaphors	✔ predicting	✔ storytelling	✔ manipulatives
— visual analogies	✔ logic games	— choral speaking	✔ physical education
✔ visual puzzles	— data collecting	— rehearsed reading	✔ crafts
— 3-D experiences	— serialing	✔ bookmaking	✔ drama
✔ painting	— attributes	✔ speaking	
✔ illustrations	✔ experimenting	— nonfiction reading	
— story maps	✔ puzzles	— research	
— visualizing	— manipulatives	— speeches	
— sketching	— scientific model	✔ presentations	
— patterning	✔ money	✔ listening	
— mind maps	✔ time	✔ reading	
✔ color	✔ sequencing	✔ read-aloud	
✔ symbols	— critical thinking	— drama	

(continued)

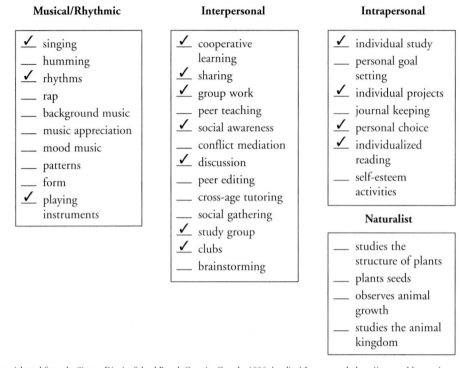

Musical/Rhythmic	**Interpersonal**	**Intrapersonal**
✓ singing	✓ cooperative learning	✓ individual study
___ humming	✓ sharing	___ personal goal setting
✓ rhythms	✓ group work	✓ individual projects
___ rap	___ peer teaching	___ journal keeping
___ background music	✓ social awareness	✓ personal choice
___ music appreciation	___ conflict mediation	✓ individualized reading
___ mood music	✓ discussion	___ self-esteem activities
___ patterns	___ peer editing	
___ form	___ cross-age tutoring	**Naturalist**
✓ playing instruments	___ social gathering	___ studies the structure of plants
	✓ study group	___ plants seeds
	✓ clubs	___ observes animal growth
	___ brainstorming	___ studies the animal kingdom

Source: Adapted from the Simcoe District School Board, Ontario, Canada, 1996. [on-line] Internet path: http://www.scdsb.on.ca/

Referenced to INTASC Standards 1–8

Brain Research Suggestions for Examining a Curriculum Guide

Examining the curriculum guide of the school, district, or state for the grade level and/or subject area you are observing can help you better understand the materials that are used in the classroom and the methods of instruction that are employed.

You might also want to examine the guide to see how brain research has influenced the type of instruction. Brain research suggests that the curriculum should have and be the following:

- Experiential, inquiry-based, and hands-on.
- Active with students doing, talking, and collaborating.
- Emphasis on higher-order thinking and learning a discipline's key concepts and principles.
- Deep study of a smaller number of topics so that students internalize the discipline's method of inquiry.
- More time devoted to reading whole, original, "real" books and materials.
- Responsibility for learning transferred to students (i.e.: goal-setting, record-keeping, monitoring, and evaluation).
- Choice for students (i.e.: selecting their own books, writings topics, team members, research projects).
- Democratic, allowing students to enact and model the principles of a democracy.
- Focus on affective needs and a variety of cognitive styles.
- Cooperative and collaborative, developing the classroom as an interdependent community.
- Heterogeneously grouped classrooms where individual needs are met through inherently individualized activities.
- Delivery of special help to students in the regular classroom.
- Varied and cooperative roles for teachers, parents, and administrators.
- Teachers' descriptive evaluation of student growth, including qualitative and anecdotal observations (Moffett, 1998, 6).

SAMPLE FORM 20   Form for Examining a Curriculum Guide

NAME OF OBSERVER: Sam Ruloff

DATE AND TIME OF OBSERVATION: November 22, 20—, 2:00 p.m.

OBJECTIVE OF EXAMINATION: To examine a curriculum guide and relate it to classroom curriculum

Instructions to the Examiner: Select a curriculum guide for the grade level and/or subject you will be observing. Complete this short answer survey.

1. Title of the guide: _The Visual Arts Curriculum Guide_

2. Check one: The guide is from the school ____; the school district ____; the state _✓_; other (specify) _____

3. Date of the guide: _2001_

4. Grade level(s) of the guide: _(7–9)—(10–12)_

5. Subject area(s) of the guide: _Art-Painting, Printing, Graphics, Ceramics, Jewelry,_ _Sculpture, Commercial Design, Weaving_

Answer the following yes/no or as indicated:

6. The guide includes: objectives _Yes_, student activities _Yes_, resources _Yes_, examples _Yes_, bibliographies _Yes_, computer software sources _No_, test banks _No_, discussion questions _No_, material for making transparencies _No_, content outlines _No_, other (specify) _Procedures—Slides, Films, Visiting Artists_

7. The guide suggests appropriate textbooks (specify): _Drawing with Ink, Creative_ _Embroidery, The Picture History of Painting_

8. The guide suggests appropriate supplemental books. _Yes_

9. The guide suggests appropriate references. _Yes_

10. The guide suggests appropriate educational media and technology. _Yes_

11. The guide suggests appropriate references. _Yes_

12. The guide suggests activities for different levels of students (i.e., learning disabled, gifted, advanced, basic, etc.). _Provides choices, in some areas. Suggestions for advanced/gifted._

Referenced to INTASC Standards 1–8

Examining Multicultural/Antibias Education in the Classroom

Examining multicultural/antibias education reflects a commitment to diversity and equity in the classroom. As you observe in your classroom, look for this commitment.

SAMPLE FORM 21 Checklist for a Multicultural/Antibias Education Evaluation

NAME OF OBSERVER: Loyola Hanks

DATE AND TIME OF OBSERVATION: March 6, 20—, 10:30 a.m.

SCHOOL: South Central Middle School

GRADE LEVELS OF SCHOOL: Fourth through seventh

OBJECTIVE OF OBSERVATION: To examine multicultural/antibias education in the classroom

Instructions to the Observer: After examining the school's curriculum (using Forms 18 and 20) and observing in numerous classrooms, complete the following evaluation checklist. Place a checkmark below the word or phrase that best describes your observations. Respond only to those items that were observable by you.

	Not at all	Some	Large Amount
1. The classroom environment is reflective of diversity.	____	____	X
2. Curriculum focuses on discrete pieces about cultures of various racial and ethnic groups.	____	____	X
3. Multicultural activities are added on to the "regular" curriculum (i.e., celebrating various holidays of other cultures).	____	____	X
4. Families or caregivers are asked to provide information about the most visible aspects of their cultural heritage (i.e., food, music, and holidays).	____	X	____
5. Languages of children (other than English) are used in songs or other communication.	____	____	X
6. The curriculum explores cultural differences among the children's families.	____	X	____
7. Staff members actively incorporate their children's daily life experiences into daily curriculum.	____	X	____
8. Curriculum and teacher-child interactions meet the cultural as well as individual developmental needs of their children.	____	____	X
9. Parents' or family caregivers' knowledge about their native cultural background is utilized.	____	X	____
10. Staff members intentionally encourage the children's development of critical thinking and tools for resisting prejudice and biased behaviors directed at themselves or others.	____	X	____
11. Staff members reflect the cultural and language diversity of the children and families they serve.	____	____	X

Source: Adapted from Louise Derman-Sparks. 1999. "Markers of Multicultural/Antibias Education." *Young Children.* 54(5) 43.

Referenced to INTASC Standards 1–8

A Survey of Media

In 1984 the national student-to-computer ratio was 125-to-1. In 2004 it was 5-to-1 (*Education Week*, May 6, 2004, 8, 9). No school today seems complete without a full complement of desktop (and even laptop) computers as well as other forms of technology. There has been a revolution in how students and teachers gather information. Only a few years ago almost all research was conducted through library searches. Today students can access information on almost every topic while sitting at desktop computers through the Internet.

The look of classrooms and the speed at which information can be acquired has changed dramatically in the last decade. The major reason for these changes is the type and amount of technology. In a survey of 500 teachers and media specialists conducted by Philips Electronics, they reported that the most common technology utilized in schools included: television, VCR's, computers, tape recorders, and overhead projectors. In the next five years the respondents indicated that they expect to see a growth in the use of DVD players, the wireless Internet, and interactive white boards (de Groot, 2002, 18-24).

Technology has assisted in the inclusion of special needs students into the classroom. Handheld computers allow some students who could not previously function in the classroom to succeed. In addition, all students' learning can be enhanced through the use of this technology (Bergen, 251).

Since so many teachers use multiple forms of technology in their classrooms, it is helpful for student observers to learn a methodology for examining them. Below are some forms that you can use to examine and evaluate some of the technology used in the classroom.

SAMPLE FORM 22   Form for Types and Uses of Media/Technology in the Classroom or Lab

NAME OF OBSERVER: Martha Henderson

DATE AND TIME OF OBSERVATION: May 15, 20—, 11:45 a.m.

SCHOOL: Westside Elementary School

TEACHER: Doris Kemp

GRADE LEVEL AND/OR SUBJECT: Fourth grade; social studies

OBJECTIVE OF OBSERVATION: To observe the types of technology available in the classroom and how it is being used in the instructional process

Instructions to the Observer: It is important to determine whether technology is used to augment instruction in subject areas for the students or whether it is used to teach students technological skills and/or how to use particular applications. Answer the following questions to help identify how technology is being used in the class you are observing.

1. List the types of media/technology you observed.

Computers, software, overhead and movie projectors, TV, laser printer, VCR, DVD.

(continued)

2. What is the objective(s) of the lesson being observed?

   To increase children's interest in reading books that support the social studies curriculum.

3. Does the use of technology match or reflect the learning objectives for the lesson?

   Yes.

4. How does the use of technology enhance the opportunity for students to meet the lesson's objectives?

   The software program allows students to explore over seventy-five novels, biographies,

   and other texts that support the social studies curriculum in American history.

5. Is technology used as a teaching tool by the teacher to present concepts and information in a particular subject area?

   Yes.

6. Is technology used to teach computer skills? If so, what skills?

   No.

7. Is the teacher's role during the lesson to guide students as they use technology or is his/her role to present information/skills?

   The teacher presented the database of books for use in social studies.

8. Is the use of the technology appropriate for the age and skill of the students?

   Yes.

9. Is equitable time provided for all students to use technology?

   Yes.

10. When technology is used, are students engaged in cooperative learning?

    No.

11. Is technology introduced for independent use, small-group use, or whole-class use?

    Independent or small-group work.

12. Does the lesson using technology provide an opportunity for student evaluation or feedback? If so, describe the opportunity. If not, ask the teacher why not.

    No. The teacher will ask for feedback at the end of the social studies unit.

Adapted from:: Jean Camp, Instructional Technology Coordinator, The University of North Carolina at Greensboro. Unpublished. Courtesy of Mary Olson, The University of North Carolina at Greensboro.

Referenced to INTASC Standards 1–8

A Survey of Computer Software

As computer software has become more readily available at affordable prices, it is increasingly important that teachers assess and evaluate the software not only in terms of its content, but also in terms of its appropriateness to the curriculum and the age and ability of the students. Likewise, student teachers should examine the software to determine if its maturity level and accuracy warrant its use with individuals, small groups, or the entire class. Recently assistive software, such as Braille printers and audible text readers, has been used to assist disabled children to succeed in the classroom. Sample Form 23 is a simple guide for examining computer software.

SAMPLE FORM 23   Software Evaluation Form

NAME OF EXAMINER: Jean Smith

DATE AND TIME OF EXAMINATION: March 17, 20—, 10:45 a.m.

SOFTWARE TITLE: Sounds and Letters

PUBLISHER: Software Support Publishing Company

PUBLICATION DATE: 1996

OBJECTIVE OF OBSERVATION: To increase students' knowledge of programs that focus on the Alphabetic Principle and Phonemic Awareness

Instructions to the Examiner: Determine the parameters of the software package by checking the appropriate blank. Answer the questions related to rating the software. Then rate the product on a scale of 1 to 4 (1 is the lowest and 4 is the highest).

I. Basic Background Information

A. Computer Platform:

IBM _____   Mac __X__

B. System Requirements:

Stand Alone _____   Hard Drive Memory __X__

Networked _____   RAM Memory __X__

Both _____

C. Format (check one):

Disk-Based __X__

CD-ROM _____

Laserdisc _____

D. Audience:

PreK–1st __X__   9th–12th _____

2nd–5th _____   Adult _____

6th–8th _____   Other _____

E. Software Type:

CAI/Drill and Practice   _____

Simulations   _____

(continued)

Problem-Solving Applications ___X___
Game Applications ___X___
Tool Applications _____
  Database _____
  Word Processing ___X___
  Spreadsheet _____
Tutorials ___X___
Grading/Student Information ___X___
Electronic Portfolio Assessment _____
Electronic Books ___X___
  Skill level accommodations ___X___
Multimedia authoring _____
Telecommunicating _____

F. Graphics: B/W _____ Color __X__ Animation __X__

G. Price: $375.00

H. Preview Policy: None _____ 30-day __X__ Other _____

II. Educational Objectives

A. State Purpose: To increase children's ability to hear phonemes within words

B. Subject Area Focus:

Math	_____	Reading	__X__	Art	_____
Foreign Language	_____	Social Studies	_____	Science	_____
Music	_____	Literature	_____	Other	_____

III. Questions to Consider When Evaluating Software

A. Does the content of the program reflect a sound learning theory? If so, which one? Is the program's subject matter accurate and logically presented?

Yes. The program reflects Vygotsky's beliefs. The content is sequenced logically and is accurate.

B. Does the program promote exploration and critical thinking?

Yes. Children have to make decisions about phonemes while using specified criteria.

C. Does the software span a range of skill abilities?

Yes.

D. Do students have control of the program? (i.e., Is it self-paced? Can they navigate through the program easily?)

Yes.

E. Can the program be adapted to large groups, small groups, and individual instruction?

Yes.

F. Does the program accommodate different ability levels?

Yes.

(continued)

G. Does the program provide supportive and positive feedback to students?

Yes.

H. Are teaching materials provided to accompany the program? If so, describe them.

Yes; puppets, games, rhymes, and stories to use in the classroom.

I. Is the program sensitive to multiculturalism? In what ways?

The program is neutral. It deals with sounds and letters.

J. Are the program directions clear enough to be used independently, or does the program require teacher support?

Requires teacher support initially and at identified sections prior to student self-pacing.

K. Does the school, classroom, or lab have the technical and educational support necessary to maximize the use of the program?

Yes.

L. Does the program have multimedia features? If so, do they enhance learning?

The program has multimedia features that increase the children's interest and motivation.

IV. Rating (Rate items on a scale of 1 to 4; 4 is the highest.)
   A. Usability   4
   B. Content   4
   C. Design   4
   D. Difficulty   4

Source: Designed by Jean Camp, Instructional Technology Coordinator, The University of North Carolina at Greensboro, Unpublished. Courtesy of Mary Olson, The University of North Carolina at Greensboro.

....
Referenced to INTASC Standards 1–10
....

A Study of the School and School Services

An excellent way to get to know how a school functions and what services it provides to students is to conduct interviews of school personnel using an interview checklist. The procedures for good interviews discussed in Chapter 2 of this guide, pages 41–42, should be carefully followed.

SAMPLE FORM 24   Checklist for School Personnel Interviews

NAME OF INTERVIEWER: Ramona Machung

DATES OF INTERVIEWS: November 6, 20—, December 20, 20—

SCHOOL: Mills River High School

OBJECTIVE OF OBSERVATION: To find out how a school functions and what services it provides

Instructions to the Interviewer: Schedule a conference with an appropriate person from each administrative division of the school. If a specific service is not identified, discuss with the principal or assistant principal how the school provides such a service or otherwise meets the needs of the students. Use checklists I–VI below to (1) formulate your questions and (2) ensure that you ask appropriate questions. You may add some of your own topics to the list. Check off each item for which you obtain an answer. Take notes in the space provided.

I. Guidance, Testing, Evaluation, and Reporting

NAME OF PERSON INTERVIEWED: Mr. Armstrong

TITLE OF PERSON INTERVIEWED: Guidance Counselor

DATE, TIME, AND PLACE OF INTERVIEW: December 3, 20—, 11:30 a.m., Mr. Armstrong's office

APPROXIMATE LENGTH OF INTERVIEW: 15 minutes

__X__	1.	Purpose of guidance program
__X__	2.	Procedures for obtaining services
__X__	3.	Services of guidance program (individual and group)
__X__	4.	Referral services
__X__	5.	Services for pregnant students and single parents
__X__	6.	Teachers' role in guidance
__X__	7.	Students' role in guidance
__X__	8.	Parents' role in guidance
__X__	9.	Standardized tests and purposes
__X__	10.	School's grading/reporting policies
__X__	11.	School's promotion/retention policies
__X__	12.	Academic advising and placement of students

Notes:
Serves students, teachers, administrators, and parents. Works with administrators and teachers on academic, psychological, and social placement and testing of students.

Tests: Group and individual IQ tests, state competency tests, reading and Iowa Tests of Basic Skills. Individual students come for help with social/behavioral problems, help with scholarships, and college selection. Helped develop sexuality education classes and set up daycare for single parents. Worked with social workers regarding the health of pregnant girls.

(continued)

II. Library or Media Center/Instructional Materials and Equipment

NAME OF PERSON INTERVIEWED: Mr. Andrade

TITLE OF PERSON INTERVIEWED: School Librarian/Media Specialist

DATE, TIME, AND PLACE OF INTERVIEW: December 6, 20—, 3:45 p.m., Library/Media Center

APPROXIMATE LENGTH OF INTERVIEW: 15 minutes

   X   1. Available library materials related to subject and/or grade level

   X   2. Library or media center hours for students and teachers

   X   3. Procedures for using library or media center (class/students/teachers)

   X   4. Vertical file and appropriate contents

   X   5. Computer indexing of library materials

   X   6. Equipment and media available for teachers' library/media center use

   X   7. Checkout policies for students, teachers, and classes

   X   8. Equipment and media available for classroom use

   X   9. Procedures for instructing students in library/media center use

   X 10. Assistance available for use of equipment and media

   X 11. Availability and procedures for computer use by students and teachers

   X 12. Procedures for selection and review of library materials and media

Notes:

Explained where fiction, nonfiction, and reference materials were for all curricular areas for sixth grade. Library open 8:10–3:30 daily for students, 7:30–4:30 for teachers. Both computer and vertical file indexing. Equipment: 3 movie projectors, 6 overhead projectors, 5 slide projectors, 1 opaque projector. Checked out first-come, first-served basis, but for 35 minutes at a time. Seven computers for student use in small room off media center. Chart of instructions about computer indexing and library and computer use.

III. Health Services

NAME OF PERSON INTERVIEWED: Mrs. Ginette Cortez

TITLE OF PERSON INTERVIEWED: Home-School Coordinator

DATE, TIME, AND PLACE OF INTERVIEW: December 13, 20—, 12:00 p.m., Health Clinic

APPROXIMATE LENGTH OF INTERVIEW: 20 minutes

   X   1. Available health services at school

   X   2. Services available through school referral

   X   3. Sex education and condom distribution

   X   4. Services for pregnant students

   X   5. Procedures for teacher with ill/injured child

   X   6. Procedures for dealing with HIV-positive student

   X   7. School safety precautions, policies, and regulations

   X   8. Other county/community services available to students

   X   9. Health and related issues taught in classes

(continued)

Notes:

First aid, cot for resting—eye and ear exams at community clinics. Flu shots at county clinic, work with guidance counselors, teachers on sexuality education—no condoms distributed as yet, but it has been discussed. School secretary calls parent/caregiver when child is ill at school. When HIV positive, refer for second opinion, student can come to classes. No smoking/drugs, guns, pushing, and running in halls allowed. Teach diet, nutrition, exercise, sexuality education.

IV. Curriculum Resource Person or Assistant Principal for Curriculum

NAME OF PERSON INTERVIEWED: Mr. Roger Maldonado

TITLE OF PERSON INTERVIEWED: Assistant Principal

DATE, TIME, AND PLACE OF INTERVIEW: November 25, 20—, 9:15 a.m., Mr. Maldonado's office

APPROXIMATE LENGTH OF INTERVIEW: 30 minutes

   X   1. School, district, county, or state curriculum guides

   X   2. Multicultural aspects of the curriculum

   X   3. School's organization for instruction:

        X   3a. grouping

        X   3b. departmentalization

        X   3c. chain of command

        X   3d. curricular offerings

        X   3e. extracurricular offerings

        X   3f. scheduling for teachers and students

   X   4. Planning and reflection requirements for teachers

   X   5. In-service and other opportunities for teachers

   X   6. Observation and evaluation of teachers (Standards for Teaching, pp. 37–39)

   X   7. Procedures for selection and review of textbooks and classroom materials

   X   8. Teachers' role in curriculum development and implementation—May suggest ideas—not always implemented

   X   9. Community's role in curriculum development and implementation—None

   X 10. Procedures for dealing with controversial issues and/or materials—None

   X 11. Special-education teachers

   X 12. Reading teachers

   X 13. Speech pathologists—None

   X 14. Gifted-program teachers

   X 15. Social-adjustment teachers, including drop-out prevention and in-school suspension—Started 1990–1991 year—seems to be helping

   X 16. Dean of boys/girls—Yes

   X 17. Music, art, and drama teachers—Yes—once a week

   X 18. Other special teachers (bilingual, physical education)

   X 19. Procedures for mainstreaming students

(continued)

Notes:

Have county and state curriculum guides. Ability grouping for reading and mathematics, otherwise heterogeneous. Basic skills curriculum. Teachers plan week ahead, hand in plan books, planning time 30 min. daily. Principal observes new teachers 5 times a year; others 3 times—lets teachers know approximate days he will observe. Discusses programs, i.e.: learning disabilities, reading, and G.T. programs. Students mainstreamed for music, art, social studies.

V. Person in Charge of Student Discipline

NAME OF PERSON INTERVIEWED: Mr. Roger Maldonado

TITLE OF PERSON INTERVIEWED: Vice Principal

DATE, TIME, AND PLACE OF INTERVIEW: December 16, 20—, 3:40 p.m., Mr. Maldonado's office

APPROXIMATE LENGTH OF INTERVIEW: 15 minutes

- __X__ 1. School policies/regulations regarding student behavior and appearance
- __X__ 2. Student handbook
- __X__ 3. Procedures for severe discipline referrals
- __X__ 4. Substance-abuse programs
- __X__ 5. Dropout prevention programs
- __X__ 6. School-administered discipline
- __X__ 7. Referrals to other agencies
- __X__ 8. Involvement of law enforcement in the school

Notes:

Policies on drugs, guns, crime, smoking, all substance abuse in student and parent handbooks. Discipline rules in all classrooms. Severe discipline problems referred to guidance counselor/principal/parent. Law officers can search lockers for suspected contents. When failing grades, placed in low student/teacher ratio—dropout prevention programs. School does not use corporal punishment as of this year. Have individual group therapy meetings with guidance counselor.

VI. Principal or Assistant Principal

NAME OF PERSON INTERVIEWED: Mrs. Elizabeth Andrews

TITLE OF PERSON INTERVIEWED: Principal

DATE, TIME, AND PLACE OF INTERVIEW: December 16, 20—, 4:30, Mrs. Andrews's office

APPROXIMATE LENGTH OF INTERVIEW: 40 minutes

- __X__ 1. School policies/regulations regarding teacher behavior and appearance
- __X__ 2. Faculty handbook. Yes
- __X__ 3. Faculty meetings (time and how used) Weekly, 3:30, Discuss Parent's Day, Routines, Curriculum-Testing
- __X__ 4. Organizational pattern of local schools (i.e., board, central office, and/or school)
- __X__ 5. Specialized type of school, such as magnet
- __X__ 6. Specialized programs, such as before- and after-school programs and preschool or childcare programs
- __X__ 7. Information about the community served by the school

(continued)

   X   8. Community and parent involvement in the school

   X   9. Business involvement in the school

   X   10. Professional organizations (union and/or academic)

   X   11. Teachers' extra responsibilities

   X   12. Student employment opportunities and procedures to follow

Notes:

Appropriate, neat dress for males/females—may wear jeans, sweaters, sneakers. Teachers must sign in/out and be there from 7:30–4:15. There are 3 feeder elementary schools, 2 middle schools, and 1 high school served by one county-elected board of education.

One elementary and one county middle school are magnet schools. There is a before- and after-school program. Breakfast is served to low-income families. Daycare provided for babies/young children of single teens. Teachers have bus, hall, and lunch duties. Children are bussed in across town for integration but still 65 percent white, 35 percent minority. Attendance at PTAs varies—if children involved most parents come. If it is a decision about playground expansion, raising money—about half come. Parents do respond to notes, some help with homework. Local business gave 20 computers and 10 typewriters. Most teachers belong to a professional organization as well as NEA or AFT and the state teacher's association. When ready to be certified, teachers need to complete application at county office, provide résumé, and make appointment with principal for an interview.

Referenced to INTASC Standards 5–8 and 10

SAMPLE FORM 25   Reflective Observation of Classrooms, Schools, and Curriculum

NAME OF OBSERVER: Tiffany Johnson

DATE AND TIME OF OBSERVATION: May 24, 20—, 10:50 a.m.

TEACHER/SCHOOL: Mr. McCormack; Hargrove School

GRADE LEVEL AND/OR SUBJECT: Sixth Grade

OBJECTIVE OF OBSERVATION: To think carefully and reflect about your observation of classrooms, schools, and curriculum. Below are some guiding questions/statements related to each of the five steps in the reflection cycle (Chapter 1, pp. 14–16 of this guide). The questions/statements are directly related to the ten principles from the INTASC Standards (Chapter 2, pp. 43–47 of this guide).

Instructions to the Observer: Use Form 25 to respond to the following questions/statements when you have completed your observations.

1. Select

  a. What did you observe about the classroom that was different from and/or similar to your past experience?

(continued)

b. What did you observe about the school that was different from and/or similar to your past experience?

c. What did you observe about the curriculum that was different from and/or similar to your past experience?

d. What principles did you use from the INTASC Standards?

2. Describe

a. Briefly describe your anecdotal observations of the school.

b. Briefly describe your structured observation of strategies that challenge students' multiple intelligences.

c. Did the school have the resources/materials that you expected it to have? Describe.

3. Analyze

a. How has the curriculum changed since you were in elementary/high school?

b. How did your observation of multicultural/antibias education compare/contrast to your own school experience?

4. Appraise

a. What did you learn from these observations?

b. How effective were you in completing the forms related to curriculum and technology?

c. What sources of information about schools, classrooms, and curriculum were most helpful to you?

5. Transform

a. What did you learn about technological resources that can help you in your teaching?

b. What new knowledge and skills will you incorporate in your teaching?

Source: Adapted from North Carolina State Department of Public Instruction. *Performance Based Licensure.* Raleigh, NC, 1998–1999.

Referenced to INTASC Standards 1–10

Chapter Four
Observing Students

Anecdotal Observations of Students

Anecdotal observations of students can reveal many things. One student can be observed over a long period of time in a variety of situations, or several different students can be observed on different occasions in the same classroom. Over a long period of time, changes can be seen in a student. It would be interesting to note, for example, differences in how Sammy, in the sample anecdotal record below, responds in his mathematics class of average-ability students as compared to his history class of above-average students. It would also be beneficial to note how his behavior in the history class changes from day to day and month to month. It might also be useful to observe several students of differing abilities in Sammy's history class. What is the ability level of Jennifer, the girl who helps Sammy? How does she respond in class? What are her interactions with other students in the class? What about the boy who rolls his eyes at Sammy? What is his ability level, and how does he interact with other students?

Another important thing to observe is the diversity of the classroom. The 21st century classroom is one of unparalleled diversity. This diversity can be an attribute or it can pose a problem. Perceiving diversity as a strength and creating an environment in which all students can succeed is the key to successful teaching and learning. How do teachers do this?

You may notice that the classroom in which you observe has students who speak no English; perhaps there are three or more languages represented. You will also note that students learn differently; maybe only a few flourish in the learning style that is most comfortable to you. Likewise, the physical, social, emotional, and intellectual attributes of the students are many and varied. Some students may leave the classroom for a part of the day to work in resource rooms. Other students, perhaps some that could be helped by special instruction, are in the classroom the entire day. There is no doubt that this diversity presents challenges, but as with all challenges it is also an opportunity. Observing the diverse classroom and teachers who are successful in capitalizing on its strengths is a beginning step to creating your own diversely successful classroom.

SAMPLE FORM 26   Anecdotal Record for Observing Students

NAME OF OBSERVER: Sally Reider

DATE AND TIME OF OBSERVATION: October 18, 20—, 2:05–3:00 p.m.

LENGTH OF OBSERVATION: 55 minutes, one class period

PERSON AND/OR EVENT OBSERVED: Sammy Hayes, student

GRADE LEVEL AND/OR SUBJECT: Tenth grade; American History

OBJECTIVE OF OBSERVATION: To see how an average-ability tenth grader responds in a history classroom

Instructions to the Observer: Write a detailed account of your subject, noting his or her appearance, background, abilities, interaction with others, habits, class responsiveness, behavior, and so on. Try to be as objective as possible.

According to his teacher, Sammy Hayes is an average-ability tenth grader. Although he is average in ability based on standardized test scores, Sammy is one of those students who works diligently. I am observing Sammy's tenth-grade history classroom. His teacher suggested that today would be a good day to observe Sammy because the students are working in small groups, and Sammy usually contributes well to the group. So that Sammy does not know I am particularly observing him, I will sit outside the group, but in a place where I can hear the students' interactions.

The bell rings. Sammy comes into the room quietly. The teacher pointed Sammy out to me yesterday so that I could quickly spot him. He's an average-looking kid: average height, slight build, teenage complexion (but no acne), medium-length brown hair—looks a bit greasy today. His clothes are typical, too: bleached blue jeans and a white T-shirt, running shoes without socks. Sammy does not stand out. He is neither attractive nor unattractive. Although he does not appear to be particularly outgoing, he is also not shy. He looks like the kind of kid who could easily get lost.

He sits down at his desk while many of the students mill around the room, but he is not a loner. He is talking to the boy sitting next to him, and the girl in front has turned around to ask him something. It appears she's asking him something about the assignment, since she's finding a page in his textbook.

The bell rings. Most of the students go to their seats. The teacher must remind a few of them that it's time to sit down. Sammy continues to talk quietly to the girl in front of him, but looks up and becomes quiet when the teacher looks at the class and says, "All right, class, today we're going to work in our groups to prepare for our oral presentations. But, before we do so, hand your homework up to the person in the seat in front of you. Yes, Sammy?" Sammy says, "Katie and I were just talking about our homework, and we don't know what numbers we were supposed to do. I thought it was 1, 3, and 7 and Katie thought it was 1, 3, and 9." A boy in the front says, "That's because we had a choice for the last question!" "That's right," the teacher says to Sammy, "You and Katie are both right. Now will you hand in your homework?" Sammy hands his to Katie.

I should probably say here that Sammy's teacher told me that this is a college prep class, and Sammy is one of the less able students in the class, but he tries so hard that the guidance office decided to place him in it. However, the teacher says he thinks Sammy is beginning to get frustrated. For all his trying, he's only getting C's. In his other, less competitive classes, he gets A's.

The teacher tells the students to get in their groups as they did on Monday and to have one group member go to the bookshelves and pick up the material they were working on. He reminds them that they should take all their material with them and move only the desks nearest where their group is supposed to meet. He also reminds them that this group project counts for a third

(continued)

of their grade for this unit. These are good kids and they follow his instructions, although there seems to be some confusion at the bookshelves. The teacher goes over to straighten it out.

Sammy has moved to his group and is asking another student what they are supposed to be doing today. The student rolls his eyes and says, "We're supposed to finish what we started on Monday." Sammy still looks puzzled, but doesn't pursue it.

The room is noisy, and the teacher says, "O.K., folks, you should have your materials. Now, get back to your group and get started. If you have questions, have one group member raise a hand and I'll get to you as soon as I can." Three groups already have hands up. No one in Sammy's group has raised a hand.

The girl who was getting the group's materials returns to Sammy's group and begins to hand things out from the box she has picked up. She gives Sammy a book. Sammy frowns. "What am I supposed to do with this?" he says. "Wait, Sammy," the girl says, "We haven't started yet." Most of the group members begin looking things up. One boy is drawing a map of what appears to be a battlefield. Several others are talking and laughing. Sammy is just sitting, staring at the book. Leadership seems to be lacking in this group. Finally, one of the boys says to Sammy, "Hey, Sammy, you're supposed to be looking up information about the Battle of Gettysburg." Sammy's eyes light up in recognition, and he immediately gets busy. I can't help but notice that he does not appear to know how to look things up in an index; he's looking in the table of contents. After some time, he finds an appropriate chapter and turns to it. He begins thumbing through the chapter. When he finally finds something, he calls out, "Wow, did you know how many Union soldiers were killed at Gettysburg?" One student looks over Sammy's shoulder at the passage and says, "Wow!" Another student says, "Sammy, you're supposed to be writing those things down. Remember the handout from Monday? You need to fill it out so we can compile all the information for our chart. Remember?" "Oh, yeah," says Sammy. He begins looking for the sheet. The girl who'd looked over his shoulder says, "I think it's in the box, Sammy; mine was." Sammy goes to the box to look and finds his sheet way on the bottom. His name is on it, but little else. Several of the students who are doing other battles are nearly through. Sammy begins diligently searching. Some of the other students begin to report their data to put on the chart. One boy says to Sammy, "Who was the commanding officer for the South at Gettysburg?" Sammy says, "I haven't found that yet." The boy rolls his eyes, but the girl next to Sammy says, "I've finished most of mine; your battle is harder. Let me help you look for it." Sammy smiles, and they begin to work together. The teacher walks by, sees the group is working, and starts to move on. He looks at Sammy's paper and sees that he's barely begun. "What's the problem, Sammy?" he asks. Sammy shrugs. "Can I help?" the teacher asks. "No, I can do it," Sammy says, looking down. The girl says to the teacher, "Sammy's got the hardest battle; I'll help him because I finished." "Thank you, Jennifer," the teacher says. (I like this Jennifer girl; I'll need to ask the teacher about her.) Sammy and Jennifer continue to work together. Sammy is now smiling. The rest of the group is ignoring them as they continue to list on the chart facts from the other battles.

(The observation continues in this fashion.)

OBSERVING SIXTH GRADE STUDENTS IN THE LUNCHROOM:

Many of the students at Madison Middle School know me through the community and through Youth League Basketball and Softball, so I chose to observe as a parent visiting her child at school. The Assistant Principal approved this approach.

On Thursday I sat in the lunchroom at a table with my daughter and observed sixth graders in general but focused on two specific students seated at other tables. While the children ranged from child-sized to adult-sized in general, the girls are taller than the boys. In motion the boys are more awkward than the girls, although neither group is graceful. All the children are animated and constantly moving, I observed them gesturing broadly with their hands as they spoke, fidgeting with dollar bills or change in their hands, rocking on their heels, swinging their feet under the table, and shifting their bodies in the chairs.

My daughter Kelsey explained that this was a special day: as a reward for good behavior the children were allowed to sit where they chose. Ordinarily they are required to sit "on assigned sears" with their class. Girls sat at tables with girls, and boys sat with boys. The only mixed-gender tables I saw were the table where a few boys sat with their female teacher and the table occupied by teachers and exceptional children, where one child required adult assistance with his meal. A few times a boy at his table would speak to the girls at another table. I was unable to determine what he said, but the girls either laughed or rolled their eyes. The atmosphere was relaxed and playful, and I was amazed at the volume of the noise in the lunchroom.

I focused on one girl at a table to my right and one boy at a table directly in from of me. The girl spoke to the whole table, gesturing as she told a story. She seemed focused on the group of six at the table with her, making and maintained eye contact with them as she spoke. She touched her face or hair at least twenty times during my observation, but seemed unconscious of this behavior. She moved in her seat constantly, from seated with feet in front of her, to sitting on one foot then the other, to half standing and leaning across the table, although she didn't stand completely until the end of her meal

The boy, on the other hand, stood at his table for most of his meal. At the beginning of the meal he was seated. Within minutes he was perched with one foot on the seat and one on the floor, squatting in the seat. Then he stood fully upright, first with one foot still on the seat, then finally with both feet on the floor.

While he did speak to the boys at his table, he didn't converse with them. His dialogue was along the lines, of, "Hey look," as he shoved half of a hot dog in his mouth, and three or four work statements followed by raucous laughter. Most of the boys talked this way, using gestures and arm-punches instead of sentences. The boy also seemed concerned with his appearance, but unlike the girl he seemed more interested in whether people were watching him. His head rotated constantly, as if he were on patrol. He touched his body, chest, and legs, instead of his face and hair.

The lunchroom appears to be designed for the middle-level child. At the middle school the chairs and tables are freestanding to accommodate various body sizes, unlike the attached benches at the elementary level. (I was as comfortable at the middle school as I was uncomfortable at the elementary school table.) The children enter with their class, each class about fifteen minutes after the one before. The two food lines are self-serve and the menu offers a limited variety. In addition to the menu items, children may purchase fruit, ice cream, "slushies," cookies or beverages. There are two snack machines that contain "junk food," and two beverage machines with sport drinks and juice.

Hansen, Kelly (September, 2001). Observations of Sixth Graders in the Lunchroom. UNC-Ashville. Preservice Student. Unpublished.

....

Referenced to INTASC Standards 1–7

....

Shadowing a Student

A simple, but time-consuming, anecdotal technique for determining what it is like to be a particular student in a particular school is shadowing that student throughout an entire school day. From this process, the observer can learn how the student interacts with teachers and other students. In addition, you can discover how the student handles social and academic situations and what the student does with his or her non-class time. Most important, you can learn what a day in the life of a student in a particular school is like.

Before shadowing a student, it is essential to obtain permission from the student, since shadowing is an intrusion into his or her life. The teacher(s) of the student, the principal, and, in some cases, the student's parents or guardians should also grant permission. You should carefully explain that the goal of shadowing is not to analyze the individual, but rather to determine what it is like to be a student at his or her school. You should encourage the student to behave as naturally as possible, explaining that shadowing will not be as helpful to you if he or she acts differently than usual or tells his or her friends about the observation. You should ask the student to try to ignore you as much as possible and simply follow his or her schedule, remaining as unobtrusive as possible.

In classrooms, sit out of the line of sight of the majority of the students. In the lunchroom, sit where the student can be observed, but where you cannot be seen by the student. If possible, talk with the student at the end of the day, sharing observations, not judgments, and asking about the student's perception of school, peers, subjects, likes, and dislikes. A separate shadowing form should be completed for each lesson and/or separate time period (i.e., classes, lunch, and recess) during the day.

According to a study on the values of shadowing students, researchers Melody Jones and Martin Tadlock concluded, "As you follow students around you begin to feel you are one of them. You see yourself through their eyes. It is an unsettling type of introspection. You have to think like a student. If you're really interested in understanding students, a shadow study is a good way to do it" (1999, 61).

SAMPLE FORM 27   Shadowing Form

NAME OF SHADOWED STUDENT: Natasha Reynolds*

NAME OF OBSERVER: Sally Burke

DATE AND TIME OF SHADOW: September 4, 20—, 8:30–10:20

GRADE LEVEL AND/OR SUBJECT: Twelfth grade; German/English

OBJECTIVE OF SHADOW: To understand what it is like to be a student at East Rodgers High School

GENERAL DESCRIPTION OF LOCATION: Classrooms: German II/German III—28 students (8 girls, 20 boys); English—30 students (16 girls, 14 boys)

*The names of the shadowed student and the school have been changed.

Instructions to the Observer: Select a student to shadow for an entire school day. Use a separate page for each class period or segment of the school day you observe. Every five to fifteen minutes, record what the subject of the observation is doing; also indicate what other students and teachers are doing. At the end of the day, summarize the shadowing experience. If possible, interview the student and report the results.

(continued)

SUBJECT/CLASS: German

Time (recorded every five to fifteen minutes)	What Subject Was Doing	What Classmates and Teacher Were Doing
8:30–8:35	Talking to neighbor	T. told class to be quiet for morning announcements. Most students talked.
8:35–8:45	Translated sentence into literal English—sounded bizarre	T. tried to help students correct quiz from day before.
		T. told personal anecdotes. Most of class amused.
8:45–8:50	Put head on desk	Classmates wrote translated sentences into literal English.
8:50–9:00	Answered question	T. asks a classmate to help subject with her translation
9:00–9:10	Talked to neighbor; put head down	'

SUBJECT/CLASS: English

Time (recorded every five to fifteen minutes)	What Subject Was Doing	What Classmates and Teacher Were Doing
9:20–9:35	Worked on quiz	T. gave quiz on assignment. All but one student worked diligently. He didn't write any answers.
9:35–9:40	Answered question # 4	T. let students correct own papers.
9:40–9:45	Head down on desk	
9:45–9:50	Appeared to listen to others reading orally	Students took turns reading orally.
9:50–10:00	Read silently, put head down, then up, then read again	T. gave directions to read William Bradford's "Of Plymouth Plantation." Most students read quietly; some talked.
10:00–10:10	Answered two questions about what she had read	T. asked questions about content of silent reading. Most students knew the answers. T. paraphrased what students had read.
10:10	Closed book: got out of seat	T. assigned questions in text for homework.

The following should be completed at the end of the shadowing experience:

1. **Overview:** Summarize how the student seemed to be involved, how the student interacted with teachers and peers, what the student seemed to learn, and how the student seems to feel about the class.

   Overview: Natasha didn't appear to be that interested in the German class. I got the impression from Natasha that she took the class because she thought it would be easy for her since her mother is German. She was more attentive in the English class, especially when she could answer questions. She did seem to lose some interest when reading silently.

2. Report of interview with student:

(Lunch time outside on picnic table) Natasha asked me several questions about college. She said she'd like to go there someday. She said history and English were her favorite subjects, but not her favorite classes. Her major complaint about school was not enough time for lunch or in between classes to socialize. Natasha said she liked horses and someday hopes to own and manage a rehabilitation horse barn.

Referenced to INTASC Standards 1–7.

Anecdotal Profile of a Student

The anecdotal profile technique is similar to, but less time-consuming than, shadowing. It allows the observer to study two or more students during a single lesson.

The goal of the anecdotal profile is to examine the attitudes and activities of several students during a specified period of time. You should select two or three students to observe for fifteen to twenty minutes each. It is helpful if these students are quite different in terms of certain key characteristics (e.g., appearance, sociability, learning style, or academic achievement). Since the observation of the students is for a limited time period, you should record the students' activities and attitudes every one to two minutes, rather than every five minutes as in the shadowing study. These observations can be kept on three-by-five-inch index cards.

SAMPLE FORM 28   Profile Card

NAME OF OBSERVER: Monica Williams

STUDENT: Jason Maxwell

DATE AND TIME OF OBSERVATION: December 5, 20—, 9:30–9:40 a.m.

GRADE LEVEL AND/OR SUBJECT: Third grade; reading group of 5

LOCATION: Classroom

OBJECTIVE OF OBSERVATION: To examine the attitude and activities of a particular student

Instructions to the Observer: Record your observations in two-minute intervals.

Time (recorded every two minutes)	Student's Activities/Attitudes
9:30–9:32	Adjusts chair; moves body left to right; whispers to friend next to him on his left.
9:32–9:34	Looks at reading chart; raises hand. Stands up, responds, "Divide between the two consonants."
9:34–9:36	Raises hand again when not called on, says, "I knew that, too." Plays with book on lap.
9:36–9:38	Opens book; appears to be reading silently; sometimes moves lips.
9:38–9:40	Raises hand again and says, "I know, I know." When not called on, appears to sulk.

Structured Observation of Students

There are many types of structured observations that can reveal specific information about students. Descriptive profile charts are more specific and focused than the anecdotal profiles discussed previously. Checklists are very specific, allowing the observer to focus on a specified list of items. A checklist does not evaluate, it documents. Coding systems allow observers to tally elements of student behavior. Informal inventories of students allow observers to gain data about students from the students' perspectives. Sociograms assist observers in plotting the interaction of students in a social environment such as a classroom.

Descriptive Profiles of a Student

Descriptive profiles are very similar to anecdotal profiles; however, they are more complete in that they attempt to record a continuing collection of facts in order to describe a particular phenomenon. The recordings are made without regard to their meaning, value, or use. A descriptive profile always begins with the date, time, and place, and includes statements and explanations about the background of the situation or setting. Descriptions tell what happened, who did or said what, and how it was done. They are noted as objectively and completely as possible. Direct quotes are recorded, posture and facial expressions are described, and gestures and voice quality are noted. However, interpretations are avoided. Thus a detailed, descriptive sentence such as "His eyes flashed, he frowned, his body became rigid, and his fist was clenched" seeks to state the facts, while a biased statement such as "He was angry" (Perkins, 1969, 28) seeks to interpret the facts and should be avoided. The descriptive profile is a lot like what a writer attempts to do when setting a scene in a literary work. The author attempts to show the readers the scene to make the readers feel as if they are there. The author attempts to keep out of the scene, and, therefore, shows rather than tells. The descriptive profile should do the same thing.

In descriptive profiles, observations should be limited to only a few phenomena at a time. Descriptive observers can make the job easier by looking for specific elements of a personality or environment. For example, the descriptive profile chart that follows outlines one student's actions during a lesson. You should look for how and when the student is actively involved in the lesson and how and when she is not.

SAMPLE FORM 29   **Descriptive Profile Chart**

PLOTTED BY: Sarah Cardinalli

DATE AND TIME OF OBSERVATION: October 28, 20—, 8:45 a.m.

STUDENT: Melissa Hernandez

SCHOOL: Smith Elementary

GRADE LEVEL: Second grade

INTERVAL: Twenty seconds

OBJECTIVE OF OBSERVATION: To record a student's involvement or lack of involvement in two different activities of a lesson

Instructions to the Observer: Record brief phrases to indicate the activities of the student during discussion and work periods. Place student activities under "application" if they show involvement in the lesson; if not, place them under "distraction."

DISCUSSION PERIOD		WORK PERIOD	
Application	**Distraction**	**Application**	**Distraction**
Listened to teacher.		Opened workbook. Looked at work.	
Raised hand.	Fiddled with pencil.	Frowned.	
Listened, shook head.			Doodled. Talked to neighbor.
	Played with fingernails.		
Looked at book.		Looked at workbook. Raised hand.	Frowned.
Answered question.			Doodled.
		Listened to teacher.	
Asked question.		Looked at book.	
Read assignment on board.			Played with fingernails.
	Looked at fingernails.	Picked up pencil.	
	Talked to student next to her.	Wrote in book.	Frowned.
Looked at teacher; raised hand.			Put head on desk.
	Looked at student.		
Asked question.			
Listened to answer.			

Source: Adapted from John Devor. *The Experience of Student Teaching,* 1964.

Referenced to INTASC Standard 2

Coding Systems of Student Participation

Another simple tool to help you limit what you are looking for in a classroom is the coding system. A coding system looks for specific elements within the classroom. Usually the observer codes the extent of the presence of these elements on three-by-five-inch index cards. The technique is most frequently used when observing students and teachers. Just as with other observational tools, you must know what you are looking for before designing the coding system.

In the example of a coding system below, the observer is looking for the extent of participation of various students in the lesson. Cards could be made to record the participation of several students during a single lesson. Over a period of time, all students' participation could be coded.

SAMPLE FORM 30   Coding System to Observe Student Participation in Lessons

NAME OF OBSERVER: Sally Reider

DATE AND TIME OF OBSERVATION: October 18, 20—, 10:45

STUDENT: Sammy Hayes

GRADE LEVEL: Tenth grade

TOPIC: Civil War

OBJECTIVE OF OBSERVATION: To observe the extent of a student's participation in a particular lesson

Instructions to the Observer: Place a slash [/] in the appropriate column to indicate student activities during a single lesson.

Important Contributions	Minor Contributions	Distracting Remarks
//	## /	///

Referenced to INTASC Standard 2

Informal Inventories of Students

Another simple technique for gathering data about students is developing inventories that list the interests of students, their favorite teachers, how students view themselves, how they view the school, and the subjects they take. Almost anything the observer wants to learn about the students can be asked on an informal inventory. Many inventories are available through educational publications. However, the inventories that are the most valuable are those designed to meet the objectives of the specific class. What follows is a simple interest inventory, designed by a student observer, to determine the student's interest in reading. Inventories can also be administered to a large group of students and tallied to learn the most common responses. You are encouraged to design an inventory appropriate to the objectives of a specific student or class.

SAMPLE FORM 31   Incomplete Sentence Inventory

Name of Observer: Irene Johnson

Date and Time of Observation: September 13, 20—, 2:00 p.m.

Student: Billy Malone

Grade Level and/or Subject: Fourth grade; reading

Objective of Observation: To determine Billy's reading interests

Instructions to the Observer: Determine the purpose of completing an informal inventory. Then design some incomplete sentences related to your objective. A sample answer for the first question should be provided in the instructions to the student. Observer can read incomplete sentences to children who are unable to read.

Instructions to the Student: Complete each sentence as honestly and completely as possible. For example, you might complete the first questions as follows: When I get home from school I usually play outside.

1. When I get home from school I usually get a snack.

2. On rainy Saturdays I particularly like to do puzzles.

3. When I am at home in the summer, I like to play ball.

4. When I go to the beach or pool, I always take with me my ball, my friend, Jim.

5. When I was a small child I remember my mother read to me.

6. When I was a small child I remember my father _____.
   (Billy did not complete this sentence.)

7. The best book I remember reading is about snakes.

8. I like to read the magazine National Geographic.

9. The last book I read was The Fascinating World of Bees.

Referenced to INTASC Standard 2

Peer Group Interaction: Sociograms

For most students, their interaction with peers is exceedingly important. In fact, by middle or junior high school, interaction with peers takes precedence over all other interactions. Therefore, it is helpful to discover ways to observe and analyze how students relate to one other. Perhaps the easiest technique for accomplishing this is the sociogram.

A sociogram graphically examines how the students in a class feel about one another. It indicates which students are most liked by other students and which are isolated from other students. "A sociogram's value to a teacher is in its potential for developing greater understanding of group behavior so that he/she may operate more wisely in group management and curriculum development" (Sherman, 2000, 1). Completing the sociogram requires the cooperation of the classroom teacher.

To complete a simple sociogram, you or the classroom teacher should have students list three classmates with whom they would like to be socially associated. For example, students can be told, "On our field trip next week, we will be in groups of four. Please list three other students, in order of preference, that you'd most like to be grouped with for the trip." It should be made clear to students that the teacher cannot guarantee that all their suggestions will be followed, but their preferences will be used as a guide in helping to form the groups. The students' choices can be tallied on a chart such as Sample Form 32. The names of students in the class are listed both vertically and horizontally. Those students who are in the vertical list are considered choosers. The order in which they have selected companions is given in the horizontal box next to the person's name. At the bottom of the form is a place to tally the total number of choices per student.

SAMPLE FORM 32   Tally Chart of Student-Group Selections

Name of Observer: Danny McKinney

Date and Time of Observation: October 26, 20—, 1:00 p.m.

School: Eastfield Middle School

Objective of Observation: To determine which students are most liked and which students are most isolated

Instructions to the Observer: List students on left side. Then tally the first, second, and third choices made by each student in the chart below.

Chosen / Choosers	Pam	John*	David	Steve	George	Brian G.	Paul	Scott F.	Scott K.	Jeff	Ruth	Marc	Libby	Sherman	Sharon	Tony	Judy	Alan	Brian S.	Jane	Wayne	Bill	Keith	Sandy	Lane
Pam													1		2		3								
John *																									
David				3	2											1									
Steve					1														3				2		
George												1				2					3				
Brian G.		1														2							3		
Paul											1	2									3				
Scott F.				2					1												3				
Scott K.					2											3							1		
Jeff			3																2				1		
Ruth												1							3						2
Marc					1													2	3						
Libby	3				2																			1	
Sherman					2											1			3						
Sharon	3								1								2								
Tony			1	2															3						
Judy	3														1										2
Alan					1														2	3					
Brian S.					2												1			3					
Jane				3							1	2													
Wayne					2							1						3							
Bill					2		3																1		
Keith		2		3																		1			
Sandy					2									1							3				
Lane												1					2							3	
Chosen 1		1	1			1	2			1	3	4	2		1	2		1				3	1	1	1
Chosen 2		1				2	7				1	1			1	2	2	1	2				1		2
Chosen 3	3			3	1				1							1	1	1	2		4	1		1	
Totals	3	2	1	3	2	3	9	0	1	1	3	5	3	0	2	5	3	3	4	0	9	4	2	2	2

* John absent

Source: Frederick J. McDonald. *Educational Psychology,* 2nd ed., Wadsworth Publishing, 1965, 634.

Referenced to INTASC Standards 1, 2, 5, and 7

In order to graphically illustrate which students are more socially popular than others, a sociogram can be constructed based on the information obtained in the tally chart. In Sample Form 33, for example, boys are drawn in circles, girls in squares. Arrows are drawn to each student selected, with the number of his or her selection marked as first, second, or third. Dotted lines indicate those students who selected one another. The larger circles and squares represent those who were selected more often than others.

SAMPLE FORM 33   Sociogram Based on Charted Student Preferences

NAME OF OBSERVER: Rebecca Talmadge

DATE AND TIME OF OBSERVATION: October 30, 20—, 2:00 p.m.

SCHOOL: Faircrest Elementary School

GRADE LEVEL AND/OR SUBJECT: fourth grade

OBJECTIVE OF OBSERVATION: To illustrate children's choices in pictorial, graphic format, showing students most liked and those most isolated

Instructions to the Observer: Use the tally chart of student-group selections to put the names of the most-selected students in a prominent place on the page. Identify males by placing their names in circles, females by placing their names in boxes. Then, put the names of students selected by those few most-selected students next to them. If they selected each other, connect them with a dotted line. If not, draw an arrow to the student selected. Proceed in this fashion until all names are represented on the form.

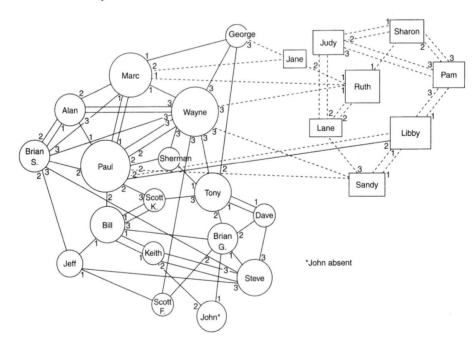

Source: Frederick J. McDonald. *Educational Psychology,* 2nd ed., Wadsworth Publishing, 1965, 635.

Referenced to INTASC Standards 1, 2, 5, and 7

Observing Diversity in the Classroom

If teachers are to be successful in meeting the needs of exceptional populations of students, they need experience in working with these students. The standards of the National Council for Accreditation of Teacher Education (NCATE) and teacher educators agree that this experience should occur during teacher training. If exceptional students, including the disabled and gifted, are included in regular classrooms, the school is responsible for creating both an environment and an Individual Educational Plan (IEP) that will allow each exceptional student to succeed. To ensure student success, it is necessary to determine the needs of each student and to create within the classroom the least restrictive environment possible so that the exceptional student can participate academically and socially and can achieve. Because of the value to the students, most educators believe that exceptional students, with and without disabilities, should be in the same educational environment and participate in the same activities as other students (Perry and Winne, 2001, 122).

Inclusive Classrooms

Increased diversity of the student population and several pieces of important federal legislation ("Education for All Handicapped Children Act," PL94-142 and "Individuals with Disabilities Education Act," PL 101-476) have led to the inclusion of all types of students in the regular classroom. Inclusion has created new challenges for educators, but has also increased learning and social opportunities for teachers and students. The law requires that schools and teachers include disabled children in the classroom by:

- Ensuring their access to the general education curriculum to the maximum extent possible.
- Strengthening the role of parents and families.
- Coordinating IDEA (Individuals with Disabilities Act) with other school improvement efforts so that special education can be a service rather than a place where students meet.
- Supporting high-quality intensive personal development so that children are prepared to lead productive adult lives (Gartner and Lipsky, 1999, 23-24).

To help encourage inclusion in the least restrictive setting possible, regular classroom teachers and special education teachers must form a partnership and share the responsibility for all students. A co-teaching model can range from one to two class periods per day to a full teaching day. In order for this partnership to continue to work and inclusion to succeed during your observation and teaching in the classroom, you will need to work with your classroom teacher to:

- Model a respect for diversity.
- Help design IEP's and/or study previously prepared IEP's for the special needs students in your classroom.
- Follow the instructional model of the IEP in your planning and teaching.
- Observe parent-teacher conferences.
- Be involved in multi-level instruction that allows for different types of learning within the same curriculum.
- Provide a variety of reading materials on different reading levels.
- Focus on key concepts to be taught and variety in the ways students can show their understanding of these concepts.
- Use advanced organizers to help students use previous knowledge and experience to relate to new concepts.
- Preteach specialized vocabulary and major concepts.
- Allow extra time for students to complete their work, as necessary.
- Summarize what has been taught.

- Provide immediate, positive, and corrective feedback.
- Use a "Circle of Friends" strategy whereby a student support team meets on a regular basis to foster friendships and help solve problems.
- Use hands-on activities, projects, thematic approaches and multimedia presentations.
- Develop a daily schedule that identifies activities by content areas, goals to be emphasized, and individual accommodations (e.g.: environment, social, curricular).
- Use specialized equipment that can help students meet specific goals (e.g. Alphasmart laptop computer to assist with spelling (Lombardi, 1999, 93-94).

Help Spills Over*

The work the school has done to create a safe environment for its special education students has paid off for Kyle Martin, a 5th grader at Lowell.

Because Kyle has severe attention deficit hyperactivity disorder, bipolar disorder, a non-verbal learning disorder, and sensory difficulties, he has trouble interacting socially with his peers and communicating appropriately, according to his mother, Michelle Martin.

"Kyle is a prime target to be picked on," she says.

When the boy started at Lowell in kindergarten, Martin says, she heard parents and even staff members complain about "that loud kid with the issues."

Most of that has changed now, she says. Martin has been assertive in speaking to Kyle's class and to parent groups about his behaviors.

Some parents wondered if it was disruptive for their children to have different teachers wandering in and out of the classroom all the time.

Martin says she tells parents, "My child's IEP is benefiting your child" because the extra help Kyle receives spills over to the rest of the class.

"If people are uninformed, that is what scares them," says Martin.

Being in a mainstream classroom forces Kyle to behave more appropriately, she adds. "The bar is lowered if you are in a room with a bunch of other kids who have issues," she says. "There is no typical model."

Still, fully including a child with severe special needs is not an easy venture.

For example, 10-year-old Patrick Vershbow, a 4th grader at Lowell, has a genetic condition called Fragile X that has affected all areas of his development.

He didn't say his first word until he was 5, relies heavily on routines, has trouble eating and drinking, and sometimes has seizures, according to his mother, Pamela Vershbow.

Having Patrick, who has a full-time aide, in your classroom "is a lot of work," Vershbow acknowledges.

Patrick would typically be placed in a very specialized school for students with severe developmental difficulties, but the environment at Lowell is "more natural," his mother says.

As a result, Patrick now knows how to read, she says, a skill that seems out of reach for some children with Fragile X.

Because special education students are mainstreamed at Lowell, Michelle Martin says, the children here have learned that "not everyone is alike, and some people have disabilities,"

"And you work with them," she says, "you don't put them in a separate room,"

*A Case Study from Lowell Elementary School in Watertown, Mass.

Source: Galley, Michelle. (1-8-2004) "No Separate Room" *Education Week, Quality Counts 2004: Count Me In: Special Education in an Era of Standards.* Vol. 23 (7) p. 31 Editorial Projects in Education. Marion, OH

SAMPLE FORM 34   Reasonable Public School Expectations for Students

NAME OF OBSERVER: Sophia Hoosain

DATE AND TIME OF OBSERVATION: October 18, 20—, 9:00 a.m.

SCHOOL/TEACHER: Highland Elementary, Mr. Byrd

STUDENT: Tikamiya Owen

GRADE LEVEL AND/OR SUBJECT: Fifth grade; self-contained

AREA OF IDENTIFICATION (DISABILITY, IF KNOWN): blind

OBJECTIVE OF OBSERVATION: To determine the extent to which a disabled student is successful in three developmental areas

Instructions to the Observer: What follows is a checklist of reasonable performance and behavior that teachers can expect from non-disabled students. In order to develop an Individual Educational Plan (IEP) for a disabled student, it is necessary to determine which of these expectations he or she is able to meet with no curriculum or classroom modifications. In the right-hand column, indicate the extent to which the student is successful in each of these categories. Note that some of this information may be available only from the student's academic file or teacher; it is important that you make no assumptions and obtain appropriate documentation.

Developmental Areas	Very	Moderate	Limited	None
A. Academic Development				
1. Reading	✓			
2. Writing		✓		
3. Mathematics	✓			
B. Social Development				
1. Interaction with other students		✓		
2. Interaction with teacher or other staff	✓			
C. Physical Development				
1. Uses regular transportation to school; walks or rides school bus				✓
2. Reports to homeroom or other central location by her/himself			✓	
3. Obeys school rules with other students	✓			
4. Goes to class with regular curriculum				
a. regular volume of curriculum	✓			
b. regular rate of presentation of material	✓			
c. at a reading level that is grade-level appropriate	✓			
5. Has homework assignments in every class		✓		
6. Changes classes when the bell rings			✓	
7. Mingles in hallway before next class			✓	

(continued)

Developmental Areas	Very	Moderate	Limited	None
8. Has lunch with other youngsters		✓		
9. Goes to gym/PE with other youngsters		✓		
10. Dresses for gym/PE			✓	
11. Goes to the restroom as classes change	✓			
12. Has recess/free time with others		✓		
13. Attends regular school assemblies	✓			
14. Takes regular tests without modifications			✓	
15. Participates in extracurricular activities		✓		
16. Goes on school field trips or outings	✓			
17. Does homework each night		✓		
18. Takes homework back to teacher each day		✓		
19. Attends school each day with very few excused absences	✓			
20. Makes up work if absent		✓		

Source: Adapted from a form used by the Asheville, North Carolina Public Schools.

....

Referenced to INTASC Standards 1–8

....

SAMPLE FORM 35 Information-Processing Categories of Instructional Modifications

NAME OF OBSERVER: Sophia Hoosain

DATE AND TIME OF OBSERVATION: October 20, 20—, 12:30 p.m.

SCHOOL/TEACHER: Highland Elementary, Mr. Byrd

STUDENT: Tikamiya Owen

GRADE LEVEL AND/OR SUBJECT: Fifth grade; self-contained

AREA OF IDENTIFICATION (DISABILITY, IF KNOWN): blind

OBJECTIVE OF OBSERVATION: To observe instructional modifications made in a regular classroom for a disabled student

Instructions to the Observer: What follows is a checklist of modifications targeted to the disabled student. Any variety of these modifications may be needed in order for a disabled student to be successful in the school or classroom environment and/or to achieve curricular goals. Observe a disabled student who is in the regular classroom and check [✓] those modifications that are currently being employed. If a modification is needed but is not currently employed, place an asterisk [*] to the left of the item.

Note: It may be necessary to interview the classroom teacher to determine whether some of these items are currently employed.

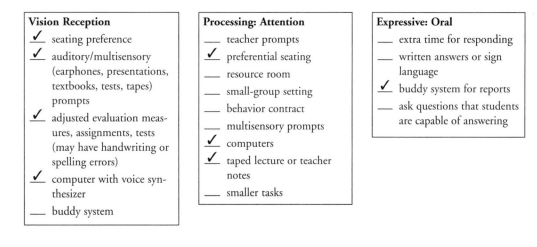

Vision Reception
- ✓ seating preference
- ✓ auditory/multisensory (earphones, presentations, textbooks, tests, tapes) prompts
- ✓ adjusted evaluation measures, assignments, tests (may have handwriting or spelling errors)
- ✓ computer with voice synthesizer
- ___ buddy system

Processing: Attention
- ___ teacher prompts
- ✓ preferential seating
- ___ resource room
- ___ small-group setting
- ___ behavior contract
- ___ multisensory prompts
- ✓ computers
- ✓ taped lecture or teacher notes
- ___ smaller tasks

Expressive: Oral
- ___ extra time for responding
- ___ written answers or sign language
- ✓ buddy system for reports
- ___ ask questions that students are capable of answering

(continued)

Reception Modifications	Processing Modifications	Expressive Modifications

Auditory Reception
- ___ seating preference
- ___ student scribes
- ___ paired oral/written prompts
- ___ visual presentation
- ✓ computers
- ✓ buddy system

Processing: Organization
- ___ teacher's outline or Xeroxed notes
- ___ highlighted text
- ✓ prepared study sheets
- ___ individual behavior contacts
- ✓ modification of assignment format
- ✓ extended time on major assignments or shorter assignments
- ___ help organizing work
- ___ interview with parent/caregiver

Expressive: Writing
- ✓ no penalty for poor handwriting
- ✓ use of word processor (or typewriter)
- ✓ test and report modifications (oral, shorter, more time)
- ✓ student scribe for notes or teacher's notes Xeroxed (tape recording)

Processing: Memory
- ___ shorter time on assignments
- ✓ prepared study sheets
- ___ paired oral and written work
- ✓ calculators and computers
- ___ answer list for fill-in-the-blank questions
- ___ no penalty for poor spelling

Source: Adapted from a form used by the Asheville, North Carolina Public Schools: *Reception Modifications.*

Referenced to INTASC Standards 1–10

SAMPLE FORM 36   Reflective Observation of Students

NAME OF OBSERVER: Angela Sexton

DATE AND TIME OF REFLECTIVE RECORD: April 26, 20—, 1:15 p.m.

TEACHER/SCHOOL: Mr. Santuro, South Central Academy

GRADE LEVEL AND/OR SUBJECT: Twelfth grade; physics

OBJECTIVE OF OBSERVATION: To think carefully and reflect about your observation of students. Below are some guiding questions/statements related to each of the five steps in the reflection cycle (Chapter 1, pp. 14–16). The statements are directly related to the ten principles from the INTASC Standards (Chapter 2, pp. 43–47).

Instructions to the Observer: Use Form 36 to respond to the following questions after you have completed your observations.

1. **Select**
   a. What anecdotal observations of students did you complete?
   b. What structured observation of students did you complete?
   c. What principles from INTASC Standards did you address?
   d. How many of the characteristics of an effective inclusive classroom did you observe?

2. **Describe**
   a. What are the unique characteristics that distinguish these students from others you have observed (e.g., needs, background, learning styles, prior experiences)?
   b. What steps did you take to assess the needs of these students?
   c. From whom and in what ways did you solicit information about the students' experiences, learning behaviors, and needs?

3. **Analyze**
   a. How will your assessment of the characteristics and needs of these students affect your planning, tutoring, and teaching?
   b. How did the cultural, ethnic, and racial characteristics of these students influence you and your interactions with them?
   c. How effective was your participation in the inclusive classroom model?

4. **Appraise**
   a. What sources of information were most helpful to you as you consider planning and teaching these students?
   b. What observation(s) improved your understanding of the diverse needs of students at this age/grade?

5. **Transform**
   a. What did you learn about the diverse nature and needs of students?
   b. What new knowledge and skills will you incorporate in your teaching?

Source: Adapted from North Carolina State Department of Public Instruction. *Performance Based Licensure.* Raleigh, NC, 1998–1999.

Referenced to INTASC Standards 1–10

PART III

Developing Successful Teaching Skills

Chapter Five
Participation: Preteaching and Planning

Preteaching Activities

Working in classrooms should proceed in a series of gradual steps from observation of children and teachers to teaching. After teacher-education students have had the opportunity to observe and reflect on their observations, they can ease into their roles as teachers by assisting the classroom teacher in a variety of noninstructional or teacher-aide duties. When the preservice teacher has mastered some of these duties, he or she can begin working with the teacher in the ongoing instructional activity of the classroom. Still later, the teacher-education student can begin to assume some limited teaching assignments that are carefully planned with the classroom teacher, such as individual tutoring and small-group instructional work. Not until the preservice teacher feels comfortable with these activities and has had time to reflect upon them and receive feedback about them should he or she move on to assume primary responsibility for a fully planned lesson. Before teaching the lesson, careful planning with the classroom teacher is essential. This step-by-step process will be discussed in this chapter and Chapter 6.

After observing and before teaching, there are numerous activities that can help student participants better understand the children, the classroom organization, and the teaching process. Michael, in the anecdotal observation in Chapter 1, discussed some of these: taking roll, bringing his pet mice to class, discussing teaching techniques with the classroom teacher, etc. Janet Joyce, in the anecdotal record of preteaching activities in this chapter, discusses others: helping the children with art projects, going to staff-development meetings, taking field trips, putting up a bulletin board, working with the classroom teacher to develop a classroom management system, discussing students with the teacher and teaching specialists, and filling out a worksheet related to a field trip students had taken. The first section of this chapter will provide you with additional ideas for preteaching activities. Tools for planning will be discussed in the second section of the chapter.

SAMPLE FORM 37   Anecdotal Record of Preteaching Activities

STUDENT: Janet Joyce

TEACHER: Ms. Bennes

GRADE LEVEL: Second grade

DATE: February 11, 20— to March 15, 20—

OBJECTIVE: To record activities I participated in prior to teaching

Instructions to Student Participant: Keep an account of the activities you participated in prior to actual teaching. Indicate how you felt about each day's events.

FEBRUARY 11, 20—
The thing I liked most about today was helping the kids with their valentine folders. I had never woven paper before. It was fun watching them do it. It was a great first day!

FEBRUARY 12, 20—
School was dismissed early for staff development. The kids were pretty excited about it. Ms. Bennes and I spent the afternoon talking with Ms. Loritch, the speech teacher, about several of our students.

FEBRUARY 13, 20—
Today was a full day! We went on a field trip to the Health Adventure. The kids learned a lesson on dental hygiene. It was great and the kids liked it too. This afternoon we had a surprise birthday party for Ms. Canty, the teacher-aide. The kids never gave the secret away (which was a miracle). Ms. Canty was surprised and the party went well.

FEBRUARY 14, 20—
The whole day was great! I helped the kids make their valentines and showed them the proper way to address them. They counted valentine candy. This afternoon they had their valentine party. It was fun, but I'll be glad when things get back to normal.

FEBRUARY 19, 20—
I found a worksheet called "Dental Insurance." I think it would be a neat activity to do as a follow-up to the Health Adventure field trip. There is math included on the worksheet. The students have to figure out the math problem in order to know what color to color a part of the picture. They will then write a letter to Dr. Trueluck, thanking him for paying their way to the Health Adventure. The letter is on the back of the picture.

FEBRUARY 20, 20—
We went on another field trip this morning. We went to see the Elephant Walk downtown. (The circus came to town.) We walked to get there. I never knew how tiring it could be to walk five blocks with 16 kids. By the end of the day, I was so tired that I didn't think I would make it home. But I did, and I was sure glad to be there.

FEBRUARY 21, 20—
I taught my first spelling lesson today. It went O.K. I think it could have been better. I never taught a spelling lesson before, and I basically did it the way Ms. Bennes does. It just wasn't me. Maybe tomorrow will be a little better.

(continued)

FEBRUARY 22, 20—

Today's lesson went a little better. I can still see where there can be a lot of improvement. I'm going to have to sit down and really think of a different twist to teaching spelling.

FEBRUARY 25, 20—

Today was pretty bad. The kids didn't want to listen, and they didn't. This afternoon I read a story to them, and they were all over the place. Ms. Bennes even said she had not seen them act this way before. Ms. Bennes and I talked to the ones who were misbehaving. I just can't imagine another day like this one.

FEBRUARY 26, 20—

Today was so much better! They listened, they were polite, they were almost little sweethearts. We did something different in spelling that they seemed to enjoy, and I think that helped a lot. This was a great turnaround from yesterday.

MARCH 6, 20—

Today we had a statewide tornado drill. It was supposed to be at 9:30, but it wasn't until about 10:15. It made the morning very disorganized, and we really didn't get a whole lot accomplished. This afternoon, I will help some of the children with their science projects for the science fair on Friday. It should be fun and interesting.

MARCH 15, 20—

I got a lot done today. I put up a bulletin board, watered the kids' lima beans, made a spelling Bingo game, and cut out positive reward incentives.

(Janet Joyce's log continues in this fashion, discussing how she helps the children make rabbit masks and helps to give an I.Q. test. She also discusses her concern about a child who threatens to run away and commit suicide, as well as her worries about how to discipline the children when they misbehave. She and the classroom teacher develop a management plan. She discusses getting ready to teach a social studies unit in which the children develop their own questions based on the table of contents of a chapter in their textbook.

Assisting the Teacher

An important, early school-based step toward the teaching process is assisting the teacher in a variety of noninstructional classroom duties, which allows education students to apply some of what they have learned in their college classes and in-school observation without taking primary responsibility for students before they are ready. Because effective teachers have an activity for students to start working on as they enter the classroom, the teacher-education student can assist in preparing and setting up this activity. Effective teachers' "students know the procedure because they have been taught to follow it, and no time is wasted directing students on what to do. Not only does this establish an orderly, efficient atmosphere, but it also forces student to take responsibility" (Shalaway, 1998, 68).

First, the student participant and classroom teacher should discuss what type of assistance would be most helpful to the teacher and valuable to the class. There are hundreds of noninstructional duties in which teachers are involved every day. They include activities as diverse as taking attendance and placing student work on the bulletin board. Although most of these duties are routine tasks, they support the important work of teaching and learning. Classroom routines usually can be placed in one of these categories: physical condition of the room, movement of the children, handling materials and papers, keeping records and reports, classroom procedures, and special drills, classes, and days.

Many student participants incorrectly assume that such tasks are demeaning and prevent active participation in the classroom. On the contrary, these routines are essential to managing the classroom, and the teacher who does not master them is rarely able to teach. Initially, routine tasks assumed by the student participants should not directly involve the children. We have provided you with a checklist of some of these activities.

SAMPLE FORM 38   Checklist of Routines for Helping the Teacher

STUDENT: Reggie Gomez

TEACHER: Mr. Downs

GRADE LEVEL AND/OR SUBJECT: Sixth grade; science

DATES: September 11, 20— to October 24, 20—

OBJECTIVE: To participate in noninstructional classroom duties

Instructions to Student Participant: All of the following duties are important to the management of the instructional environment. You will need to learn to complete these while simultaneously teaching the students and managing the class. To help you learn to do so efficiently, complete all tasks appropriate to your teaching situation and indicate the date each is accomplished. Please have the classroom teacher sign this form when all appropriate activities have been successfully completed.

Activity	Date Completed
1. Make a seating chart	September 11
2. Take attendance	September 16
3. Run errands for the classroom teacher	September 3
4. Help with classroom housekeeping	September 3
5. Organize materials needed for a lesson	September 26
6. Make copies of materials needed for the lesson	September 18
7. Help pass out materials to the students	September 4
8. Arrange a bulletin board	October 3
9. Check out books from the library to be used by students in the classroom	September 13
10. Check out media to be used in a lesson	October 14
11. Make a chart or graph	October 29
12. Make a transparency or stencil	September 16
13. Run a film, filmstrip, videotape, etc.	October 21
14. Get supplementary materials needed for a lesson (magazine illustrations, pamphlets, maps, etc.)	September 16
15. Develop a bibliography for an upcoming unit	November 4
16. Correct papers	September 19
17. Set up or help set up a lab	October 21

(continued)

18. Write news/assignments on the chalkboard . . . . *October 5*

19. Set up a learning center . . . . *November 18*

20. Set up an experiment or a demonstration . . . . *October 24*

21. Obtain a speaker to come to class, or help organize a class field trip . . . . *November 15*

22. Help gather materials for a class party . . . . *November 22*

23. Help make costumes for a class play . . . . *October 24*

24. Send out a class newsletter to parents . . . . *did not do*

25. Other (please list below): . . . . *October 26*

Supervised playground, took children to bus.

I certify that the student participant listed above has successfully completed all of the above activities that are appropriate to my classroom.

Mr. Downs
_____

(Classroom teacher's signature)

Referenced to INTASC Standards 1, 4, 7, 10

After student participants work in classrooms for a few days and begin to learn the routine and know the children, they can broaden their activities to include those that directly involve the children. We provide you with two checklists of some of these activities in Sample Form 39.1 and Form 39.2.

SAMPLE FORM 39.1   Checklist of Routines Involving Students

STUDENT: Alex Gerstenberger

TEACHER: Mrs. Caudle

GRADE LEVEL AND/OR SUBJECT: Eighth grade; social studies

DATES: September 19, 20— to November 14, 20—

OBJECTIVE: To determine students' skills, motivation, and interests in a teaching/learning situation

Instructions to Student Participant: All of the following activities are important to the instruction of the students. You will need to learn to complete these while simultaneously teaching the students and managing the class. To help you learn to do so efficiently, complete all tasks appropriate to your teaching situation and indicate the date each is accomplished. Please have the classroom teacher sign this form when all appropriate activities have been successfully completed.

Activity	Date Completed
1. Orient a new student.	*September 19*
2. Help individual students with seatwork	*September 11*
3. Work with a club or student activity.	*October 14*

(continued)

 4. Assist a small group . . . . *September 24*
 5. Work with an individual student in a lab (i.e., computer, language, or science) . . . *September 27*
 6. Assist a disabled student . . . . *October 18*
 7. Assist students with library research . . . . *October 31*
 8. Monitor a test . . . . *November 14*
 9. Collect money . . . . *September 6*
10. Hand out and collect materials . . . . *September 6*
11. Listen to an individual student read or recite a lesson . . . . *September 26*
12. Give a test or a quiz . . . . *November 11*
13. Assist young children with clothing . . . . *N/A*
14. Bring books or materials to share with the students . . . . *October 15*
15. Supervise students outside the classroom . . . . *October 21*
16. Read aloud or tell a story . . . . *September 30*
17. Help students in a learning center . . . . *November 6*
18. Accompany students to a school office, the bus, or the playground . . . . *September 26*
19. Attend a parent-teacher conference . . . . *October 29*
20. Work with the teacher in developing an IEP (Individual Education Plan)
    for a mainstreamed student . . . . *November 8*
21. Accompany students to before- or after-school programs . . . . *Daily beginning*
    September 9
22. Help monitor the hallway, lunchroom, or playground . . . . *September 9*
23. Other (please list below):
    Worked with small groups in computer lab for 30 minutes, two days a week.

I certify that the student participant listed above has successfully completed all of the above activities that are appropriate to my classroom.

Mrs. Caudle
_____
(Classroom teacher's signature)

···
Referenced to INTASC Standards 1, 4, 7, 10
···

The Kidwatching Model

Kidwatching? What is kidwatching and how does it differ from what you have been doing your entire life? How does it differ from the observations of students you have done in the past?

The kidwatching model comes from the field of psychology. The "child study movement" began in the 1930s to help preservice teachers become systematic observers of student behaviors. Throughout this text you have been practicing kidwatching as you completed anecdotal observations, structured observations, and interviews. You may remember Sally Reider's anecdotal observation of Sammy in Chapter 4. Sally was participating in kidwatching.

Today the kidwatching most commonly employed focuses on the observation and assessment of the student's oral and written development. Sample Form 39.2 is a simplified version of the kidwatching model. As you plan for your tutoring and small-group teaching, you can use the information you gain from kidwatching. The Checklist for Kidwatching can be a helpful tool as you target the specific needs and strengths of your students' oral and written language.

SAMPLE FORM 39.2   Checklist for Kidwatching

STUDENT: Frederic Gaddis

TEACHER: Mr. Gaberra

GRADE LEVEL AND/OR SUBJECT: Grade 4

DATES: September 20, 20— to October 20, 20—

TIME: 20 minute periods over a period of a month.

OBJECTIVE: To observe the oral and written language development of a student over a period of time.

Instructions: Become familiar with the statements below. Check activity observed and record the date(s) you observed the activity, then write a brief statement of what you <u>specifically</u> observed.

Check	Date	Activity Observed

1. ✓   9/20   Participates in group talk (discussions about books, stories/plays, science experiments, math problems).

EXAMPLE: Told the class about the book he had just read: **Z is for Zamboni: A Hockey Alphabet by Matt Napier.**

2. ✓   9/20   Asks teacher questions (for assistance, about language, about content).

EXAMPLE: Asked for help in multiplication problem. Asked how to spell "believe" and "interesting."

3. ✓   9/25   Leads conversations.

EXAMPLE: Talked often one-to-one, but said only a few words during group discussion on assigned problem.

4. ✓   9/25   Participates and takes turns appropriately in conversations.

EXAMPLE: Talked frequently (to those sitting nearby) while others were focusing on the topic. Interrupted frequently to contribute to the topic.

5. ✓   9/27   Builds on what others say.

EXAMPLE: When the Autumnal Equinox was being discussed by the class, Frederick's comments were only vaguely related, e.g., "My Dad goes bear hunting this time of year."

6. ✓   10/1   Speaks clearly and audibly; used comprehensible speech.

EXAMPLE: Noted he dropped his voice or left off entirely the endings of words, such as "ed", "er", "ing".

7. ✓   10/3   Listens when others speak.

EXAMPLE: Listened attentively during the reading of a story entitled, "Loser" by Jerry Spinelli, but did not listen when peers discussed this story about a kid who was a loser.

(continued)

8. ✓ 10/5   Demonstrates understanding of oral directions.

EXAMPLE: Did not listen to directions for solving the assigned math problem on multiplication of fractions. He played with pencil and rubber band when the teacher was showing them how to work similar problems on the blackboard.

9. ✓ 10/7   Explains how to do or make something.

EXAMPLE: In science class, Frederick gave a good explanation while demonstrating with jar, candle and water in dish that fire needs oxygen. He handled the materials well while talking.

10. ✓ 10/9   Writes for a specific purpose on an assigned topic.

EXAMPLE: Wrote down one main idea about "Living near the Arctic Circle", but gave only two details.

11. ✓ 10/11   Demonstrates knowledge of punctuation (spacing, commas, period, question marks, and capitalization).

EXAMPLE: Writing today (turned in to teacher) was missing needed commas, periods and question marks. Caps were appropriately used.

12. ✓ 10/11   Writes sentences in appropriate grammatical form.

EXAMPLE: Incorrect verb tenses, e.g., "He come" instead of "He came". "He done" instead of "He did". "He seen" instead of "He saw".

13. ✓ 10/13   Expresses interest in specific book(s), character(s), magazine(s).

EXAMPLE: Read about race horses, breeding and training, during free time today. Talked to me about jockeys, Kentucky bluegrass and the Kentucky Derby.

14. ✓ 10/15   Attempts to read unknown (sounding out, context clues).

EXAMPLE: Asked help with sounding out "explanation" and "development". Knew what "explanation" meant and guessed meaning of "development" by context clues.

15. ✓ 10/17   Demonstrates understanding of what has been read.

EXAMPLE: "Pioneers" was topic read by the teacher. Demonstrated understanding and interest. Showed me a map of the "Oregon Trail" and told me the dangers in traveling, e.g., Indians, wagons, rough trails, fording streams, etc.

Referenced to INTASC Standards 1–10

Preparing to Teach

Most uninitiated observers of the teaching process believe that teaching is lecturing to a large group of students. Many contend that anyone who has knowledge and can speak, can teach. These contentions are based on the assumption that the teacher must be perpetually on stage. Today the best teaching practices take the teacher off the stage. Rather the teacher acts as a moderator, facilitator, coach, designer, observer, and assessor (Zemelman, Daniels, and Hyde, 1998, 156).

Teaching involves employing many activities at once. In addition to the routine tasks described previously, classroom teachers frequently find themselves teaching small groups of students while they are instructing individuals within the group.

At the same time, they may be observing the activities of other students in the classroom. If a teacher, for example, knows that four students are at the math center, and that one of them is likely to have difficulty with the new word problem added today, he makes a mental note to see if the student needs help as soon as he finishes with another group. The teacher is also aware of the students working on a science experiment at the back sink, and listens carefully for any sound that might indicate that playing with water is more interesting than using it in the experiment. The teacher hears beeps and burps from the computers, so he knows that the students are busily engaged. He is also aware that in fifteen minutes he must interrupt all of this activity so that there is time to introduce the children to the new social studies unit before lunch. When he hears a knock on the door he is not surprised; he knows that the door monitor will open it. Jacob Kounin describes the teacher's simultaneous involvement in dozens of activities as "withitness" (1970). Being able to focus on so many activities at once is not easy, nor does it come naturally to the beginner. "Withitness" is a skill learned from considerable experience with the variety of activities that occur in the classroom.

To help develop this essential skill, student participants should begin their teaching experiences with the smallest unit of classroom instruction—tutoring a single student in a single skill or concept. From here, they can proceed to working with a small group of students, initially using the classroom teacher's plan, as Janet Joyce does, and later using their own plans. After all of this has been successfully accomplished, they can tackle teaching a lesson to the entire class. At first, teaching might be done using the teacher's plan; afterward, with the help of the teacher, it might be done by developing more independent plans. After significant practice using all of these teaching skills, the student participant should begin developing "withitness."

Planning to Teach

Before any teaching is done, whether it be tutoring a single child or teaching a lesson to the entire class, planning is essential. Planning for anything—a social function, what college to attend, where to go on vacation—can be a difficult task. All planning requires reflecting on the past and anticipating the future. We recommend that preservice teachers practice their planned lessons prior to presenting them to students in the classroom. The consequences of failing to plan are usually more painful than the labor of planning. Thus, for the teacher, the consequences of an unplanned or poorly planned lesson may include embarrassment, preoccupation with discipline, loss of control, and a poor evaluation by a superior. Similarly, the student may also suffer such consequences as loss of interest, disruptive behavior, and limited or no learning. The table that follows gives one teacher's account of a lesson with little or no planning.

TABLE 5.1   Running Account of an Unplanned Lesson

AIM: To discuss digestion

PROCEDURE: A pupil will give a report that will lead to a class discussion

MATERIALS: Mimeographed drawing of the digestive process in hands of the pupils, and a sketch on the board of the same process.

Teacher	Pupils	Supervisory comment
	"Mr. Gale, the diagram on the board says it takes four days for digestion to take place. Isn't that wrong?"	
The boy who copied it down for me made a mistake.	"But. Mr. Gale, the mimeographed sheet you gave us reads the same way."	Teacher loses respect by failing to admit his error.
"Well, then, it's wrong. It should be four hours. Let's forget that until I take the roll." (Calls off names one by one.)		Uneconomic use of time. Should have a seating chart.
"John, get up here and give your report."	(Report, obviously copied from an encyclopedia, is read in three minutes.)	Pupils are evidently not taught how to make or give a report.
"Is that all? Read it again."	"Do we have to take notes on this? Will we be tested on this?"	Indicates lack of any organized procedure.
"Certainly, everything we do here is important. Joan, you come to the board and take down important data in John's report."		Yet notebooks of pupils around me contain no science notes.
"John, read your report."	"I've read it twice." (Girl at board is not clear on what to do.)	Introduces a new procedure without preparing the class.
"We'll finish this tomorrow. Get out some paper. I'm going to give you a quiz. Copy down these questions."	(Class is very noisy.)	Teacher improvising. Had no alternative plan worked out.
"All right, not too much talking."		
"There is too much noise here. There is no need for it."		
"Now look! What is all this chattering about? Stop it."	"You didn't teach us any of this."	Quiz evidently not prepared beforehand.
"This is supposed to be a quiz. Would you mind moving apart a little?"	(Pupils unconcerned and talk throughout the quiz.)	Teacher's lack of planning and procedure is leading to chaos.
"Do you know what you can put down on this paper - zero."		

(continued)

Teacher	Pupils	Supervisory comment
"Look! I'm getting fed up. Come to detention this afternoon."		Threats ineffective. Class does not respect or fear teacher.
"Do you realize that you people cannot keep quiet for five minutes?"		
"All right. I'll collect the papers, and we will go into tomorrow's lesson."		Collects papers one by one.
"Anybody know what a spectrum is?"	"Something like a color wheel." (Aimless discussion for about ten minutes.)	Teacher improvising.
"Read this chapter for tomorrow."		Assignment nebulous.
"Quiet now! I am going to open the door to see if classes have been dismissed."		School has a bell system. Teacher cannot wait to escape from the noise.

Source: Adopted from Thomas J. Brown. *Student Teaching in a Secondary School,* 1968.

When teaching, successful planning requires thorough knowledge of the content, an understanding of a variety of methods for presenting the content, and knowledge of the psychological readiness of the pupils. Any teacher who assumes that learning ends with the baccalaureate degree is not likely to be very successful. This was acknowledged when the Interstate New Teacher Assessment and Support Consortium (INTASC) developed standards recognizing that all teachers, at every career stage, must possess core knowledge and skills. As a teacher's career matures, his or her knowledge and skills must also become more sophisticated. Some subjects and skills that today's teachers teach were not a part of the curriculum when they attended school. For example, many teachers have had neither courses nor even instruction in computers, but they now must teach word processing, using the Internet, computer graphics, computer programming, and even computer ethics. Likewise, they use CD-ROM technology and PowerPoint presentations to teach their lessons. For some teachers, the information superhighway allows their students to communicate with students at universities around their state and even children in Japan. None of this was even a remote possibility during their years in school and in some cases even during their undergraduate, teacher-education programs. Likewise, the world of teacher education is continually developing and changing. Many classroom teachers did not focus on teaching standards, teaching styles, multiple intelligences, multicultural education, reflection, or kidwatching during their college careers. Today, knowledge of each of these areas and an ability to integrate the knowledge into the curriculum and teaching is critical to effective teaching. Therefore, one of the most important steps to success in planning to teach and in teaching is continuous study.

The 2003 report from the National Commission on Teaching and America's Future lists the following criteria for a highly qualified beginning teacher:

- Possess a deep understanding of the subjects they teach;
- Evidence a firm understanding of how students learn;
- Demonstrate the teaching skills necessary to help all students achieve high standards;
- Create a positive learning environment;
- Use a variety of assessment strategies to diagnose and respond to individual learning needs;
- Demonstrate and integrate modern technology into curricula to support student learning;

- Reflect on their practice to improve future teaching and student achievement;
- Pursue professional growth in both content and pedagogy; and
- Instill a passion for learning in their students. (National Commission on Teaching and America's Future, 2003, 7)

Developing Plans

Although planning is always time-consuming, it is not a difficult process. Planning is a skill involving a series of steps that can be taught and learned. Assuming the teacher has knowledge of both the content to be taught and the students, the steps in planning are as follows:

PREPLANNING

1. Examine the ten principles of teaching standards.
2. Examine the technology standards.
3. Consider the ability levels, learning styles, and multiple intelligences of the students.
4. Examine school district, county, or state curriculum guides.
5. Examine the results of your observation of students ("Kidwatching").
6. Determine which goal(s) you will address in the lesson. (A goal is a learning end.)
7. Select the topic of the lesson.
8. Research your lesson topic on the Internet
9. Gather materials and examples. Be sure you have selected ones that are appropriate for the pupils (e.g., Do you need left-handed scissors? Can your kindergarten students do a print that requires multiple colors of paint in a single class session? Have you included materials that represent the ethnic, cultural, racial, and religious background of your students?).
10. Identify what students already know about the topic.
11. Determine the duration of the lesson.

PLANNING

1. Write the goal(s) you plan to address at the top of your plan.
2. Develop specific, short-term objectives for your lesson. (Objectives are what you hope the pupils will accomplish by the end of the lesson.)
3. Select the materials you will use.
4. Identify an appropriate teaching methodology (or a variety of methodologies).
5. Arrange the materials and/or steps in a logical sequence. (Ask yourself: Is the amount of material and number of steps appropriate for the maturity of the students and length of the class period?)
6. Choose appropriate teaching activities and experiences.
7. Decide how learning will be assessed.

PRETEACHING

1. Prepare class handouts, audiovisuals, etc.
2. Review or preview any materials you will be using in the lesson. (Be sure that if students will be using materials individually you have previewed them as well.)
3. Review your plan.

The following plan was developed by a student participant who used the steps outlined above to meet a state literal comprehension goal for tenth graders. This student used the lesson plan format in Chapter 2, pp. 39–40, to design her lesson and meet the state goal: "The learner will identify [the] *sequence* of events." This and other lesson plan formats can be used to design lessons follow.

SAMPLE FORM 40.1   Lesson Plan Form 1

STUDENT: Juan Gomez

TEACHER: Mrs. Ricardo

GRADE LEVEL AND/OR SUBJECT: Tenth grade; English

DATE AND TIME: December 9, 20—, 8:30 a.m.

OBJECTIVE: To prepare a seven-step lesson plan to be used in teaching a specific lesson.

Instructions to the Student Participant: Whether your plan covers several classroom sessions or only one, each lesson should include an outline of your goal, objectives, materials, and expected lesson duration in addition to the seven steps listed below:

Goal: To teach the learner to identify sequence of events

OBJECTIVES:

1. The learners will identify the sequence of events in a videotape of a popular television show, "Murder She Wrote."
2. The learners will identify the sequence of events, using the format established by the class, in the short story, "Four and Twenty Blackbirds," by Agatha Christie.

MATERIALS:

1. Videotape player and television.
2. The videotape of an episode of "Murder She Wrote."
3. Chalk.
4. Twenty-five copies of "Adventures in Appreciation," the literature text containing the Christie story.
5. Five sheets of newsprint, five magic markers, and masking tape.
6. Overhead projector, blank transparency, and marker pen.

Duration: Two sixty-minute class periods.

(continued)

FIRST CLASS

1. Anticipatory Set

Today we're going to be seeing a videotape of a recent episode of "Murder, She Wrote." (This alone will provide the motivation.)

How many of you have seen that show on T.V.?

Who is the main character on the show? (Jessica Fletcher, a mystery writer/detective.)

What usually happens in the show? (List responses on chalkboard. Be sure students determine the following: Murder usually occurs early in the show. During the remainder of the show, we are introduced to various suspects to learn their motives and alibis. Jessica spends her time researching such clues as the murder weapon. Throughout the show, we are presented with many "red herrings," which attempt to lead us to the wrong conclusion. By the end of the episode the murder is solved.)

Write SAVE on the board; this information will be needed tomorrow. (5 minutes)

2. Objective

We will be looking for the exact sequence of events in today's episode. You'll need a notebook and a pen. Put everything else under your chairs. Write down each event as it occurs; you might want to use the outline on the board to assist you in the process. Remember, you are looking for the exact sequence of events. Be sure to take careful notes because you will need them in class tomorrow. (Wait for students to have notebook and pen on desk and everything else under their chairs.) (5 minutes)

3. Teacher Input

View the video of "Murder, She Wrote." (Watch video from rear of the room to monitor students' attention and notetaking.) (45 minutes)

SECOND CLASS

4. Checking for Understanding

Take out the notes you took yesterday on the "Murder, She Wrote" video. Put everything else under your chairs.

Let's review the sequence we recorded on the board yesterday. (Call students' attention to SEQUENCE written on board.)

Did you see a similar sequence in this episode? (5 minutes)

Did you find any "red herrings"? (5 minutes)

5. Guided Practice

You will be outlining the specific events of this episode in your activity groups. (Note: This assumes students are assigned to long-term activity groups, and they know the procedure to be used in completing group-work.) The assignment for your group-work is written on the board.

ASSIGNMENT ON THE BOARD AS FOLLOWS:
Group-Work Assignment

1. Select a recorder.

2. List on the newsprint provided, the sequence of events in the episode of "Murder, She Wrote." Be sure to include all elements outlined on the board.

3. You have ten minutes to complete this task. When you have finished, post your newsprint on the side wall, using the masking tape provided.

   (While students are working in groups, place a copy of the literature anthology under each chair.)

(continued)

After groups have completed their sequence-of-events charts, compare each sequence chart with the class. On the overhead projector, create a class sequence of events. Discuss why some groups sequenced the events of the story differently. (25 minutes)

6. Independent Practice

Now we will independently read Agatha Christie's "Four and Twenty Blackbirds," found in your literature anthology on page 16.

Have any of you heard of Agatha Christie before? Have you read anything by her? (She is a famous British mystery writer, known particularly for her murder mysteries. The detective in this story is one of her two famous detectives, Hercule Poirot, who is always investigating cases in London. Note: The other famous detective is Miss Marple.)

As you read this story, outline the sequence of events just as we did for "Murder, She Wrote." I'll leave the original outline of the sequence of events we did yesterday on the board to help you. I'll also leave the one we just completed on the overhead to help you. You'll need to do this in your notebook. We'll have about 20 minutes to read today in class. If you do not finish the story, you'll need to finish it for homework. I will be collecting the sequence you do for this story tomorrow at the beginning of class. (This will be used to assess the students' understanding of the sequence-of-events concept as well as their understanding of Christie's story.) Any questions? (As students are reading, put homework assignment on the board.)

ASSIGNMENT ON THE BOARD AS FOLLOWS:
Homework Assignment

1. Finish reading "Four and Twenty Blackbirds" by Agatha Christie ("Adventures in Appreciation," pages 16-25).

2. On notebook paper, list the sequence of events of the story.

3. The assignment will be collected tomorrow at the beginning of class. (25 minutes)

7. Closure

Five minutes before the end of the class, ask the students to stop reading and pay attention to a brief discussion.

Summarizing questions to involve the students in synthesizing the lesson:
How was this story similar to the episode of "Murder, She Wrote?"
Did the sequence follow the model we put on the board?
How did the story differ from the episode of "Murder, She Wrote?"
Did Christie present you with any "red herrings"?
Your assignment for tomorrow is on the board.

Source: Lois Sprinthall. *A Strategy Guide for Teachers: Guidebook for Supervisors of Novice Teachers.* Unpublished manuscript. Based on the work of Madeline Hunter.

Referenced to INTASC Standards 1–10

Because there are so many different formats you can use in planning lessons, we have included two additional ones below. You, your school-based cooperating teacher, or your university supervisor can select any one of these formats, or you might want to try both of these to see which one works best for you. It is also likely that your cooperating teacher or university supervisor has another format he or she would like you to try. It doesn't matter which lesson plan format you use as long as it gives you all the information you need to teach and evaluate your lesson effectively. Likewise, it is also important that the lesson plan format you select makes articulation between other lessons within a unit or across subject areas easy to accomplish. A lesson should not stand alone, but rather be a part of an entire curriculum.

SAMPLE FORM 40.2   Lesson Plan Form 2

STUDENT: Jennifer Davis

TEACHER: Mrs. Bragg

GRADE LEVEL AND/OR SUBJECT: k, 1, 2 (MULTI-GRADES) MATHEMATICS

TOPIC: SYMMETRY

DATE AND TIME: March 16, 20—9:10a.m.

Background: One of the North Carolina Mathematics Standards for first and second grade is that student will understand the meaning of "symmetry." The kindergarten children will develop some initial understanding.

Instructions to the Student Participant: This plan will cover one or two days, depending on the levels of maturity in a multi-age/multi-grade class. Hands on and interactive approaches will be used.

Objectives

1. The students will pronounce the work, "symmetry".

2. The students will be able to point to the line of symmetry in a circle, triangle and rectangle on the blackboard.

3. The students will relate that symmetry means the details are same on either side of a line (axis).

4. The students will be able to fold their own cut out—circles and rectangles, to make a line (axis) of symmetry.

5. The students will use geo reflector mirrors to observe symmetry in pictures.

6. The students will finish the incomplete image of a tree and then decorate the tree symmetrically.

Key Concepts
Symmetry, Equal, Exact, Triangle, Square Reflection, Rectangle.

Materials
Different colored circles, squares, rectangles, and a circle that has been divided symmetrically, geo reflector mirrors.

Procedures

1. Write symmetry, equal and exact on the blackboard and discuss their meanings.

2. Discuss how the line of symmetry divides the image equally.

3. Have students fold cut-out of circles, squares, and rectangles to identify lines of symmetry.

4. Have first and second grade students use geo-reflector mirrors to observe symmetry in pictures. Have kindergarten children use pattern blocks to identify symmetry.

5. Have students finish drawing, then coloring the incomplete image of a tree.

(continued)

Evaluation

1. All of the students completed the incomplete image of a tree.

2. The first and second graders made lines of symmetry by folding cutouts of circles, squares and rectangles.

3. The kindergarten children matched pattern blocks that fit lines of symmetry.

4. The first and second graders were able to relate that "symmetry" meant equal and exact in detail on each side of the line or axis.

5. The students took their completed trees and folded circles, squares and rectangles home to share with their parents.

Referenced to INTASC Standards 1–10

SAMPLE FORM 40.3   Lesson Plan Form 3

DATE/TIME: 2/2/04 – 1:30 PM

TIME: 1:30–3:00

STUDENT: Margaret Lee

TEACHER: Mr. Tucker

GRADE LEVEL/SUBJECT: Eleventh grade; American Literature

Objective: Students will learn information on the literature produced during the Revolutionary Period, focusing on Paine's Crisis No. 1" and the "Declaration of Independence."

INTASC STANDARDS	Lesson Objectives
Standard 1: Content Pedagogy Standard 2: Student Development Standard 4: Multiple Instructional Strategies Standard 7: Planning Standard 8: Assessment Standard 9: Reflective Practice	1. Students will learn characteristics of revolutionary literary period. 2. Students will read Thomas Paine's "Crisis No. 1" and focus on his persuasive techniques. 3. Students will read "The Declaration of Independence" and study the structure of the document and imitate it with their own declaration.

Materials

"Crisis No. 1" and "Declaration of Independence," a reading quiz, handout: facts about Revolutionary Period and writers of Period.

Warm-up Activity

Reading Quiz on "Crisis No. 1" & "Declaration of Independence"

(continued)

Lesson

1. Get vocabulary from reading.
2. Give background information on revolutionary period. Compare with colonial period. Ask students to see differences. See handout for information.
3. Discuss Paine's "Crisis No. 1." Have students look at the persuasive techniques Paine uses to get his reader to support the war. Why is that significant? Have students pick out a line in the essay that could stand alone. Share responses with class. See handout for additional questions and comments.
4. Discuss "The Declaration of Independence." What is significant about the changes that the Congress made? Why did Jefferson include the rights he did and the reasons for Americans wanting independence? What is the logical structure of the document? Deductive Reasoning. Show example.
5. Give students a copy of the women's Declaration of Independence. Ask students to find similarities.
6. Have students write their own declaration of independence about something they believe in, modeled after Jefferson's. Have students share their responses if they want. Share own example first.

Assessment

Reading quiz grades will be added to their final grade. An informal evaluation of their writing their own "Declaration of Independence".

Homework Assignment

Students will read Poe's "Tell Tale Heart" and "The Raven." Their reader response drafts are due tomorrow, too.

ESL/EC Strategies

- Write information about period on the board for visual learners.
- Give example of a declaration of independence for students before they write their own.
- Use questions from all levels of Bloom's taxonomy to motivate students

Lesson Evaluation/Changes (Reflection)

good quiz grades, responded more to Jefferson that Paine, need to relate Paine to current war situation, look more at persuasive techniques, worked hard on their declarations (very creative)

Source: Adapted from Robert Ventura, Nancy Reid and Margaret Lee: (2001) State Department of Public Instruction Raleigh, NC 27602

....
Referenced to INTASC Standards 1–10
....

The student participant, Juan Gomez, who taught the lesson in a tenth-grade English class (Sample Form 40.1) understood, after reflecting on it with the classroom teacher, that it would lead to several more complex lessons. A unit (a series of lessons addressing a single topic) on mystery writing was planned for several weeks later, and the lesson described in this chapter was used as an advance organizer for the unit to help students understand the plotting techniques used by mystery writers. During the unit, the tenth graders would also write their own narratives, learning to employ sequencing techniques. Likewise, they would examine plot sequence in a variety of other literary genres, including fantasy, historical fiction, and adventure/suspense.

Sequencing lessons in an entire program is a very important part of teaching. Therefore, it is necessary for student participants to examine teaching standards and curriculum guides designed by the district, county, or state (as discussed in Chapters 1 and 3) so that they can begin to understand how their lessons fit into the entire curriculum. Likewise, it is essential that student participants work with classroom teachers to develop lesson plans, so that the teacher can help them understand this sequence of objectives, goals, lessons, and units. A sample unit plan is presented next.

SAMPLE FORM 41   Unit Plan Format

STUDENT: Heather Harbison

TEACHER: Mrs. Sinclair

GRADE LEVEL AND/OR SUBJECT: Twelfth grade, British Literature

DATE: November 13, 20—

UNIT: 17th Century British Poetry

DURATION: 5 days, 90 minute periods or adapted as needed

Objective: To plan a series of related, sequential lesson plans on 17th Century British Poetry, for five, 90 minute class periods.

Overview

Kenneth Rexroth, writer, poet, Special Lecturer at the University of California, Santa Barbara, writes, "…mankind is one species, with a common fund of general experience. Egyptian scribes, Soviet bureaucrats, and junior executives in New York City live and respond to life in the same ways; the lives of farmers or miners or hunters vary only within narrow limits. Love is love and death is death. So the themes of literature have at once an infinite variety and an abiding constancy." (1973 p. 1044)

Therefore, themes of love and death in a study of selected seventeenth century British poets/poetry is relevant to high school students today.

Since this study involves group discussions, analyses, reflections, and written work, based on state and INTASC standards, the unit is planned for an extended period of time.

Purposes

The main purpose of this activity is to develop a deeper appreciation of 17th Century British poetry by analyzing the themes of love and death and how these relate to students' lives.

Another purpose is vocabulary development, particularly word identification, meaning and etymology.

A third purpose is having students work in selected heterogeneous groups over a period of time so they can examine their opinions and beliefs and better understand the perspectives of others.

A further purpose is to involve students in planning, organizing, exercising creative thinking, and using innovative software and varied activities.

Competency Goals

The Learner:

- Will express reflections and reactions to selected poems on love and death to personal experience.
- Will analyze and critique poems from various perspectives and approaches.
- Will deepen understanding of 17th British poetry through exploration and extended engagement.
- Will understand important issues of technology-based society and will exhibit ethical behavior in the use of computer and other technologies.
- Will select and demonstrate knowledge and skills in the use of technological tools for research, class assignments and presentations.
- Will use a variety of technologies to access, analyze, interpret, synthesize, apply, and communicate information.
- Will use word processing and/or desktop publishing for a variety of writing assignments/projects.
- Adhere to Fair Use and Multimedia Copyright Guidelines, citing sources of copyrighted materials in papers, projects, and multimedia presentations.

(continued)

Specific Objectives for this Unit
Students will be able to...

1. Develop vocabulary and word identification skills by writing unfamiliar words from poetry in their literature logs.
2. Use a variety of reading strategies such as Poetry Circles to comprehend poetry.
3. Increase knowledge of death customs in other cultures.
4. Analyze literary elements of poetry by comparing works of poetry.
5. Express and support responses to poetry by discussion and writing in their literature logs.
6. Read and interpret 4/5 poems by British poets of the 17th Century.
7. Express understanding through music, art, speaking and listening and writing in their literature logs.
8. Dissect a poem by creating graphs using the software program "Inspiration 6".
9. Discuss 7-10 British poets and the roots of civil conflict in 17th Century England.

Calendar of Activities

Day 1—   Poems: "To His Coy Mistress" by Andrew Marvell and "Sonnet 130" by Shakespeare.
Theme: Love.
Background Music: "Could Not Ask for More" Edwin McCain
Students will record their individual thoughts about love, then have discussions in small groups. Discussion will center upon comparing, contrasting the two poems and choosing favorite lines. Each student will record unfamiliar words (i.e., coy, hue, parley) w/meanings in their literature logs.
To check understanding: appropriate discussion questions and/or a prepared worksheet should follow.

Day 2—   Poems: "A Valediction: Forbidding Mourning" by John Donne and "Holy Sonnet 14" by John Donne
Theme: Death.
Background Music: "No Man Is an Island" from novel by Ernest Hemingway
Students work in pairs, researching Donne and the 17th Century in which he lived. Research results will be given orally. Unfamiliar vocabulary words from his poems will be discussed and meanings recorded. Working in small groups, the poems will be analyzed: looking for similes, metaphors, personification, symbolism and other poetic devices.
To check understanding: appropriate discussion questions and/or prepared worksheet should follow.

Day 3—   Poetry Circles
Poems: "Holy Sonnet 14" by John Donne; "When I Consider How My Life is Spent" by John Milton; "Virtue" by George Herbert; "On My First Song" by Ben Johnson; and "To the Virgins, To Make Much of the Time" by Robert Herrick.
After orally reading the poems, the students work in groups of five, with each assigned a role: discussion director, vocabulary enricher, interpreter, illustrator and connector (how the poem relates to their lives). Unfamiliar vocabulary w/meanings is recorded. Each group prepares a written summary and makes a collage to help explain the poem. The summary and collage are presented to the class.

Day 4—   Group Work
Poem: "Holy Sonnet 14" by John Donne.
Students work in groups using the Poetic Analysis Template from the software program, "Inspiration 6", on the Internet (See reference list) to analyze (diagram and outline). Unfamiliar vocabulary with meanings are recorded. Each group presents their

(continued)

analysis of this to the class and records their diagram of the poem in their literature log. Students are introduced to the ethical use of computers and The Fair Use of multimedia and copyright guidelines.

Day 5—   Debate

The debate serves both as summary and as an evaluation of the previous 4 days.

The class will be divided into 2 groups for a debate about a poet/poem they have studied. The purpose of the debate is to determine which poet/poem has stood the test of time (which one is a Survivor?) They will examine the poet's accomplishments, literary style, meaning of the poem, vocabulary development and how relevant the poet's theme is to modern life. Each student must participate at least one time in the debate. At the end of the debate, the class votes on the modern life. Each student must participate at least one time in the debate. At the end of the debate, the class votes on the "poet/poem survivor" and each student will record in his/her literature notebook the points which support the group's resolution that their poet/poem has better stood the test of time.

Suggested Assessment

Literature logs	15%
Poetry Circle	25%
Debate	15%
Donne/17th Century	10%
Poetry Analysis	25%
Participation	10%
Total	100%

Referenced to INTASC Standards 1–10

The Rubric: A Quantitative and Qualitative Assessment

Heather used a quantitative assessment to evaluate the students' understanding of 17th Century British Poetry. Another assessment tool is a rubric.

A rubric assigns numbers to levels of quality of achievement from excellent to poor. The criteria to reach each level is clearly indicated on the rubric, thus making it easier for the teacher to assess the students' work and for the students to understand the teacher's evaluation.

Teachers, students, and parents like well designed rubrics for the following reasons:

- Defines more clearly the quality of teaching and learning, showing students more clearly how to meet teacher expectations. The performance of students can be monitored.
- Demonstrates improvement in the quality of student work and in learning. Helpful in students becoming a better judge of their own and others' work.
- Provides a working guide for teachers and students before instruction.
- Reduces the amount of time teachers spend evaluating student work.
- Provides students with more immediate informative feedback about their strengths and areas of need.
- Provides parents with better understanding of exactly what their child needs to be successful. (Andrade, 2002, 2-3)

TABLE 5.2 A Rubric for Assessing Student's Work in Seventeenth Century British Poetry

Criteria	Quantitative Assessment			
	4	3	2	1
Poet's Accomplishments	Records all of the volume of the poet's works and lists from literature text the most well known work/works. Compare/contrasts volume of his work with that of another poet.	Records half of the volume of the poet's works and lists most well known works of the poet.	Records one fourth of volume of poets works. Lists from literature text the most well-known of poet's work.	Records one poem written by a poet
Literary Style	Compared/contrasted poet's style with 2 other poets in 17th Century British literature. Use of imagery Has thematic element Reflection of poet's life	Compared/contrasted poet's style with one other 17th Century British poet Use of imagery Has thematic element Reflection of poet's life	Has thematic element. Reflection on poet's life	Stated why he/she did not like the poet's style.
Meaning of Poem	Wrote a 5 sentence paragraph, recording the use of similes, metaphors, adjectives and work meanings to relate meaning of poem in 17th Century England.	Wrote a 3 sentence paragraph, recording the use of similes, metaphors, adjectives and work meanings to relate meaning of poem in 17th Century England.	Wrote a 2 sentence paragraph using adjectives and word meanings.	Wrote one sentence about what the poem meant.
Vocabulary Development	Recorded all the unfamiliar words and their meanings from each of the eights poems. All meanings were expressed in context.	Recorded unfamiliar words and their meanings from seven of the poems. 3 meanings were expressed in context. Listed synonyms for 3 meanings.	Recorded unfamiliar words and their meanings from 5 of the poems. Synonyms were written for the 5 words.	Unfamiliar words from two of the poems were recorded—no meanings were given.
Relevancy to Modern Life	Recorded four reasons why it was relevant. Two for him/herself and two to older adults.	Recorded three reasons why it was relevant to modern life.	Recorded one reason why it was relevant to modern life.	Recorded it was relevant but did not explain how it was relevant.

Referenced to INTASC Standards 1–10

SAMPLE FORM 42   Reflective Observation of Preteaching and Planning

NAME OF OBSERVER: Richard Blackburn

DATE AND TIME OF REFLECTIVE OBSERVATION: May 22, 20— 1:15 p.m.

TEACHER/SCHOOL: Mr. Romano; Ellenboro Elementary

GRADE LEVEL AND/OR SUBJECT: Fifth grade

OBJECTIVE OF OBSERVATION: To think carefully and reflect about your participation, preteaching, and planning. Below are some guiding questions/statements related to each of the five steps in the reflection cycle. The questions/statements are directly related to the ten principles from the INTASC Standards.

Instructions to the Observer: Respond to the following questions on this form after you have completed participation, preteaching, and planning.

1. **Select**
   a. What preteaching activities did you complete?
   b. What kind of planning did you do before your teaching?
   c. What principles from INTASC Standards did you address in your plan?
   d. What can a rubric help you do?

2. **Describe**
   a. List the steps you used in the planning process.
   b. Describe the parts of your lesson plan.
   c. Describe the parts of your unit plan.
   d. Describe Kidwatching.

3. **Analyze**
   a. How do you relate planning a lesson to teaching a lesson?
   b. How did your preteaching and planning prepare you for your future teaching?
   c. Which preteaching activities were most helpful to you?
   d. Compare/contrast a rubric scoring with the scoring listed at the end of the unit.

4. **Appraise**
   a. What planning techniques were most helpful to you?
   b. How effective were you in checking classroom routines?
   c. How effective were you in checking students' routines?
   d. How does Kidwatching influence teacher planning?

5. **Transform**
   a. What lesson and/or unit planning techniques will you use in your future teaching? Why?
   b. What additional planning skills would you like to develop?
   c. What did you learn about planning for using the Internet that you can use in your classroom teaching?
   d. How will you incorporate rubrics in your future teaching?

Source: Adapted from North Carolina State Department of Public Instruction. *Performance Based Licensure,* Raleigh, NC, 1998–1999.

Referenced to INTASC Standards 1–10

Chapter Six
Teaching

Initial Teaching Experiences

Your initial teaching experiences should be successful ones. To ensure their success, you should plan carefully and begin slowly. A good place to begin is working with a single student. The first session should be devoted to getting to know the student and letting the student get to know you. Your objective for that session might be simply, "The learner will discuss something about himself or herself with the tutor." If the student you will be tutoring speaks English as her or his second language (ESL), you may want to focus on the student's cultural, linguistic, and family background.

Most preservice students are nervous when they face a student or a class for the first time. These jitters are normal, but once you have examined the management and discipline standards and principles in the classroom and have developed your lesson plan, you will feel more confident. To ensure that your plan will be successful, discuss it with the classroom teacher prior to implementing it.

Try to begin each new teaching experience with something you enjoy. For example, you might spend an early session reading and discussing a story you love. Or, you might do part of a lesson in which you discuss a trip you took. If the fifth-grade social studies class is studying Mexico and you recently visited Mexico, your first short lesson plan might include some Mexican music, a few slides you took, sharing a Mexican story, discussing Mexican food, etc.

In order for you to develop your teaching skills, it is essential that you increase your understanding of teaching standards, management principles, and students. It is also important that you learn to reflect on your actual teaching experiences, and share these reflections with classroom cooperating teachers and college or university supervisors. As you work through this chapter, we advise you to review the reflective process described in Chapter 1, pp. 14–16 and the ten performance-based teaching principles outlined in Chapter 2, pp 6–9.

The Importance of Teaching Standards

Just as it is important to set high standards for our students in order to encourage learning, it is critical that we have high standards for ourselves as teachers. You were introduced to the concept of standards in Chapter 1. You have used the standards established by the Interstate New Teacher Assessment and Support Consortium (INTASC) in the reflections you have completed. It is our hope that your understanding of the standards and their importance to your growth as a teacher will deepen as you work through the forms in this chapter.

According to researcher Linda Darling-Hammond, the INTASC standards hold promise for mobilizing reforms in the teaching profession—reforms that will lead to higher-quality teaching. In addition, the standards will help structure the learning process of preservice and inservice teachers by articulating the complex nature of teaching through the ten performance-based principles. These principles capture the interactive nature of teaching. In addition, the common core standards acknowledge that teachers must grow and develop throughout their careers. Therefore, the forms suggested for use by preservice teachers could continue to be used throughout the teacher's career.

Researchers have found that using the INTASC standards during preservice observation and teaching helps teacher-education students gradually integrate them into their practice. Likewise, the more they are used to reflect on what has been observed, planned for, and taught, the more likely preservice teachers are to develop awareness of and appreciation for them. This leads to principled decision making and an ability to plan approaches to or make changes in their own teaching (Bliss and Mazur, 1997). This, then, is what we hope for you.

The Importance of Classroom Management and Discipline

Just as there are academic standards and principles for quality teaching, there are also standards and principles for quality classroom management and discipline. Quality teaching and effective classroom management and discipline are interdependent. In Chapter 1, you learned that the 2001 research from the Center for the Study of Teaching and Policy (CTP) reported that beginning and experienced teachers found that learning about classroom management was one of the most significant elements in classroom-based preservice teaching. (CTP, 2001, 1-3).

Many preservice students and also inservice teachers are highly motivated to teach but they fear students' misbehavior. C. M. Charles, Professor Emeritus at San Diego University, and renowned researcher in classroom management, concludes that even though "classroom misbehavior is the bane of most teachers everywhere, it need not be so and can be reduced dramatically" (Charles, 2002, 207).

We have synthesized the following principles of classroom management and discipline from research and from our own experiences in K-12 classrooms.

- Determine that synergetic teaching and synergetic discipline can't be separated in practice.

    The focus is on effective ways of teaching that motivate students and produce energy and excitement and remove or reduce causes of classroom misbehavior. Synergetic teaching includes teacher ethics, trust, charisma, communication, interest, cooperation, class agreements, and procedures for problem resolution.

    Synergetic discipline involves teacher recognition of students' seven needs that motivate their behavior: security, hope, acceptance, dignity, power, enjoyment and competence (Charles, 2002, 206, 207).

- Have a vision of your classroom plan for management and discipline that reflects your commitment for developing good character traits and the skills needed for democratic living.

    If one values democracy, being an unsympathetic dictator in the classroom is out of the question (Pohan, 2003, 372).

- Spend sufficient time the first days for establishing classroom procedures/rules/consequences Pohan (2003, 372).
- Involve students in the process of establishing and reviewing rules and consequences (i.e. why are rules necessary, Pohan, 2003, 372).

- Hold and communicate high expectations for student learning and behavior. Your personal warmth and encouragement, along with established classroom requirements, allows students to know they are expected to learn well and behave appropriately.
- Understand that behavioral rules and classroom routines are taught in much the same way as instructional content is taught. They must be reviewed periodically and usually are posted (Cotton, 2002, 224).
- Specify consequences and their relation to student behavior. Explain the connection between students' misbehavior and imposed sanctions. This, too, is taught and reviewed as needed (Cotton, 2002, 225).
- Enforce classroom rules promptly, consistently and equitably, regardless of gender, race or other personal characteristics of misbehaving students (Cotton 2002, 225).
- Provide students with physical, mental, emotional and social handicaps any added necessary individualized classroom rules.
- Work to inculcate a sense of belonging and self-discipline rather than something imposed from the outside (Cotton, 2002, 226).
- Plan effectively, maintain a brisk pace of instruction and make smooth transitions. This not only increases learning but reduces the likelihood of misbehavior (Cotton, 2002, 226).
- Provide feedback and reinforcement for appropriate classroom behavior using verbal, symbolic or tangible rewards.
- Use cooperative learning structures in small groups, showing students the benefits of working together and thus easing tensions that sometimes arise among racial, ethnic and limited English students (Brophy, 1984, 6).
- Use humor to hold student interest and to reduce classroom tensions (Ornstein, 1990, 36).
- Communicate to the student that you still care for him/her, even though his/her misbehavior didn't follow classroom rules and procedures (Hymes, 1978, 32).
- Look for cause of misbehavior and attempt to correct it. Ask, "Is there a problem I can help you with?" Or "Can you help me understand why this is happening? I'd like to help fix the problem." Show you are not interested in punishing, but only in helping. (Charles, 2002, 207).
- Inform parents of your principles of management and discipline the first week of school, inviting their support (Pohan 2003, 373).

A Case Study: Getting It All Together

Date: March 19, 2003

Today, I observed Dina Mancini's fifth grade class as Maiden Elementary in Catawba County, N.C. I had heard excellent things about this young, enthusiastic teacher, and I wanted to see her instruct a Language Arts lesson. The classroom setting was ideal. The desks formed a square U with some desks in the middle. Ms. Mancini's desk was easily accessible to all her students. My favorite part of the classroom was the reading corner where students are allowed to work. There is a couch, recliner, lamps, plants, and many books. This setting could really help students become more avid readers because instead of feeling like they have to sit straight up at a desk, they can relax and enjoy their academics in a "home-like" setting. She also has a music area where she plays music while the students are working independently.

Ms. Mancini has her students' work posted all over the room and the hallway also, demonstrating how competent her students are. This can ensure more confident students. I also thought how she collected work was a neat idea and one I probably will adopt. She has a crate at the back of the room with folders labeled for each subject. When the students get finished with their work, they put it into the folder of that subject. This way, her desk does not overflow with papers, and it also teaches the students they are responsible for turning in their work.

Ms. Mancini began the lesson by saying, "Today we are gong to work with contractions that use the word 'not'. "Can someone tell me what a contraction is?" Many students raised their hands. She called on a student, and he replied, "A contraction is a shortened from of two words." She praised him and moved on to the next question. "What punctuation mark goes into a contraction?" Students respectfully raised their hands; she called on a student, and the student answered, "An apostrophe." "Very good Erika," said Ms. Mancini, so "what letter does the apostrophe represent?" Not as many students raised their hands for this answer, but one student said, "an o."

Ms. Mancini sat down at the overhead and began writing contractions. For example, she wrote 'aren't' and said, "what two words make up this contraction?" She called on several students to answer her contraction examples. She also had students come up to the overhead and they would write the contraction for the two words she provided. She always gave affective praise to each student.

Ms. Mancini then asked, "Who has not participated in this language arts lesson yet?" Ten students raised their hands. Ms. Mancini paired them up, and told them to go to the board and write down their own examples of contractions. "If your partner does it incorrectly, please respectfully tell them," replied Ms. Mancini. Before they moved on to a practice worksheet, she asked if there were any questions. She handed out the worksheet and said, "Put your pencils down or behind your ears until I have given the instructions." Not every student did this, so she started counting to ten. By six, every student's pencil was down or behind his or her ear, so she said, "Since I only got to six, each of you can put four stars beside your name at the end of class."

The students began to work independently on their worksheets, and she went to the music station and played music softly while they worked. Students were also allowed to go work in the reading corner as long as they worked quietly.

Even though I will not be working in an Elementary School, I had heard great things about this teacher and wanted to see her in action. She is probably the best teacher I have ever seen, especially with younger adolescents. She is one of these teachers that colleges try to teach you to be like. She never raised her voice or missed a beat. She had to tell a couple of students that they would need to put up a strike beside their name after class, but she never interrupted her pace during the instruction. It was like she never even took a breath to fuss at them. Ms. Mancini spoke to them like they were adults, and it was obvious they respected her.

The things I enjoyed the most about this teacher and classroom was how she played music while they worked and allowed them to sit in the reading corner. Providing a comfortable setting and joyful atmosphere will ensure avid readers. I loved it! I asked her at the end of class how she maintained such great control, and she said, "I didn't come in being their buddy. They knew from the start that I was in charge." I completely understand this concept because it is something I have had trouble with in student teaching – refraining from being their buddy. What a wonderful teacher and experience!

Source: Harbison, Heather (March, 2003) Observations of a Teacher. UNC-Asheville Preservice Student, Unpublished.

Tutoring

Tutoring, teaching, or guiding—usually an individual child—is a very important function of the classroom teacher. Unfortunately, little time is available in most large, public-school classrooms to work with students one-to-one. Therefore, the student participants who act as tutors are not only developing teaching skills, but are also providing an important service for the classroom teacher and the students they are tutoring.

Types of Tutoring

Two major types of tutoring are (1) short-term and informal, and (2) long-term and planned. Student participants can experience the first kind of tutoring while assisting the teacher. For example, while pupils work on individual projects, the student participants might be wandering around the classroom, bending down to the eye level of the children, reading their stories, making comments, and asking questions. This is informal, short-term tutoring. The kind we will emphasize in this chapter, however, requires planning.

Tutoring that requires planning includes teaching skills in language, mathematics, social studies, science, computers, art, music, health, physical education, etc. Usually, though not always, this type of tutoring is done with pupils who are experiencing difficulty learning the skill or have missed learning class skills due to absence.

Tutoring may also involve diagnosing specific strengths and weaknesses. For example, as the pupil reads aloud to the tutor, the tutor might be looking for specific reading problems. Sometimes tutoring is used to remedy these weaknesses. A kindergarten teacher might notice that one student is unable to hold his scissors and cut a simple outline. The teacher has noticed other problems in this child's motor skills when the child is doing physical activities. Since the teacher suspects problems in eye-hand coordination, the tutor will select activities to help the child develop these skills.

Sometimes tutoring is used to give certain students individual attention. For example, a student may be experiencing home problems or may have a special talent that is not encouraged during the regular class. He or she may be disabled, or the teacher may simply feel the child has been neglected because so many other pupils require special attention. To help you determine the tutoring activities in which *you* can be involved, a checklist is provided below.

SAMPLE FORM 43   Checklist of Tutoring Activities

STUDENT: Nicholas Rapparlie

NAME OF PUPIL(S) TUTORED (IF APPROPRIATE): Frank Mozolic

TEACHER: Mr. Sulinski

GRADE LEVEL AND/OR SUBJECT: Fourth grade; reading/language arts/math

DATES: September 6, 20— to October 30, 20—

OBJECTIVE: To develop teaching skills and to determine students' interests

Instructions to Student Participant: Listed below and on the following pages are several types of short-term and long-term tutoring activities in which you can participate. As you complete these activities, indicate the date each is accomplished. At the end of each section there is space for your comments about what you learned from the tutoring activities. Please have the classroom teacher sign this form when your activities have been completed.

(continued)

Short-Term, Informal Tutoring Activities	Date Completed
1. Ask individual students questions about something they are reading or writing, a picture they are drawing, or a project they are working on.	September 17
2. Discuss with individual students, stories they have read.	September 19
3. Help students with their seatwork.	September 6
4. Answer questions students have about their individual work.	September 23
5. Assist students with learning computer skills	

6. Comment on what you learned from these activities:

I learned that fourth graders seem to forget a lot over the summer. Some needed help with easy words like "master," and some needed help with simple multiplication. Many liked to draw about outer space and tell me about their Nintendo games. A few liked to read stories about racing cars and Antarctica.

Long-Term, Planned Tutoring Activities	Date Completed
1. Teaching skills that have not been mastered by individual students (grammar, composition, reading, mathematical computations, times tables, word problems, word processing, using a computer program, using a table of contents, reading a textbook for meaning, cutting out objects, using a microscope, etc.). List the skill(s) you taught: Syllabication—dividing between two syllables; after prefixes and before suffixes	October 22
2. Diagnosing a student's strength or weakness (administering a specific individual test, listening to a student read, asking a student questions on a variety of levels, watching a student do a mathematical computation, observing a student using a computer program, watching a student use a piece of equipment, etc.). List the method(s) you employed and what you were attempting to diagnose: Had student read six passages from grade levels 1–6 silently; then had student respond to five questions of varied levels of difficulty after each passage. I wanted to determine the student's comprehension level. It was fifth grade.	September 27

(continued)

3. Remedying a weakness (helping a student learn to cut out a shape with scissors, assisting a student with rules of phonics or grammar, drilling a student on vocabulary, showing a student how to find meaning in a paragraph, demonstrating for a student how to use a piece of equipment safely, etc.). List the method(s) you employed and the weakness you were attempting to remedy:

October 30

—Listed Halloween words for student to divide into syllables and use those words to write a Halloween story.

—Wanted to determine if student could apply syllabication rules.

4. Developing a special talent (teaching the student a technique of drawing, reading a piece of student writing and providing support and suggestions, listening to a student read and discussing what has been read, talking to a student about a historical event, working with a student on a science project, helping a student complete a woodworking project, teaching basic computer programming, taking the student to a museum, etc.). List the method(s) you employed and the talent you were attempting to develop:

September 11

Wanted to motivate student to read about current events from newspapers/journals, not just hear them on TV. We read reports of unemployment, the war in Iraq, and the presidential campaigns, hoping this would motivate him to read further.

5. Other. List specific long-range tutoring activities in which you have participated:

October 17

Helped student do research on controlled burning in national parks. Student needed a lot of help finding and using a variety of reference/media material. He did write a good outline and a fairly good paper.

6. Comment on what you learned from these activities:

Students at this age need to practice library skills and use them in their writing.

I certify that the student participant listed above has successfully completed those tutoring activities indicated above.

Mr. Sulinski

_____

(Classroom teacher's signature)

Planning for Tutoring

To ensure that tutoring is as valuable as possible to the tutor as well as to the pupil, it is essential that careful planning is done prior to every session. The student participant should discuss with the classroom teacher the specific goals for the tutoring sessions. Then the tutor should check the INTASC standards and the ten performance-based principles. Next, the tutor should examine district, county, or state curriculum guides to determine where these goals fit in with the sequence of goals to be accomplished during the school year. In addition, review the principles of management and discipline. Finally, the tutor should set specific objectives for each tutoring session.

For example, if the teacher's goal is to provide a child with more practice in reading aloud, the tutor checks the state curriculum guide and finds the following related goals: The learner will (1) demonstrate adequacy of *oral expression,* (2) demonstrate adequacy of *auditory discrimination* and *memory,* (3) develop *oral vocabulary,* and (4) demonstrate adequate *comprehension skill.* Likewise, the tutor discovers many goals in the areas of phonics and comprehension that might relate to the pupil's oral reading. In addition to these goals, the tutor examines INTASC standards related to diversity of learners, multiple intelligences strategies, motivation, and management.

The tutor decides to continue kidwatching and to begin with those goals directly related to reading aloud. Therefore, after a well-planned introductory session in which the tutor and pupil talk about themselves, the tutor begins the next session by asking the pupil to pick one of three stories she would like the tutor to read to her. The tutor has made sure that each of the stories relates to the unique characteristics of the child. Her selection might tell the tutor some things about the child with whom he is working. The tutor reads the story to her, stopping at appropriate points to discuss it. After they have completed the story, the tutor asks several questions about it, mentally noting areas of weakness in aural (listening) comprehension. Next, the tutor asks the pupil to read the story to him. He hopes that she will find this less threatening than reading a new story, since the story is already familiar to him or her. As the child reads, the tutor looks for specific problems she is experiencing. Immediately following the session, the tutor makes a list of these problems, discusses them with the classroom teacher, and uses them as the basis for some subsequent sessions. Finally, the tutor reflects on what has been accomplished and notes that in future sessions he will ask the child to do some art activities related to the story they are reading. What follows is a checklist you can use as you plan for tutoring.

SAMPLE FORM 44   Checklist for Planning a Tutorial

STUDENT: Robert Jones

NAME OF PUPIL(S) TUTORED: Billy Fields

GRADE LEVEL AND/OR SUBJECT: Fourth grade

DATES: September 26, 20— to October 20, 20—

OBJECTIVE: To develop teaching skills: diagnosing, planning, finding materials, conferencing, evaluating with the teacher

Instructions to Tutor: As you complete each of the following in your tutoring plans indicate the date completed.

(continued)

Planning Activity	Date Completed
1. Discuss the student you will tutor with the classroom teacher.	September 26
2. Discuss possible tutoring topics and techniques with the classroom teacher.	September 26
3. Carefully plan an initial "getting-to-know-you" session with the student.	September 27
4. Diagnose student strengths and weaknesses as necessary.	September 30
5. Check INTASC standards and performance-based principles.	October 2
6. Check available curriculum guides to determine skills to be taught and their sequence.	October 3/4
7. Review management and discipline procedures with classroom teacher.	
8. Set a specific objective for each tutoring session.	October 7
9. Develop a plan for each tutoring session (appropriate plan formats can be found in Chapter 5, pp. 121–126).	October 7 to October 15
10. Develop strategies that utilize your knowledge of multiple intelligences.	October 16
11. Discuss special needs of mainstreamed or English as Second Language (ESL) student, if appropriate, with teacher.	October 16
12. Consult appropriate resources for teaching techniques and materials.	October 17
13. Make sure all necessary materials are available and copied prior to each tutoring session.	October 18
14. Monitor the pupil's progress by keeping a log of each day's tutoring.	October 19
15. Discuss student's progress with the classroom teacher. Ask for additional suggestions for helping the student.	October 20

The basic elements of a tutoring lesson are the same as the elements of a lesson taught to a class. The tutor must:

1. Get the attention and interest of the pupil.

2. Relate the objective for the session.

3. Relate to INTASC and to state and district standards.

4. Attempt to determine prerequisite learning, ask questions, and fill in gaps.

5. Guide the student through what is expected and model the learning to be accomplished.

6. Allow the student to attempt the skill/concept on his/her own.

7. Provide feedback.

8. Tie together the lesson by discussing what has been learned, what the pupil needs to do next, and what will be done in the next tutoring session. In addition, each session should provide some means of assessing the pupil's progress.

These steps are roughly parallel to the steps in a lesson plan (see Chapter 5, pp. 121–126) for an entire class and can be used, with limited modifications, for any type of tutoring. Following the tutoring you should reflect on the session using the following form.

SAMPLE FORM 45   Reflections on Tutoring Activities

NAME OF TUTOR: Richard Karpinski

DATE AND TIME OF RECORD: April 26, 20—, 10:50 a.m.

TEACHER/SCHOOL/GRADE: Mrs. Strablow, Miller Middle School, Seventh grade

OBJECTIVE OF OBSERVATION: To think carefully and reflect about your tutoring activities. Below are some guiding questions/statements which you can use for your reflection.

Instructions: Use this form to respond to the questions after you have completed your tutoring.

1. **Select**
   a. What kind(s) of tutoring activities did you complete?
   b. Why did you decide to do the kind(s) of tutoring you did?
   c. How did the tutoring activities relate to the student(s) age(s)?
   d. What performance-based standard(s) (the ten principles) did you address?

2. **Describe**
   a. Briefly describe the pupil you tutored (age, gender, background, etc.).
   b. What special needs/interests did you consider when you planned the tutoring activity(ies)?
   c. What resources did you use?
   d. How did you monitor student progress?

3. **Analyze**
   a. How did your preplanning with the classroom teacher help you in planning for your tutoring sessions?
   b. How did the characteristics of the student affect your planning and tutoring?
   c. Did your tutoring plan allow for modification due to unanticipated student input? How?
   d. Why did you select the teaching strategies you incorporated in your lesson?
   e. What management and discipline principles did you implement?

4. **Appraise**
   a. How different/similar were your objectives for each tutoring session?
   b. How effective were you in using available resources for your tutoring?

5. **Transform**
   a. What did you learn about planning for tutoring?
   b. How did you adjust your teaching as a result of student assessment?
   c. What did you learn about the synergy of teaching and discipline?

Source: Adapted from North Carolina State Department of Public Instruction. *Performance Based Licensure,* Raleigh, NC, 1998–1999.

Referenced to INTASC Standards 1–9

Small Groups

After student participants have worked successfully with one student in a tutoring situation, they may direct their teaching to a small group of students. Frequently, small groups of students work together without direct instruction to complete a task. However, the small group we will emphasize is a small instructional group, similar in many respects to the tutorial-teaching situation discussed previously. In fact, small-group instruction is frequently called multi-student tutoring.

Advantages and Functions of Small Groups

Small groups allow students more opportunity to participate. However, it is critically important that the teacher using the small-group instructional model recognize that developing a management and discipline system for small groups is critical to their success. In the small group you can see the synergy of teaching and management and discipline more than anywhere else.

Small-group instruction and learning accomplishes many goals. Below you will find a synthesis from the research on small groups, their functions, advantages, and goals.

Small-group instruction has many advantages, including:

- Increased participation of both articulate and shy students.
- Improved motivation due to reduced inhibition and more personal involvement in learning.
- Encourages active learning, through task-centered activities such as learning centers, experiments, and discussions (Ur, 1981, 8).
- Frees the teacher from roles of instructor and controller, allowing her or him to move around and focus attention on those students most in need of assistance.
- Allows for peer teaching as students play the role of the teacher as well as the learner thereby increasing teaching time and teaching techniques.
- Involves students in the decision-making suggestions, criticizing, listening, agreeing, disagreeing, and making joint decisions (Cohen, 1994, 3, 6).
- Greater opportunity for the teacher to observe and analyze students' abilities and weaknesses (kidwatching) in oral and written language.
- Enhances student cooperation and social skills; encourages democratic principles.
- Provides an environment in which students can progress at their own rate.
- Provides special attention to special needs students, students with low self-esteem, and those with limited English.

Small groups can:

- Facilitate learning by allowing students to work together on basic skills, such as reading or math, that members are having difficulty mastering on their own.
- Allow students to read different books/articles/stories, according to their ability or interest, related to a project or research topic.
- Encourage completing laboratory experiment or laboratory reports.
- Serve as an audience for student writing ("Writing Circles"), helping each other improve skills.
- Allow students to practice dramatic performances.
- Complete bulletin boards on topics or themes in such subjects as Social Studies, Science, and English.
- Provide opportunities for developing new computer skills.
- Encourage more student participation in brainstorming to develop creativity and rational thinking skills.
- Be randomly assigned to complete a specific activity or to serve a management or classroom governance function, such as planning a class trip.

- Encourage learning over the long-term by grouping to address diverse student needs, abilities, intelligences, and backgrounds.

Structures of Small Groups

According to Alan Ornstein (1990), groups function best when they have from five to eight students. With fewer, the students tend to pair off rather than interact within the group. Other educators suggest that younger children tend to perform better in even smaller groups.

Frequently, first and second graders work better in pairs or in trios. However, the more experience the learners gain in group-work, the larger the group they can work in effectively. The student population included within the group will depend on the particular function of the group. As a general rule, Ornstein suggests that groups should be racially and ethnically mixed. Likewise, most groups function better if they have both male and female members. Finally, it is a good idea for preservice teachers to take into account behavior problems when forming groups, particularly those that will function independently. In most groups, the preservice teacher should mix ability and skill levels. It is not a good idea to formulate groups randomly or by "counting off." On the contrary, creating a group that will function effectively requires good preplanning. The sociogram (Sample Form 33) is a particularly useful tool to use prior to planning student groups.

The structure of any group varies according to its function. Frequently, small groups involve students working independently of the teacher on a project or problem arising from classroom work. At other times, groups may work with the teacher for a short period of time while the task or assignment is explained or guidance is given, and then work independently. Or the teacher may instruct one small group while other students in the class work without the teacher's direct guidance. In order to provide preservice teachers experience working with small classroom groups, we will focus on teacher-led groups in this chapter. Preservice teachers will want to include independent small groups in units and lessons planned and taught to the entire class.

Small-Group Instruction

Since classroom teachers frequently recognize a need to instruct small groups of students but have only limited time to do so, preservice teachers can meet an instructional need by assuming the responsibility for one small group. In an instructional group, the teacher's guidance is required to assist students in completing their task. Therefore, the small-group instruction designed by the student participant should be work that the students are unlikely to be able to complete successfully without instruction. This would include such things as skills they are having difficulty developing, new topics, introduction of new skills, and discussion of difficult topics or stories in order to bring learners to higher levels of cognition.

Planning for Small-Group Teaching

The sequence of the lesson plan is nearly the same as that for tutoring, but in this case several students are involved in the learning. Therefore, the preservice teacher must consider the needs and abilities of all group members to develop assessment instruments that can measure the progress of several students simultaneously. A rubric is a good assessment tool for assessing small group learning. See a sample rubric in Table 5.2 (p. 130).

SAMPLE FORM 46   Preplanning Small-Group Checklist

STUDENT: Kim Andrews

TEACHER: Shirley Walrod

GRADE LEVEL AND/OR SUBJECT: Eighth grade; science

DATES: November 3, 20— to November 12, 20—

OBJECTIVE: To practice my planning skills for small group instruction

Instructions to Student Participant: As you complete each of the following in planning for your small group, indicate the date completed.

Preplanning Activity	Date Completed
1. Discuss possible types of small-group teaching with the classroom teacher.	November 3
2. Discuss the assignment of students to the small group.	November 3
3. Discuss the classroom teacher's goal for the small group.	November 3
4. Consider the needs, interests, abilities, and intelligences of the students who will participate in the instructional group. Discuss these issues with the classroom teacher.	November 5
5. Develop an assessment tool or technique that can measure the progress of several students simultaneously. (e.g., Students complete mathematics problems that begin slightly below their level of achievement and continue beyond their level of achievement. Students answer questions about reading samples that are below their reading level and continue beyond their reading level. Students complete multiple-choice items on a leveled vocabulary list. Students attempt to perform part of a one-act play. Students read parts orally in a short play, etc.) A rubric can be a good tool to measure this type of achievement.	November 6
6. Determine a specific objective for each small-group session.	November 7/8
7. Determine which of the INTASC standards principles can be addressed in the small-group lesson.	November 9
8. Review management and discipline procedures	November 9
9. Develop a plan for each small-group session. (Appropriate plan formats can be found in Chapter 5, pp. 121–126.)	November 9
10. Consult appropriate resources for teaching techniques and materials.	November 11
11. Make sure all necessary materials are available and copied prior to each small-group session.	November 11
12. Monitor the pupils' progress by having them complete individual practice exercises related to each session's objective.	November 3 to November 11
13. Discuss the students' progress with the classroom teacher. Ask for additional suggestions for helping the students.	November 12

The student participant must be sure that all students in the group possess prerequisite knowledge for learning the concepts or skills to be taught. For example, if the students are grouped together to find the least common denominator, each student must already possess the prerequisite concepts of numerator, denominator, factor, and multiple, as well as know how to multiply and divide small whole numbers and how to add fractions with identical denominators. Therefore, an important part of planning for small-group instruction is determining each student's level of prerequisite knowledge.

To determine if students possess prerequisite skills and knowledge, you might want to begin the lesson, after you have gained the students' attention and explained the objective of the group-work, with a task you are sure they can accomplish. For example, the small group has been assigned to complete research on the Civil War from the perspective of various groups of Southerners (i.e., plantation owners, small planters, merchants, government officials, slaves). In order to accomplish this task, students will need to possess some basic research skills. Therefore, you decide to teach the lesson in the library. Early in the lesson, each student is required to find a reference book or article in a maximum of five minutes. If one or more of the students have problems finding the reference materials, you and the group members might discuss the problem. If most of the members seem unable to accomplish the task, you might decide to either teach library skills or obtain for them the reference material needed to complete the research. If the classroom teacher's goal is for the group to complete the research within a short period of time, the student participant, with the help of the librarian, might locate the materials for the students and then report to the classroom teacher the students' apparent weakness in library skills. A checklist of activities for small-group lessons follows.

SAMPLE FORM 47   Small-Group Teaching Checklist

STUDENT: Loretta Connor

TEACHER: Mr. Lebowitz

GRADE LEVEL AND/OR SUBJECT: Ninth grade; history

TOPIC: The Constitution

DATE AND TIME: November 20, 20—, 10:15 a.m.

OBJECTIVE: To implement a well-planned lesson and practice teaching skills

Instructions to Student Participant: Use this checklist while planning and teaching your small group. To be sure that your lesson includes each of the following, check [✓] each item off as it occurs.

Teaching Activity	Appears in Lesson
1. The students' attention is grabbed.	✓
2. The objective of the lesson is related to the students.	✓
3. Prerequisite knowledge is ascertained through questions and answers, a quiz, completion of an exercise, etc.	✓
4. If appropriate, gaps in needed information are filled in.	✓

(continued)

5. New information, skills, or materials are presented through explanation,   ✓
   demonstration, discussion, etc.

6. Individual tasks are assigned to each group member.   n/a

7. Student performance is elicited and monitored through independent work.   ✓

8. Teacher feedback is provided to each student.   ✓

9. Student work is related to previous and future learning.   ✓

10. Students review what they have learned in the lesson.   ✓

11. The objective for the next small-group lesson is determined and   ✓
    communicated to the students.

Although the small-group instructor must remain flexible to meet the needs and abilities of the students, a well-planned lesson is essential. Without careful planning, little or inadequate learning is likely to occur. For example, if you were a preservice teacher working with the Civil War activity described above and had not carefully planned the group work, you might stray from the objective—"the students will examine the Civil War from the perspective of various groups of Southerners"—to teach skills that students don't really need to complete the assignment. Although library skills are essential if the students are to find their own references, they are not required if the references are located for the students by the teacher and librarian.

This is part of the reason why reflecting on teaching is critically important. During your reflection, you can remind yourself of what the objective of the lesson had been and assess if it were achieved. If not, you might discover that in the name of flexibility you deserted the objective and inserted a new one—teaching library skills—that might have been more appropriately addressed at another time.

SAMPLE FORM 48   Reflections on Small-Group Teaching

NAME OF PRESERVICE TEACHER: Nezerdine Williams

DATE AND TIME OF RECORD: May 10, 20—, 1:10 p.m.

TEACHER/SCHOOL/GRADE: Mr. Duque, Cliburn Elementary School, Third grade

OBJECTIVE OF LESSON: To think carefully and reflect about your teaching of a small group. Below are some guiding questions/statements you can use for your reflection.

Instructions: Use this form to respond to the following questions after you have completed your small-group teaching.

1. **Select**
   a. What were the characteristics (age, gender, background) of the pupils in your small group?
   b. What concepts/skills did you address?
   c. What INTASC standards did you address?
   d. What technique(s) did you use to "grab" students' attention?

(continued)

2. **Describe**
    a. What diverse student needs did you consider in your planning to teach the small groups?
    b. Briefly describe the resources/materials you used.
    c. How did you address multiple intelligences?
    d. What teaching strategies did you incorporate in your lesson?

3. **Analyze**
    a. How did your assessment of prior student learning influence your lesson?
    b. How did the characteristics of the pupils affect your planning and teaching?
    c. What performance modes did you use (e.g., writing, speaking, art)?
    d. How did you modify your plan and teaching to adjust to the unexpected?

4. **Appraise**
    a. How successful was your teaching? What was most effective? What was least effective?
    b. What did the students learn?
    c. How successful was your management and discipline?

5. **Transform**
    a. What did you learn about selecting and using varied teaching strategies?
    b. What did you learn about planning for teaching a small group?
    c. How could you improve your management and discipline?

Source: Adapted from North Carolina State Department of Public Instruction *Performance Based Licensure,* Raleigh, NC, 1998–1999.

Referenced to INTASC Standards 1–9

Large Groups

After student participants have successfully instructed individuals and small groups of students, they are ready to work with a large group or the entire class. Due to the variety of individuals in a large group of twenty or more students, instruction is not as precise as with individuals and small groups. Learning theorist Robert Gagne in *Principles of Instructional Design* (1979) refers to the teacher's amount of control over instructional events as the "degree of precision" (258). According to Gagne, precision decreases as numbers of students in the instructional group grow. This lack of precision occurs because each student in the large group learns differently, possesses varied prerequisite knowledge, has had different experiences, works at different skill levels, has had varied instructional experiences and successes, possesses differing attitudes about education, has different interests and needs, etc. To increase the teacher's control over classroom events, careful planning that addresses student differences is required.

Getting Started

The more prepared you are to teach a large-group lesson, the less nervous you are likely to be. Confidence comes from knowledge of the subject content, an effective management and discipline plan, and access to and understanding of quality materials. In addition, the prepared preservice teacher knows the students as a result of observation, tutoring, and small-group work that has previously occurred. Further, he or she has planned well and has reflected on those plans and on prior teaching experiences, transforming instruction based on those reflections. Finally, the confident student participant has shared and discussed those plans with the classroom teacher and university instructor. Many successful preservice teachers have practiced and previewed their teaching on video- or audiotape and discussed these presentations with instructors or other trusted mentors or friends.

An excellent way to get started is planning to teach a lesson (or parts of a lesson) on a concept or skill that is particularly familiar to you. For example, if you have spent a semester in Great Britain, a lesson introducing students to the country through slides, music, oral reading, and discussion can be a good initial lesson. The students have an opportunity to learn something about you, and your first teaching experience is likely to be more rewarding since you are already comfortable with the material.

Planning for the Large Group

M. Lee Manning in *Developmentally Appropriate Middle-Level Schools* (1993) suggests that large-group instruction requires careful and effective planning of teaching strategies to match the diverse learning styles within the large group. In other words, teachers must consider the needs of the individual while attempting to help large groups achieve lesson objectives. According to Manning, successful individualization within the large group includes the following:

- questions that progress from requiring factual information to higher levels of synthesis and value judgment
- varieties of advanced organizers (also called "anticipatory set" or "focus") that prepare and motivate students for the new concept or skill
- multisensory experiences that allow students to utilize multiple intelligences such as reading aloud, reading silently, music, artwork, journals, notetaking, computer graphics, etc.
- multiple-review and reflection strategies such as debates, simulations, time-lines, computer software, or journal entries

Many components of the large-group lesson plan are similar to tutoring and small-group plans. However, the large-group plan must recognize the wide variety of learners in the classroom. Here are some steps in the large-group plan.

1. Gaining the attention of the learner is even more important in large-group instruction than in tutoring or small-group instruction, since lack of attention by one or more students in the large group can lead to serious discipline problems. There are many ways to gain the attention of students. Demonstrations, oral readings, audiovisual presentations, provocative questions, and dramatic monologues are a few commonly used techniques.

2. Informing students of the lesson's objective(s) gives the learners a sense of direction and a common goal.

3. Stimulating recall of prerequisite learning is of critical importance, but it is very difficult to do successfully in a large group. Although no approach to helping students recall previous learning can be successful with all students, you can help by:
   - reviewing material covered in the previous class
   - asking students probing questions
   - having students complete short activities or exercises
   - requiring students to review their notes early in the class period and frame questions or write a summarizing paragraph based on their notes
   - reviewing homework assignments from previous classes, etc.

4. Presenting the new material to be learned should emphasize distinctive features of the new concept or skill (Gagne, 1979, 254). For example, if the students have been working in the

library to develop research skills and have just completed using the card catalog to locate books on a particular topic, the new lesson might involve using the *Guide to Periodical Literature* to discover information about their topic.

5. Particularly, care in presenting new material in classes in which special students are included is critical. Student participants must be aware of whether these learners lack the background information or have the skills they need to complete a task or assignment. Within the lesson, the student participant must provide for the needs of these learners by including definitions or descriptions, providing examples or sets of procedures, providing visuals to reinforce the concept, providing computer reinforcement, or repeating key information so that it can be communicated to the learner.

6. Using a variety of techniques to provide learning guidance for all kinds of learners and multiple intelligences is a necessary part of lesson planning. For example, if the new concept deals with a historic event, there are numerous ways to help learners understand the event. These include:

- showing pictures (still or motion) of it
- placing it on a class-constructed timeline
- having the students research various aspects of the event on the Internet and in the library.
- conducting a simulation of the event
- having small groups prepare dramatic episodes
- orally reading eyewitness accounts of the event, etc.

If learners use all of their senses in dealing with a new skill or concept, they are more likely to retain it. The use of all the senses requires active participation by each learner during a significant part of every lesson. During periods of time in which learners are working in small groups or independently, the student participant must be aware of the needs of special students. It may be necessary to provide:

- peer tutors
- special books
- computer-assisted instructional programs
- cassette recordings or CD's of instructions
  - CD's of DVD's of related music, stories, or movies
  - Books on tape

These instructional modifications should be described in each special student's Individualized Educational Plan (see Sample IEP Form Chapter 4, pp. 103–104).

7. Providing feedback in each lesson lets learners know if they are reaching the objective. This can be accomplished by using a variety of techniques such as quizzes, student boardwork, exercises, activities, tests, assignments, question-and-answer sessions, small-group or individual oral reports, student-teacher conferences (these can be as short as a few seconds as the teacher circulates throughout the room commenting on each student's work), etc.

8. Assisting the learner in retention and transfer of concepts and skills is an important part of effective teaching. This can be done through techniques such as reviews; written student summarization of major concepts (precise writing); student notetaking and instruction in how to take effective notes; construction of appropriate timelines, charts, or graphs, and a rubric.

Following is a checklist of additional helpful hints for teaching large groups.

FORM 49   Checklist for Working with Large Groups

STUDENT: Amy Poulimenos

TEACHER: Mrs. Garner

GRADE LEVEL AND/OR SUBJECT: Eleventh grade; biology

DATES: October 17, 20—, October 19, 20—

OBJECTIVE: To practice my teaching/management skills with a large group

Instructions to Student Participant: As you complete each of these activities, place a check [✓] in the right-hand column.

Activity	Completed
Management of the Classroom	
1. Discuss management rules with the classroom teacher.	✓
2. Ascertain consequences for infractions with the classroom teacher.	✓
3. Use only the discipline methods sanctioned by the classroom teacher and the school.	✓
4. Communicate the rules and consequences to the students so that they know you will enforce them.	✓
5. Enforce rules and apply consequences consistently.	*didn't work one time*
6. Do not threaten if you do not intend to carry through on the threat (e.g., "If you aren't quiet, I'll keep you all after school.").	✓
7. Make eye contact with as many students as possible.	✓
8. Call students by name. (Make a temporary seating chart to help you learn names or have the students make, wear, or display name tags.)	✓
Teaching	
1. Carefully plan lessons and divide them into clear segments. (Use a planning format such as those in Chapter 5, pp. 121–126)	✓
2. Be sure all materials are copied and ready to distribute.	✓
3. Preview all materials prior to using or showing them.	✓
4. Preread anything you intend to use.	✓
5. Maintain instructional momentum (i.e., Keep up the pace; do not spend too long on any one element of the plan; do not overexplain).	✓
6. Be certain that students understand what is expected (i.e., Ask them to explain to you what they are to do; place assignments on the chalkboard prior to the lesson; make sure instructions and printing on handouts are clear; provide clear examples).	✓
7. Be sure students know how to perform and are capable of accomplishing the task. (Beware of asking students to do tasks for which they do not have prerequisite knowledge or skills; check with the classroom teacher to be sure they will be able to accomplish what you expect.)	✓
8. Review previous lessons and prerequisite knowledge or skills required for this lesson.	✓
9. Actively involve the students in the lesson.	✓

Activity	Completed
10. Use teaching methodology appropriate to the subject and the maturity of the students (e.g., labs in science classes, oral reading and independent writing in English and language arts, problem solving in mathematics, research in social studies, etc.).	Tried, the teacher said I did
11. Employ a variety of teaching techniques so that all types of learners can achieve (e.g., audiovisuals, hands-on activities, problem solving, student-designed charts and graphs, laboratories, demonstrations, the Internet).	✓
12. Assess students' level of mastery of skills and concepts as often as possible (e.g., classwork that requires demonstration of mastery, observation of students completing classwork, homework that is not merely drill, quizzes, journal entries, writing assignments, use of a rubric).	✓
13. Expect mastery of skills and concepts after a period of teaching, practice, coaching, assessing, reteaching, etc.	n/a
14. Do not expect all students to master all concepts and skills in the same way or at the same time. Group students to provide additional assistance to those who have not mastered important concepts and skills. Use different teaching techniques with these students, or allow those who have mastered the skills or concepts to tutor those who have not.	✓

Referenced to INTASC Standards 1–9

After teaching the lesson you will want to reflect on what was successful and what was less than successful. To help you do this, we have provided a reflection form on p. 153.

HOMEWORK

We mentioned homework in the checklist above. Do you think the students that you are teaching have too much homework? Recently there have been some complaints by students and parents that student have too much homework and not enough free time.

Responding to the complaint, the 2003 Brookings Institute study found that "students don't have substantially more homework to-day than they did twenty (20) years ago." (Education Week, October 8, 2003, 4) Some disagree with the Brookings Institute results, stating that the study doesn't measure the quantity of the homework assigned; it measured the amount of hours students actually spent doing the homework—a big difference. Student can be assigned six hours of homework, but can find only four hours a day to complete it (Morales, 35).

As you plan homework related to your teaching, we suggest the following guidelines:

• Confer with your cooperating teacher about the quantity and quality of the homework you plan to assign.
• Consider if all students in the class should have the same quantity and quality of the homework each day.
• Determine if the directions for completing the homework are clear and relevant to your current curriculum.
• Consider having students read a story/book that is related to the theme of your lesson/unit.
• Consider having small groups of students plan any related art, music or drama projects that augment the theme of the lesson/unit.
• Coordinate the quantity and quality of your homework assignments with other teachers that share the same students you have.
• Survey/discuss the quantity and quality of assigned homework as related to other student activities, i.e. band, chorus, music lessons, sports.

SAMPLE FORM 50   Reflections on Large-Group Teaching

TEACHER: Inez Jenkins

DATE AND TIME OF RECORD: May 22, 20—, 10:50 a.m.

GRADE LEVEL AND/OR SUBJECT: Eleventh grade; chemistry

OBJECTIVE: To think carefully and reflect on your teaching a large group. Below are some guiding questions/statements you can use for your reflection.

Instructions: You will use this form to respond to the questions.

1. **Select**
   a. What concepts/skills did you address in the lesson?
   b. Why did you address these concepts/skills?
   c. How do these concepts/skills relate to the students' ages and ability levels?
   d. What management techniques did you use?

2. **Describe**
   a. Briefly describe the characteristics of the students (gender, age, race, ability, disability levels).
   b. What resources/materials did you use?
   c. What multiple intelligences did you address?
   d. What role(s) (coach, audience, facilitator) did you play to encourage student learning?
   e. What teaching strategies did you incorporate?
   f. What student assessment technique(s) did you use prior to planning your lesson?
   g. What assessment of students' learning did you apply at the conclusion of your lesson?

3. **Analyze**
   a. How did the characteristics of the students affect your lesson plan?
   b. How did you utilize different performance modes (writing, speaking, reading, doing experiments, solving puzzles)? Why?
   c. Did you modify your plan because of unanticipated events? How?
   d. Why did you select the particular teaching and assessment strategies you incorporated in your lesson?
   e. Evaluate the assessment strategies you used in your lesson.
   f. How did the students respond to your enforcement of rules and application of consequences?
   g. How do you incorporate INTASC, state, and district standards in your lesson?

4. **Appraise**
   a. How successful was your lesson? What was most effective? Least effective?
   b. How did your choice of teaching strategies increase the students' opportunities to engage in critical thinking and problem solving?
   c. What changes will you make in your management and discipline plan?

5. **Transform**
   a. What did you learn from planning your lesson? What did you learn from teaching the lesson?
   b. What did you learn about the teaching strategies you used?
   c. How did you adjust instruction as a result of the assessment of student learning?
   d. What did you learn about homework?

Source: Adapted from North Carolina State Department of Public Instruction. *Performance Based Licensure,* Raleigh, NC, 1998–1999.

Referenced to INTASC Standards 1–9

PART IV

The Portfolio

Chapter Seven
Keeping a Portfolio

Definition of a Portfolio

Portfolio development is common to many professionals. Artists, designers, architects, authors, entertainers, scientists, university faculty, and K-12 teachers are some of the professionals who keep records of their work and achievements in a portfolio. The portfolio may contain items such as pictures of or actual samples of the individual's work. In addition, audio or videotapes documenting the work may be included. Letters commending the individual's achievements, copies of articles either written by or about the individual, and testimonials from those familiar with the work may also be prominent in the portfolio. Results of laboratory experiments may be included as might solutions to difficult mathematical problems. Finally other displays, problems, solutions, etc., designed to show the quality of the work can be included. In short, you might think of a portfolio as a professional scrapbook, or as educator and researcher Sandra M. Murphy says, a "collection" that illustrates your history and your success (1998, 7).

It is important to note that a portfolio is a professional document designed to highlight an individual's professional development and achievement. Therefore, many items that would be found in a personal scrapbook are inappropriate in a portfolio. In addition to illustrating an individual's career, a portfolio exhibits the person's ability to reflect, appropriately assess professional strengths, and organize.

Until recently, teachers who kept portfolios kept them for personal reasons much as one would have a scrapbook or a diary. However, with the advent of teacher accountability, assessment, and national licensure of teachers, professional portfolios are increasingly important in the teaching profession. Because development of a portfolio is time consuming, difficult, and important to your career advancement, we have included this chapter in the text.

In Chapter One, we told you that the portfolio designed for this guide, was the "end product of your field experience" and that it was the "compilation of your completed work." For the most part, the portfolio you complete during this course will be the compilation of all your observation, participation, teaching and reflection activities completed for Chapters 2 through 6. However, if you have already completed a portfolio for previous teacher preparation courses, you may choose to include applicable activities from these courses in your portfolio for this course.

You may be asked to complete additional portfolios during your professional development. Some of these might include: a portfolio of your student teaching experiences, local and state assessment during your initial years of teaching, and a portfolio for certification by the National Board for Professional Teaching Standards (NBPTS). Each will be more comprehensive than the proceeding portfolio. And, the experience you gain from completing previous portfolios will make the process easier when you are required to complete more extensive portfolios.

Educator and researcher Lee Shulman of Stanford University introduced the idea of portfolio development in teacher education and assessment in the early 1990s. According to Shulman, "A teaching portfolio is the structured, documentary history of a set of coached or mentored acts of teaching substantiated by student work and fully realized through reflective writing, deliberation, and serious conversation" (1994, 37). Educators Diane Hood Nettles and Pamela Bondi Petrick have developed a similar definition for use by preservice teachers. "Preservice education portfolios are collections of authentic, learner-specific documents that give evidence of growth and development toward becoming teachers. The portfolios are also an acknowledgment that teacher development is an individualized process. They reflect a student's progress over time, and help document if goals are being met in teacher preparation" (1995, 10).

In this chapter we will provide you with guidelines to make the process of organizing a portfolio easier. According to Jo Ann Phillian, Professor of Education at Purdue University, "A professional portfolio is a collection of documents that represents one's understanding of teaching and learning as it unfolds over a period of time, from entrance to teacher education through the development of a teacher's career. A portfolio is a way to document not only what a preservice teacher and her students do but also how she thinks and makes decisions as a teacher. Like an art exhibit, a professional portfolio will contain several entries, each entry contributing to a vision of teaching as a whole" (Authors, 2003,1).

Purpose of a Portfolio

First and foremost, a portfolio is used to document professional growth. Keeping a portfolio should be viewed as a rewarding activity. Like most rewarding tasks, it is complex, perplexing, and time-consuming. A portfolio should not be looked at as something that can be quickly thrown together.

(1) **A teaching portfolio is an organizational and assessment tool.** It allows you to integrate the INTASC performance-based standards; your work in observation, participation, and teaching; and reflections about your work. Completing a portfolio requires you to work toward becoming a reflective practitioner. (Note: You might want to review the Reflection Cycle, Figure 1.1 in Chapter 1 to assist you in completing your portfolio.) Many of the forms you have completed as you have worked through this text can be placed in your portfolio to illustrate your progress in becoming a teacher. Your portfolio should not be designed to illustrate a finished product but rather to reflect a work in progress. That work is your professional development as a teacher. Keep in mind that the standards under which you will be evaluated for much of your career assume that teaching is developmental in nature. Part of that development involves keeping a portfolio that allows you to document, and others to examine, your growth as a professional.

(2) **A teacher portfolio requires you to describe what you did.** Description answers the question, "What happened?" Your portfolio is a clear, logical and complete picture that sets the stage for what follows. A strong description shows rather than tells what happened. What did you do? What did the students do? (Mack-Kirschner, 2003, 102). The Case Studies throughout this text are good examples of descriptions that show rather than tell what happened.

The forms you have completed are what you did. The letters you wrote to parents, the bulletin board, projects, performances, videos, lesson and unit plans are also what you did. The description is comprised of your selection of appropriate documents and artifacts that relate to each of the ten INTASC standards.

(3) **A teaching portfolio requires analysis.** You must analyze which of the many artifacts and documents related to your teaching and your students' learning should be included in your portfolio. Through this process, you are developing a rationale of what is important to you as a teacher. Analysis is the "why" of what you did. The evidence you provide supports your analysis. Analysis must be specific so that the reader will understand what you mean. For example, avoid

such phrases as "the student understood"; instead write, "the student demonstrated understanding when she/he wrote the following: ."

(4) A teaching portfolio is a reflective tool. As you collect and organize artifacts (samples and examples of your work and your students' work) and documents (lesson plans, management strategies, teacher-designed tests, etc.), you will begin to see patterns related to your teaching. You may discover, for example, that you have successfully documented student diversity. However, you may have failed to successfully take into account diversity in your teaching. Reflection on and discussion of this problem with your mentors may lead you to conclude that you need to transform your planning to include, for example, unit plans that incorporate multiple strategies, modes of learning, and varieties of materials over a period of time.

(5) A teaching portfolio leads to an understanding of the importance of reflective practice. If you have been a good student, you have reflected on how a final exam or project has assisted you in tying together what may have previously appeared to be disparate concepts and skills within a subject. The same type of synthesis occurs in the process of developing a portfolio. You will begin to understand the importance of the observation that you have completed and reflected upon. Likewise, you will understand why you first worked with individual pupils, then small groups, and finally the entire class. You will know why you conducted assessments of your students. In short, you will begin to understand the importance of your entire teacher-education program.

(6) A teaching portfolio leads to the development of a rationale and philosophy. Philosophers have told us for centuries that it is the purposeful, reflective life that is worth living. We know that we are happiest and most fulfilled when we are striving toward clearly understood goals. When we reach those goals, we must have new ones in order to remain truly happy. In addition, goals by themselves are not motivators—there must be a reason to achieve the goal. The same is true in our professional lives—whether teaching or any other career. It is critical that we know why we are teaching and what we plan to achieve. Portfolios will help you focus on what is truly important. By focusing on important issues, ideas, artifacts, and documents you will begin to develop a real rationale for teaching and a philosophy of learning.

Getting Started

It is critical that you remember that portfolio preparation is an ongoing project. Even though this is the final chapter of the text, you have been preparing your portfolio from the day you completed your first observations. The process now is an organizational one. Below are some suggestions to help you get started.

- Save all completed observation, participation, teaching, and reflection activities.
- Save copies of students' assignments, tests, rubrics, reports, and schedules.
- Save copies of letters to parents.
- Save special materials from: holidays, field trips, performances.
- Save evaluations from supervising classroom teacher(s), university supervisors, and others.
- Save whatever you think will describe your preservice teacher preparation.
- Save your analysis and reflections.
- Take and save photos of bulletin boards, projects you created, and student involvement.
- Select a container (cardboard file) for your documents and artifacts.
- Obtain plastic non-glare page/photo protectors.
- Have a separate folder of the forms from Chapters 2-6.
- Talk with your students about what they think was most helpful in promoting learning.
- Review the INTASC standards.

- Have separate folders for ancillary documents and artifacts, such as: letters to parents, descriptions of field trips, science experiments, examples of students' work, tests, projects, photos, videos, etc.
- Write a statement of your philosophy of teaching and learning.

Writing Your Philosophy of Teaching and Learning

The first item in your portfolio should be a written reflective essay of your philosophy of teaching and learning. You can think of it as a way of introducing yourself and what you believe to your readers.

You should reflect on your beliefs regarding teaching and learning now that you have completed this stage of your preservice training. Writing down your beliefs will help you to articulate them later to peers, supervisors, administrators, and future employers.

You should consider the following as you write your philosophy of teaching and learning. Is your philosophy:

- A succinct and cogent well-written essay of one or two pages in length?
- A description of how your beliefs about teaching, i.e. standards, curriculum, planning, teaching and learning styles, classroom management, technology, and classroom social environment, can facilitate the student learning process?
- A description of how you believe learning occurs in general within a certain grade and subject?
- A description of how learning occurs in specific situations such as field trips, the cafeteria, sporting events, the arts, play, and holidays?
- A description of your goals related to: learning to appreciate and enjoy particular grades or subjects, developing critical thinking, and working in small groups?
- A description of your beliefs about classroom management and discipline?
- A brief explanation of areas of teaching and learning that you would like to learn more about or experiment with in the future?

Organizing Your Portfolio

1. Use the ten INTASC standards to organize your portfolio (Chapter 1, pp. 7–9). Use one notebook or folder for each principle. The principles will not only serve as an organizational tool, but also as criteria for the selection of artifacts and documents to keep in your portfolio.

2. Sort through all of the forms from this text that you have completed during your observation, preteaching, planning, and teaching experiences. If you have been assigned other forms to complete, sort through those as well. Place each form in its most appropriate standard and folder or notebook. This process involves reflection and consultation with peers, classroom teachers, university professors and/or supervisors, and other trusted mentors.

3. Select documents or artifacts to illustrate important aspects of your development as a teacher. Documents might include: participation activities, lesson plans, and unit plans. Artifacts might include photographs taken of the classroom and students, samples of student work, examples of tests you designed, results of student assessments, letters to parents, PowerPoint presentations, illustrations of how the students or you utilized computers and the Internet, etc. If you have audio- or videotaped your teaching, you may also want to include those tapes in your portfolio. **WARNING:** Do not attempt to include everything you and your students have done. An important part of this process is reflecting on what is most important and

illustrative. Keep in mind that people do not want to examine your entire life's history; rather, they want you to help them understand what is important to you.

4. Write a brief rationale for each notebook or folder explaining why you have selected the particular forms, documents, and artifacts. Also, analyze why the items you have chosen fit into the particular performance-based standard. (Note: It is possible that some items might be illustrative of more than one standard. This is why your rationale is important.) Refer to Table 7.1 below as an example.

5. Write a reflection on what you have learned about teaching and learning. You might want to include one reflection for each of the ten principles, or your reflection might be the conclusion of the entire portfolio.

6. Write an introduction to your entire portfolio. This introduction might be the beginning step toward developing a philosophy of teaching and learning.

7. Prepare a Table of Contents and use index tabs for each standard, folder, notebook, and/or section.

8. Discuss your portfolio with your cooperating teacher, professor, supervisor, peers, or other mentors. Consider the discussion to be a part of the portfolio development process.

9. Present your portfolio to your teacher-education class or seminar. Learning how to present it requires additional reflection. The presentation will be terribly boring if you simply go through your portfolio saying, "And then . . . and then . . ." Instead, you must select the most important items illustrating your growth as a teacher and present those in an entertaining manner. Oral presentation is a reflection of you as a teacher.

Models for Designing Your Portfolio

There are various ways you can design your portfolio. The National Board of Professional Certification has its own workbook on how to prepare a portfolio for inservice teachers deciding to become nationally certified. Several universities require preservice students to complete a portfolio as part of their teacher education course work.

We have given you one model using steps 1-7 above. This may be the least time-consuming for you. Another model is to use Table 7.1 below for each of the ten INTASC standards.

TABLE 7.1   A Template for Portfolio Design

Standard	Description	Analysis	Reflection

This model is illustrated in Table 7.2, using the <u>first</u> INTASC Standard. For this model, you follow steps in 1 through 3 above and then rewrite your description, analysis, and reflection for your selected items as related to each of the 10 INTASC standards.

This model portfolio design used the <u>first</u> INTASC Standard as an example. It is based on the Unit Plan of Heather Harbison (Chapter 5, pp. 127–129). You would complete a similar design for each of the ten standards. In addition, you would need to add supporting illustrations and artifacts, such as an example of the students' literature logs, completed Poetic Analysis Templates, and collages. Also, you would begin the portfolio with an introduction and your philosophy. You would organize it with a Table of Contents and dividers for each INTASC standard.

TABLE 7.2   Model One for Organizing a Portfolio

1. Content Pedagogy
The teacher understands the central concepts, tools of inquiry, and structures of the discipline he or she teaches and can create learning experiences that make these aspects of subject matter meaningful for students.

KEY INDICATORS:
- Demonstrates an understanding of the central concepts of his or her discipline
- Uses explanations and representations that link curriculum to prior learning
- Evaluates resources and curriculum materials for appropriateness to the curriculum and instructional delivery.
- Engages students in interpreting ideas from a variety of perspectives.
- Uses interdisciplinary approaches to teaching and learning
- Uses methods of inquiry that are central to the discipline.

2. Describe what you did:
- Planned and taught a unit on 17th Century British Poetry (See Chapter 5, pp. 127–129), having themes of love/death, using poems by Andrew Marvell, William Shakespeare, John Donne, John Milton, George Herbert, Ben Johnson and Robert Herrick with background music by Edwin McCain.
- Students compared/contrasted and interpreted the poems in small groups and recorded new vocabulary in their literature logs. Students worked in groups using the Poetic Analysis Template from the Internet to analyze the poems. Class was divided into two groups and debated the accomplishments, literary style and meaning of the poem, then made a collage to illustrate the poems.

3. Analysis/Explanation
- A study of 17th Century British poetry is one of the North Carolina Standards for 12th grade literature.
- I chose poems with themes of love and death because these themes are relevant to 12th grade students today.
- One of my instructional goals was to have students work in selected heterogeneous groups over a period of time so they could examine their opinions and beliefs and better understand the perspectives of others related to these universal human experiences.

4. Reflection
- I would like to have taught this unit in 60 minute daily periods over a two week period rather than 90 minute periods in one week. About half of the class didn't have time to reflect on the interpretations of the poems and the new vocabulary.
- Lesser ability students said, "I liked the music and art part the best and then next, listening to what other kids said in our group."
- Higher ability students said the best thing they liked was using the Poetic Analysis Template from the Internet to analyze the poems.
- I really enjoyed preparing and teaching this unit. I could hardly wait for the class to begin. If I teach it again I will have them use some of the new vocabulary in a different context and will use more music, art and perhaps drama to augment the group work.

TABLE 7.3   Model Two for Organizing a Portfolio

1. Divide your portfolio according to the main topics in this guide: Participation, Activities, Planning, Preaching, Tutoring, Teaching, Management and Reflections.
2. Choose your completed artifacts and insert them under the appropriate main topic.
3. Reference your artifacts to the appropriate INTASC standard(s).
4. Write your philosophy of education
5. Write a reflection about your experiences with each of the main topics.

SAMPLE FORM 51   Reflections on Keeping a Portfolio

NAME OF PRESERVICE TEACHER: Angela Harris

NAME OF CLASSROOM TEACHER: Mrs. Jones

NAME OF SCHOOL: Meredith Elementary

DATE(S) OF PREPARING THE PORTFOLIO: November 11, 20— through December 15, 20—

OBJECTIVE: To think carefully and reflect on the planning and preparation of a portfolio.

Instructions: Make a list of the ten performance-based standards (Chapter 1, pp. 7–9). Refer to them as you respond to the statements/questions as given below. After you have completed your portfolio, respond to the statements/questions on this form.

1. Select
   a. What was your objective for preparing a portfolio?
   b. How did you organize your portfolio?

2. Describe
   a. List the observation, participation and teaching forms, documents, and artifacts which you selected for inclusion in your portfolio.
   b. Briefly describe assistance you received from classroom teachers, university professors, and peers.
   c. Briefly describe any problems/concerns you experienced.

3. Analyze
   a. How did your reflections on completed observations, participation, and teaching help or hinder you as you prepared your portfolio?
   b. How did you decide which forms, documents, or artifacts related to each performance-based standard?

4. Appraise
   a. How effective were you in relating your work to the ten performance indicators from the INTASC standards?
   b. How successful were you in keeping a portfolio?

5. Transform
   a. What did you learn about teaching from keeping a portfolio?
   b. What did you learn about yourself as a preservice/future classroom teacher?
   c. How is your philosophy of teaching and learning reflected in your portfolio?

Source: Adapted from North Carolina State Department of Public Instruction. *Performance Based Licensure,* Raleigh, NC, 1998–1999.

Referenced to INTASC Standards 1–10

The Portfolio and Your Future Career

There are many reasons why keeping a portfolio during your preservice teaching is important to your future. First, a portfolio, rather than a résumé, is far more illustrative of who you are as a professional. The fact that you have compiled a portfolio puts you ahead of those candidates for teaching positions who have not completed one. It illustrates your ability to describe, analyze, and reflect upon what you have accomplished during your field experiences as well as what you have taught and your students have learned. It shows school administrators that you are a reflective practitioner. It also tells administrators that you are on your way to achieving national licensure that requires portfolio development. (Remember: If you present the portfolio during the interview process, prepare your presentation so that you highlight the portfolio's key elements. If the interviewer wants more information, he or she can request to review your portfolio. Of course, you must be prepared to leave it with the interviewer for a reasonable amount of time.)

Although a well-done portfolio is an important job-search tool, there are other more important reasons for preparing one. The process of portfolio organization increases your chances of professional growth during your preservice training. The processes of organizing a portfolio and writing rationales require you to reflect on your practice. In addition, the process helps you see clearly what your students have learned and what you have accomplished. In addition, it assists you in tying together numerous bits and pieces of important information, documents, and artifacts that can be lost in the day-to-day pressures of observing, planning, and teaching. After a few years as a licensed teacher, you may decide to seek National Certification. This requires the completion of a portfolio. Keeping a portfolio in the very beginning stages of your preparation to teach will give you a distinct advantage in gaining National Certification.

Just as you must decide what techniques to use in encouraging the development of skills in your students, so, too, your university professors and supervisors must do the same. They know what you will come to understand: Portfolio preparation requires the utilization of high-level, cognitive skills. In preparing a successful portfolio, you are analyzing, making decisions, categorizing, organizing, reflecting, creating, and interacting with others about your work. If you present the portfolio, you are honing these skills even more. Likewise, you are improving your oral communication. All of these skills are critical for high levels of achievement as a teacher.

In addition, your portfolio gives you something to take with you when you begin teaching. Many of the successful unit and lesson plans you created may be able to be adapted to your first classroom. Some of the materials you used may also be applicable. The assessment tools may be transferable to new situations. Even if none of what you created is useable in your new environment with a new, diverse student population, your reflections and the habits you have formed will be.

Finally, the portfolio gives you tangible evidence of your work and professional growth during the semesters you spend observing, planning, and finally teaching. It allows you to share your experiences with friends, family, mentors, and professional colleagues.

PART V

Forms

FORM 1   Anecdotal Record Form for Observing Teachers or Instructional Events—1

NAME OF OBSERVER: _____

DATE AND TIME OF OBSERVATION: _____

LENGTH OF OBSERVATION: _____

PERSON AND/OR EVENT OBSERVED: _____

GRADE LEVEL AND/OR SUBJECT: _____

OBJECTIVE OF OBSERVATION: _____

Instructions to the Observer: As completely and accurately as possible, describe the person or the event. If appropriate, include direct quotes and descriptions of the location or individual. Try to avoid making judgments.

FORM 2   **Anecdotal Teacher-Student Interaction Form**

NAME OF OBSERVER: _____

DATE AND TIME OF OBSERVATION: _____

LENGTH OF OBSERVATION: _____

TEACHER: _____

STUDENT: _____

GRADE LEVEL AND/OR SUBJECT: _____

OBJECTIVE OF OBSERVATION: _____

_____

Instructions to the Observer: As completely and accurately as possible, describe the interactions between the teacher and one selected student. Include direct quotes and descriptions of the teacher and the student, including facial expressions, gestures, and voice quality. However, be careful to avoid making judgments.

Time	Teacher	Student

FORM 3   Anecdotal Record Form for Observing Teachers or Instructional Events—2

NAME OF OBSERVER: _____

DATE AND TIME OF OBSERVATION: _____

LENGTH OF OBSERVATION: _____

PERSON AND/OR EVENT OBSERVED: _____

GRADE LEVEL AND/OR SUBJECT: _____

OBJECTIVE OF OBSERVATION: _____

Instructions to the Observer: As completely and accurately as possible, describe the person or the event. If appropriate, include direct quotes and descriptions of the location or the individual. Try to avoid making judgments.

FORM 4   Anecdotal Record Form for Grouping Patterns

NAME OF OBSERVER: _____

DATE AND TIME OF OBSERVATION: _____

LENGTH OF OBSERVATION: _____

PERSON AND/OR EVENT OBSERVED: _____

GRADE LEVEL AND/OR SUBJECT: _____

OBJECTIVE OF OBSERVATION: _____

_____

Instructions to the Observer: As completely and accurately as possible, describe the different groups in the classroom. If appropriate, include direct quotes and descriptions of locations or individuals. Try to avoid making judgments.

FORM 5   Observation Form for Rank Ordering

NAME OF OBSERVER: _____

DATE AND TIME OF OBSERVATION: _____

LENGTH OF OBSERVATION: _____

TECHNIQUES OR TYPES OF EVENT OBSERVED: _____

GRADE LEVEL AND/OR SUBJECT: _____

OBJECTIVE OF OBSERVATION: _____

_____

Instructions to the Observer: Over a period of one week list a variety of possible techniques or types of grouping patterns. Keep a tally of those you observe. At the end of the observation period, count the number of occurrences of each technique or type.

Techniques or Types of Grouping Patterns	Number of Occurrences
Total Number of Groups (Date:)	

To gain additional insight into the grouping patterns used in Mrs. Menotti's classroom, the percentage of times particular types of grouping patterns were used might be interesting. For example, 37 percent of the groups in Mrs. Menotti's classroom were homogeneous skill groups, and 26 percent were based on interest.

FORM 6   Coding System—Type and Tally of Student-Teacher Interaction

NAME OF OBSERVER: _____

DATE AND TIME OF OBSERVATION: _____

LENGTH OF OBSERVATION: _____

ELEMENT OBSERVED: _____

TEACHER AND/OR STUDENT: _____

GRADE LEVEL AND/OR SUBJECT: _____

OBJECTIVE OF OBSERVATION: _____

_____

Instructions to the Observer: Tally the number of times each interactive behavior occurs during your observation period. Try to record at least one example of each type of interaction. At the end of the observation period, total the number of all teacher-student interactions, and calculate the percentage of the total for each interaction.

Type of Interactive Behavior	Tally of Times Observed	Percentage
INDIRECT		
Accepts Feelings Example:		
Praises/Encourages Example:		
Accepts or Uses Student Ideas Example:		
Asks Questions Example:		

(continued)

Type of Interactive Behavior	Tally of Times Observed	Percentage
DIRECT		
Lectures		
Example:		
Gives Directions		
Example:		
Criticizes or Justifies Authority		
Example:		
STUDENT TALK		
Student Talk-Response		
Example:		
Student Talk-Initiation		
Example:		
TOTALS		
MOST FREQUENTLY USED TYPE OF INTERACTION		

Source: Adapted from Ned Flanders, 1985.

FORM 7   Observation Form for Examining Questions

NAME OF OBSERVER: _____

DATE AND TIME OF OBSERVATION: _____

TEACHER: _____

GRADE LEVEL AND/OR SUBJECT: _____

OBJECTIVE OF OBSERVATION: _____

_____

Instructions to the Observer: On a separate piece of paper or on a cassette, record all questions asked by the teacher, orally and in writing, for one lesson. Then place each question below at the appropriate level. Next, tally the number of questions at each level. Count the total number of questions asked, and compute a percentage for each level.

Type of Question	Total Number of Questions
1. Memory:	
2. Translation:	
3. Interpretation:	

(continued)

Type of Question	Total Number of Questions
4. Application:	
5. Analysis:	
6. Synthesis:	
7. Evaluation:	
TOTAL Number of Questions, All Levels:	

Percentage of Memory ____; Translation ____; Interpretation ____; Application ____;
Analysis ____; Synthesis ____; Evaluation ____

FORM 8.1 Checklist for Determining Teaching Style

NAME OF OBSERVER: _____

DATE AND TIME OF OBSERVATION: _____

TEACHER: _____

GRADE LEVEL AND/OR SUBJECT: _____

OBJECTIVE OF OBSERVATION: _____

_____

Instructions to the Observer: Prior to the observation, read over the items below. These items represent various teaching styles used by teachers. During and after the observation, place an "X" next to those items you have observed.

____ prefers teaching situations that allow interaction and discussion with students	____ has students work in small groups
____ uses questions to check on student learning following instruction	____ prefers impersonal teaching situations
____ viewed by students as teaching facts	____ uses questions to introduce topics and probe student answers
____ provides feedback, avoids negative evaluation	____ uses teacher-organized learning situations
____ strong in establishing a warm and personal learning environment	____ viewed by students as encouraging to apply principles
____ tells students the objectives of the lesson	____ gives feedback, uses negative evaluation
____ use a variety of media and technological resources	____ strong in organizing and guiding student learning

Adapted from: [online] Internet path: http://www.aismissstate.edu.\ALS/Unit9modulers.num and Dean Boyd, computer system coordinator, Mississippi State University of Starkville, MS, College of Agriculture and Life Sciences, September 22, 1999.

FORM 8.2   Checklist for Examining Teaching Practices Which Accommodate Diversity of Learning Styles

NAME OF OBSERVER: _____

DATE AND TIME OF OBSERVATION: _____

TEACHER: _____

GRADE LEVEL AND/OR SUBJECT: _____

OBJECTIVE OF OBSERVATION: _____

_____

Instructions to the Observer: Prior to the observation, read over the items below. These items represent various teaching practices used to accommodate different learning styles of students in the classrooms. During and after the observation put an "X" next to those items you observe(d).

VISUAL

____ writes directions on board as well as giving them orally

____ uses flash cards, printed in bold letters

____ uses resources that require reading and seeing

____ uses transparencies

____ uses models, graphs, charts

____ assigns written reports

____ has students write/draw comic strips related to lessons/projects

____ has students take notes on important words, concepts

____ gives a written copy of boardwork if student has difficulty copying

____ uses videos

TACTILE

____ uses manipulative objects especially when teaching abstract concepts (measurement, geometry)

____ allows students to build models, draw/paint pictures, make a display instead of written reports

AUDITORY

____ gives oral rather than written tests

____ uses lectures

____ uses audiotapes

____ uses music related to themes/holidays

____ allows students to use tape recorder to recite then play back

____ substitutes oral reports for written assignments

____ uses CD's

____ uses books on discs

KINESTHETIC

____ allows students to make multimedia production (PowerPoint)

____ allows students to use computers and calculators

____ uses role playing and simulations

____ provides opportunities for movement, games, activities

Adapted from the North Carolina Teacher Academy, North Carolina Department of Public Instruction, Raleigh, NC 2001.

FORM 9   Observation Form for Structured Observation of a Lesson

NAME OF OBSERVER: _____

DATE AND TIME OF OBSERVATION: _____

TEACHER: _____

GRADE LEVEL AND/OR SUBJECT: _____

OBJECTIVE OF OBSERVATION: _____

_____

Instructions to the Observer: As you observe in the classroom, write the elements of the lesson which fit under the categories below. (See Sample Form 9, p. 39.) A description of each category appears in italics.

1. **Anticipatory Set**—*In every lesson, the teacher provides initial motivation and focus for the lesson. Sometimes this focus takes the form of a review of previous knowledge important to this lesson; at other times it is designed to "grab" the students' attention. Key words: alerting, relevance, relationship (to previous lesson), meaningfulness, etc.*

2. **Objective**—*In almost every lesson, the teacher specifies the behaviors the students will be expected to perform. In other words, the students know what is expected of them and what they are expected to learn.*

3. **Teacher Input**—*In most lessons, the teacher will provide the students with the information needed to reach the objective successfully. Sometimes the teacher will show the students how to accomplish the task by modeling appropriate performance.*

(continued)

4. **Checking for Understanding**—*Throughout the lesson, the teacher checks to ensure that the students understand the concepts or skills being taught. This can be accomplished through random questioning or individual tutoring.*

5. **Guided Practice**—*In every lesson, students practice the expected performance. This may include exercises completed with the teacher, examples done by students on the board, students reading aloud, students working together to complete assignments, games that allow the students to exhibit understanding, etc.*

6. **Independent Practice**—*Student independently exhibit the behaviors set forth in the objective. To accomplish this, students might complete problems, write a paper, do an experiment, give a report, complete a project, do research, etc.*

7. **Closure**—*The teacher helps students review what they have learned in the lesson. This may include a summary of the lesson, questions about what happened during the students' independent practice, the students' report of their progress, an evaluation by the teacher, a discussion of the relationship of this lesson to the next lesson or the unit, or an assignment of additional independent practice.*

Source: Lois Sprinthall, *A Strategy Guide for Teachers: Guide Book for Supervisors of Novice Teachers.* Unpublished manuscript. Based on the work of Madeline Hunter.

FORM 10   Checklist of Interview Techniques

NAME OF OBSERVER: _____

DATE AND TIME AND PLACE OF OBSERVATION: _____

PERSON TO BE INTERVIEWED : _____

GRADE LEVEL AND/OR SUBJECT: _____

OBJECTIVE OF OBSERVATION: _____

Instructions to the Observer: Review this checklist prior to and after your interview. Check off those items you have completed.

1. Prior to the Interview

____ Establish the purpose for the interview.

____ Request an appointment (time and place), giving sufficient lead time for you and the person to be interviewed.

____ Plan objective, specific questions related to the purpose of the interview.

____ Prioritize questions, asking the most important first.

____ Remind the person to be interviewd of the time, place, and purpose of the interview.

2. The Interview

____ Arrive at the pre-established place several minutes before the scheduled time for the interview.

____ Start the interview by reminding the person to be interviewed of its purpose.

____ Request permission to tape the interview (if appropriate).

____ If taping is unfeasible, take careful, objective notes, trying to list direct quotes as often as possible.

____ Avoid inserting impressions or judgments.

____ Limit the interview to no more than 15-30 minutes.

3. After the Interview

____ Review with the respondent what has been said or heard.

____ Express your appreciation for the interview.

____ Offer to share the interview report with the respondent.

FORM 11   A Rating Scale for Observation of Standards for Teaching

NAME OF OBSERVER: _____

DATE AND TIME OF OBSERVATION: _____

LENGTH OF OBSERVATION: _____

TEACHER: _____

GRADE LEVEL AND/OR SUBJECT: _____

OBJECTIVE OF OBSERVATION: _____

Instructions to the Observer: Prior to your observation, read carefully over each principle and key indicators. During and after your observation, put a mark (X) on the rating scale that best describes what you observed. The check may be either on one number or between two numbers. NOTE: This rating is based on one observation and does not constitute a complete evaluation of the teacher's sophistication or effectiveness. Refer to key indicators pp. 42–47.

Content Pedagogy

Principle 1   The teacher understands the central concepts, tools of inquiry, and structures of the discipline he or she teaches and can create learning experiences that make these aspects of subject matter meaningful for students.

1	2	3	4	5
Limited Sophistication		Moderate Sophistication		High Sophistication

Student Development

Principle 2   The teacher understands how children learn and develop, and can provide learning opportunities that support a child's intellectual, social, and personal development.

1	2	3	4	5
Limited Sophistication		Moderate Sophistication		High Sophistication

Diverse Learners

Principle 3   The teacher understands how students differ in their approaches to learning and creates instructional opportunities that are adapted to diverse learners.

1	2	3	4	5
Limited Sophistication		Moderate Sophistication		High Sophistication

Multiple Instructional Strategies

Principle 4   The teacher understands and uses a variety of instructional strategies to encourage student development of critical thinking, problem-solving, and performance skills.

1	2	3	4	5
Limited Sophistication		Moderate Sophistication		High Sophistication

(continued)

Motivation and Management

Principle 5   The teacher uses an understanding of individual and group motivation and behavior to create a learning environment that encourages positive social interaction, active engagement in learning, and self-motivation.

1	2	3	4	5
Limited Sophistication		Moderate Sophistication		High Sophistication

Communication and Technology

Principle 6   The teacher uses knowledge of effective verbal, nonverbal, and media communication techniques to foster active inquiry, collaboration, and supportive interaction in the classroom.

1	2	3	4	5
Limited Sophistication		Moderate Sophistication		High Sophistication

Planning

Principle 7   The teacher plans instruction based upon knowledge of subject matter, students, the community, and curriculum goals.

1	2	3	4	5
Limited Sophistication		Moderate Sophistication		High Sophistication

Assessment

Principle 8   The teacher understands and uses formal and informal assessment strategies to evaluate and ensure the continuous intellectual, social, and physical development of the learner.

1	2	3	4	5
Limited Sophistication		Moderate Sophistication		High Sophistication

Reflective Practice

Principle 9   The teacher is a reflective practitioner who continually evaluates the effects of his or her choices and actions on others (student, parents, and other professionals in the learning community) who actively seeks out opportunities to grow professionally.

1	2	3	4	5
Limited Sophistication		Moderate Sophistication		High Sophistication

School and Community Development

Principle 10   The teacher fosters relationships with school colleagues, parents, and agencies in the larger community to support student learning and well being.

1	2	3	4	5
Limited Sophistication		Moderate Sophistication		High Sophistication

Source: Robert F. Yinger. "The Role of Standards in Teaching and Teacher Education" in *The Education of Teachers.* National Society for the Study of Education (NSSE), pp. 100-101, 1999.

FORM 12   A Rating Scale for Observation of Education Technology Standards for Teachers

NAME OF OBSERVER: _____

DATE AND TIME OF OBSERVATION: _____

LENGTH OF OBSERVATION: _____

TEACHER: _____

GRADE LEVEL AND/OR SUBJECT: _____

OBJECTIVE OF OBSERVATION: _____

_____

Instructions to the Observer: Prior to your observation, read over each standard carefully. During and after your observation, put a check on the rating scale that best describes what you observed. The check may be either on, or between, the numbers 1-5.

Note: This observation is based on one limited observation.

1. Technology operations and concepts

Teacher demonstrates a sound understanding of technology operations and concepts.

1	2	3	4	5
Limited Sophistication		Moderate Sophistication		High Sophistication

2. Planning and designing learning environments and experiences

Teachers plan and design effective learning environments and experiences supported by technology.

1	2	3	4	5
Limited Sophistication		Moderate Sophistication		High Sophistication

3. Teaching, learning, and the curriculum

Teachers implement curriculum plans that include methods and strategies for applying technology to maximize student learning.

1	2	3	4	5
Limited Sophistication		Moderate Sophistication		High Sophistication

4. Assessment and evaluation

Teachers apply technology to facilitate a variety of effective assessment and evaluation strategies.

1	2	3	4	5
Limited Sophistication		Moderate Sophistication		High Sophistication

(continued)

5. Productivity and professional practice

Teachers use technology to enhance their productivity and professional practices.

1	2	3	4	5
Limited Sophistication		Moderate Sophistication		High Sophistication

6. Social ethical, legal, and human issues

Teachers understand the social, ethical, legal and human issues surrounding the use of technology in PK-12 schools and apply that understanding in practice.

1	2	3	4	5
Limited Sophistication		Moderate Sophistication		High Sophistication

Source: National Educational Technology Project (NETS) http://www.iste.org/standards/. March 2003.

FORM 13   Reflective Observation of Teachers

NAME OF OBSERVER: _____

DATE AND TIME OF OBSERVATION: _____

TEACHER: _____

GRADE LEVEL AND/OR SUBJECT: _____

OBJECTIVE OF OBSERVATION: _____

_____

Instructions to the Observer: Use Form 12 to respond to the following questions after you have completed your observations of teachers.

1. **Select**
   a. What two types of observation did you complete?

   b. What principles from INTASC standards did you address?

2. **Describe**
   a. What grade level(s) did you observe?

   b. Briefly describe your anecdotal observations.

   c. Briefly describe your structured observations.

   d. Briefly describe the type of assessments you used.

3. **Analyze**
   a. How did your prior experience with observation of teachers influence this experience?

   b. How will your observation of different teaching styles affect your future teaching?

   c. How will your observation of educational technology standards affect your future teaching?

4. **Appraise**
   a. Describe the teacher-student interaction you observed. Was it appropriate?

   b. Did the ten principles based on the common core of standards (INTASC) influence your decision to become a teacher? Explain.

5. **Transform**
   a. What did you learn about teaching through your observation?

   b. What did you learn about types of assessment?

   c. How do you think this observation will help you in your future teaching?

Source: Adapted from North Carolina State Department of Public Instruction. *Performance Based Licensure,* Raleigh, NC, 1998–1999.

FORM 14 Form for Anecdotal Record of Classroom Organization

NAME OF OBSERVER: _____

DATE AND TIME OF OBSERVATION: _____

LENGTH OF OBSERVATION: _____

PERSON AND/OR EVENT OBSERVED: _____

GRADE LEVEL AND/OR SUBJECT: _____

OBJECTIVE OF OBSERVATION: _____

_____

Instructions to the Observer: As completely and accurately as possible, describe the organization of the classroom. Be sure to include as much detail as possible. Try to avoid making judgments.

FORM 15   Form for a Classroom Map

NAME OF OBSERVER: _____

DATE AND TIME OF OBSERVATION: _____

PERSON AND/OR EVENT OBSERVED: _____

GRADE LEVEL AND/OR SUBJECT: _____

OBJECTIVE OF OBSERVATION: _____

_____

Instructions to the Observer: First, draw a map of the classroom you are observing, including seating arrangements, placement of furniture, computers, telephone, and other equipment. Then, give a brief anecodotal description of these classroom elements: use of technology, lighting, traffic patterns, instructional displays, management, and motivational elements.

   1. Draw classroom map:

2. Anecdotal description of classroom elements:

(a) Use of Technology:

(b) Lighting and Traffic Patterns:

(c) Instructional Displays, Management, and Motivational Elements:

FORM 16   Form for Coding Scale of Classroom Social Environment

NAME OF OBSERVER: _____

DATE AND TIME OF OBSERVATION: _____

LENGTH OF OBSERVATION: _____

PERSON AND/OR EVENT OBSERVED: _____

GRADE LEVEL AND/OR SUBJECT: _____

OBJECTIVE OF OBSERVATION: _____

Instructions to the Observer: Before using the coding scale, become familiar with each of the fifteen dimensions that describe the classroom social environment found on pages 58–59.

Each dimension is divided into three elements (or statements). Each of these three elements appears in the same order, once per set, in the three sets that comprise the coding scale.

To use the coding scale effectively, you should circle the appropriate rating and average the scores *for all three statements* in any given dimension(s) you want to examine. For example, to study classroom diversity, you would compare the scores for numbers 2, 17, and 32.

The scale may also be used to determine what you might want to examine further. Thus, after one or more classroom observations, you may want to average the scores for all three sets, and then pick out those that stand out in some way.

When scoring, you should note the following: (1) some statements are phrased negatively and, thus, their ratings have been reversed, and (2) in several of the dimensions being measured (diversity, speed, difficulty, democracy, and competitiveness), a higher score is not necessarily more desirable.

Dimension Elements	Strongly Disagree	Disagree	Agree	Strongly Agree	No Information
Set 1					
1. A student in this class has the chance to get to know all the students (cohesiveness).	1	2	3	4	N/I
2. The class has students with many different interests (diversity).	1	2	3	4	N/I
3. There is a set of rules for the students to follow (formality).	1	2	3	4	N/I
4. Most of the class has difficulty keeping up with the assigned work (speed).	1	2	3	4	N/I
5. The books and equipment students need or want are easily available in the classroom (environment).	1	2	3	4	N/I
6. There are tensions among certain students that tend to infere with class activities (friction).	1	2	3	4	N/I
7. Most students have little idea of what the class is attempting to accomplish (goal direction).	4	3	2	1	N/I

(continued)

Dimension Elements	Strongly Disagree	Disagree	Agree	Strongly Agree	No Information
8. The better students' questions are answered more sympathetically than those of the average students (favoritism).	1	2	3	4	N/I
9. Some students refuse to mix with the rest of the class (cliquishness).	1	2	3	4	N/I
10. The students seem to enjoy their classwork (satisfaction).	1	2	3	4	N/I
11. There are long periods during which the class does nothing (disorganization).	1	2	3	4	N/I
12. Some students in the class consider the work difficult (difficulty).	1	2	3	4	N/I
13. Few students seem to have a concern for the progress of the class (apathy).	4	3	2	1	N/I
14. When group discussions occur, all students tend to contribute (democracy).	1	2	3	4	N/I
15. Most students cooperate rather than compete with one another in this class (cooperativeness).	4	3	2	1	N/I

Set 2

Dimension Elements	Strongly Disagree	Disagree	Agree	Strongly Agree	No Information
16. Students in this class are not in close enough contact to develop likes and dislikes for one another (cohesiveness).	4	3	2	1	N/I
17. The class is working toward many different goals (diversity).	1	2	3	4	N/I
18. Students who break the rules are penalized (formality).	1	2	3	4	N/I
19. Most of the class covers the prescribed amount of work in the time given (speed)	4	3	2	1	N/I
20. A comprehensive collection of reference materials is available in the classroom for students to use (environment).	1	2	3	4	N/I
21. Certain students seem to have no respect for other students (friction).	1	2	3	4	N/I
22. The objectives of the class are not clearly recognized (goal direction).	4	3	2	1	N/I
23. Not every member of the class is given the same privileges (favoritism).	4	3	2	1	N/I
24. Certain students work only with their close friends (cliquishness).	1	2	3	4	N/I
25. There is considerable student dissatisfaction with the classwork (satisfaction).	4	3	2	1	N/I

(continued)

Dimension Elements	Strongly Disagree	Disagree	Agree	Strongly Agree	No Information
26. Classwork is frequently interrupted by some students with nothing to do (disorganization).	4	3	2	1	N/I
27. Most students in this class are constantly challenged (difficulty).	1	2	3	4	N/I
28. Some members of the class don't care what the class does (apathy).	1	2	3	4	N/I
29. Certain students have more influence on the class than others (democracy).	4	3	2	1	N/I
30. Most students in the class want their work to be better than their friends' work (competitiveness).	1	2	3	4	N/I

Set 3

31. This class is made up of individuals who do not know each other well (cohesiveness).	4	3	2	1	N/I
32. Different students are interested in different aspects of the class (diversity).	4	3	2	1	N/I
33. There is a right and wrong way of going about class activities (formality).	4	3	2	1	N/I
34. There is little time in this class for daydreaming (speed).	4	3	2	1	N/I
35. There are bulletin board displays and pictutes around the room (environment).	4	3	2	1	N/I
36. Certain students in this class are uncooperative (friction).	1	2	3	4	N/I
37. Most of the class realizes exactly how much work is required (goal direction).	1	2	3	4	N/I
38. Certain students in the class are favored over others (favoritism).	1	2	3	4	N/I
39. Most students cooperate equally well with all class members (cliquishness).	4	3	2	1	N/I
40. After an assignment, most students have a sense of satisfactions (satisfaction).	1	2	3	4	N/I
41. The class is well-organized and efficient (disorganization).	4	3	2	1	N/I
42. Most students consider the subject matter easy (difficulty).	4	3	2	1	N/I
43. Students show a common concern for the success of the class (apathy).	4	3	2	1	N/I
44. Each member of the class has as much influence as does any other member (democracy).	4	3	2	1	N/I
45. Students compete to see who can do the best work (competitiveness).	4	3	2	1	N/I

Source: Gary Borich. *Observation Skills for Effective Teaching,* pp.113–115, 1990.

FORM 17   Checklist to Determine Student Assessments in the Classroom

NAME OF OBSERVER: _____

DATE AND TIME OF OBSERVATION: _____

PERSON AND/OR EVENT OBSERVED: _____

GRADE LEVEL AND/OR SUBJECT: _____

SCHOOL: _____

OBJECTIVE OF OBSERVATION: _____

_____

Instructions to the Observer: After structured observation or an interview with the class-room teacher, put a check in the appropriate column. List additional assessments where required next to items marked with an asterisk.

Type of Assessment	Observed	From Interview
1. Commercial Workbooks in Curricular Areas Reading Mathematics Science Social Studies Language Arts Others* (*handwriting*)		
2. Duplicated Sheets		
3. Homework Assignments		
4. Oral Presentation/Report		
5. Hands-On Performance Computers Science Experiment Construction Project Dramatic Performances/Skits Chalkboard Work Art Project Musical Production Classroom Displays/Bulletin Board School Displays Others*		

(continued)

Type of Assessment	Observed	From Interview
6. Written Work Reports Research Projects Creative Writing Others*		
7. Teacher-Made Tests		
8. Prepared Tests from Students' Texts		
9. Standardized Tests		
10. State Competency Tests		
11. State End-of-Year Tests		
12. Anecdotal Records Writing Journals/Folders Art Folders Cumulative Record Folders Portfolios Others*		
13. Others*		

FORM 18   Checklist of Goals and Objectives Covered in a Seventh-Grade History Classroom

NAME OF OBSERVER: _____

DATE AND TIME OF OBSERVATION: _____

TEACHER: _____

SCHOOL: _____

OBJECTIVE OF OBSERVATION: _____

_____

Instructions to the Observer: Use the list of goals and objectives from a curriculum guide to develop your own checklist. For an example of a checklist of goals and performance indicators in a seventh-grade history classroom, see pp. 66–68. If the competency, goal, objective and/or performance indicator is observed, place an "X" in the right-hand column.

Competency Goals	Objectives	Observed

(continued)

Competency Goals	Objectives	Observed

FORM 19   Examination of Curricular Strategies That Challenge Students' Multiple Intelligences

NAME OF OBSERVER: _____

DATE AND TIME OF OBSERVATION: _____

TEACHER: _____

SCHOOL: _____

OBJECTIVE OF OBSERVATION: _____

_____

Instructions to the Observer: A list of curricular descriptors that challenge students' multiple intelligences is given below. Place a check before each descriptor observed.

Visual/Spatial	**Logical/Mathematical**	**Verbal/Linguistic**	**Bodily/Kinesthetic**
___ charts	___ problem solving	___ stories	___ field trips
___ graphs	___ tangrams	___ retelling	___ activities
___ photography	___ geometry	___ journals	___ creative
___ visual awareness	___ measuring	___ process writing	movement
___ organizers	___ classifying	___ reader's theatre	___ hands-on
___ visual metaphors	___ predicting	___ storytelling	experiments
___ visual analogies	___ logic games	___ choral speaking	___ body language
___ visual puzzles	___ data collecting	___ rehearsed	___ manipulatives
___ 3-D experiences	___ serialing	reading	___ physical
___ painting	___ attributes	___ bookmaking	education
___ illustrations	___ experimenting	___ speaking	___ crafts
___ story maps	___ puzzles	___ nonfiction	___ drama
___ visualizing	___ manipulatives	reading	
___ sketching	___ scientific model	___ research	
___ patterning	___ money	___ speeches	
___ mind maps	___ time	___ presentations	
___ color	___ sequencing	___ listening	
___ symbols	___ critical thinking	___ reading	
		___ read-aloud	
		___ drama	

Musical/Rhythmic	**Interpersonal**	**Intrapersonal**
___ singing	___ cooperative learning	___ individual study
___ humming	___ sharing	___ personal goal setting
___ rhythms	___ group work	___ individual projects
___ rap	___ peer teaching	___ journal keeping
___ background music	___ social awareness	___ personal choice
___ music appreciation	___ conflict mediation	___ individualized reading
___ mood music	___ discussion	___ self-esteem activities
___ patterns	___ peer editing	
___ form	___ cross-age tutoring	**Naturalist**
___ playing instruments	___ social gathering	___ studies the structure
	___ study group	of plants
	___ clubs	___ plants seeds
	___ brainstorming	___ observes animal growth
		___ studies the animal
		kingdom

Source: Adapted from the Simcoe District School Board, Ontario, Canada, 1996.
[on-line] Internet path: http://www.scdsb.on.ca/

FORM 20   Form for Examining a Curriculum Guide

NAME OF OBSERVER: _____

DATE AND TIME OF OBSERVATION: _____

OBJECTIVE OF EXAMINATION: _____

_____

Instructions to the Examiner: Select a curriculum guide for the grade level and/or subject you will be observing. Complete this short answer survey.

1. Title of the guide: _____

2. Check one: The guide is from the school ____; the school district ____; the state ____; other (specify) _____

3. Date of the guide: _____

4. Grade level(s) of the guide: _____

5. Subject area(s) of the guide: _____

_____

Answer the following yes/no or as indicated:

6. The guide includes: objectives _____, student activities _____, resources _____, examples _____, bibliographies _____, computer software sources _____, test banks _____, discussion questions _____, material for making transparencies _____, content outlines _____, other (specify) _____

7. The guide suggests appropriate textbooks (specify): _____

_____

8. The guide suggests appropriate supplemental books. _____

9. The guide suggests appropriate references._____

10. The guide suggests appropriate educational media and technology. _____

11. The guide suggests appropriate references. _____

12. The guide suggests activities for different levels of students (i.e., learning disabled, gifted, advanced, basic, etc.). _____

FORM 21   Checklist for a Multicultural/Antibias Education Evaluation

NAME OF OBSERVER: _____

DATE AND TIME OF OBSERVATION: _____

SCHOOL: _____

GRADE LEVELS OF SCHOOL: _____

OBJECTIVE OF EXAMINATION: _____

_____

Instructions to the Observer: After examining the school's curriculum (using Forms 18 and 20) and observing in numerous classrooms, complete the following evaluation checklist. Place a checkmark below the word or phrase that best describes your observations. Respond only to those items that were observable by you.

	Not at all	Some	Large Amount
1. The classroom environment is reflective of diversity.	_____	_____	_____
2. Curriculum focuses on discrete pieces about cultures of various racial and ethnic groups.	_____	_____	_____
3. Multicultural activities are added on to the "regular" curriculum (i.e., celebrating various holidays of other cultures).	_____	_____	_____
4. Families or caregivers are asked to provide information about the most visible aspects of their cultural heritage (i.e., food, music, and holidays).	_____	_____	_____
5. Languages of children (other than English) are used in songs or other communication.	_____	_____	_____
6. The curriculum explores cultural differences among the children's families.	_____	_____	_____
7. Staff members actively incorporate their children's daily life experiences into daily curriculum.	_____	_____	_____
8. Curriculum and teacher-child interactions meet the cultural as well as individual developmental needs of their children.	_____	_____	_____
9. Parents' or family caregivers' knowledge about their native cultural background is utilized.	_____	_____	_____
10. Staff members intentionally encourage the children's development of critical thinking and tools for resisting prejudice and biased behaviors directed at themselves or others.	_____	_____	_____
11. Staff members reflect the cultural and language diversity of the children and families they serve.	_____	_____	_____

Source: Adapted from Louise Derman-Sparks. 1999. "Markers of Multicultural/Antibias Education." *Young Children.* 54(5) 43.

FORM 22   Form for Types and Uses of Media/Technology in the Classroom or Lab

NAME OF OBSERVER: _____

DATE AND TIME OF OBSERVATION: _____

SCHOOL: _____

TEACHER: _____

GRADE LEVEL AND/OR SUBJECT: _____

OBJECTIVE OF OBSERVATION: _____

Instructions to the Observer: It is important to determine whether technology is used to augment instruction in subject areas for the students or whether it is used to teach students technological skills and/or how to use particular applications. Answer the following questions to help identify how technology is being used in the class you are observing.

1. List the types of media/technology you observed.

2. What is the objective(s) of the lesson being observed?

3. Does the use of technology match or reflect the learning objectives for the lesson?

4. How does the use of technology enhance the opportunity for students to meet the lesson's objectives?

5. Is technology used as a teaching tool by the teacher to present concepts and information in a particular subject area?

6. Is technology used to teach computer skills? If so, what skills?

7. Is the teacher's role during the lesson to guide students as they use technology or is his/her role to present information/skills?

8. Is the use of the technology appropriate for the age and skill of the students?

9. Is equitable time provided for all students to use technology?

10. When technology is used, are students engaged in cooperative learning?

11. Is technology introduced for independent use, small-group use, or whole-class use?

12. Does the lesson using technology provide an opportunity for student evaluation or feedback? If so, describe the opportunity. If not, ask the teacher why not.

Adapted from:: Jean Camp, Instructional Technology Coordinator, The University of North Carolina at Greensboro. Unpublished. Courtesy of Mary Olson, The University of North Carolina at Greensboro.

FORM 23   Software Evaluation Form

NAME OF EXAMINER: _____

DATE AND TIME OF EXAMINATION: _____

SOFTWARE TITLE: _____

PUBLISHER: _____

PUBLICATION DATE: _____

OBJECTIVE OF OBSERVATION: _____

_____

Instructions to the Examiner: Determine the parameters of the software package by checking the appropriate blank. Answer the questions related to rating the software. Then rate the product on a scale of 1 to 4 (1 is the lowest and 4 is the highest).

I. Basic Background Information

   A. Computer Platform:

     IBM _____   Mac _____

   B. System Requirements:

     Stand Alone _____   Hard Drive Memory _____

     Networked _____   RAM Memory _____

     Both _____

   C. Format (check one):

     Disk-Based   _____

     CD-ROM   _____

     Laserdisc   _____

   D. Audience:

     PreK–1st   _____   9th–12th   _____

     2nd–5th   _____   Adult   _____

     6th–8th   _____   Other   _____

   E. Software Type:

     CAI/Drill and Practice   _____

     Simulations   _____

     Problem-Solving Applications   _____

     Game Applications   _____

     Tool Applications   _____

       Database   _____

       Word Processing   _____

       Spreadsheet   _____

     Tutorials   _____

     Grading/Student Information   _____

     Electronic Portfolio Assessment   _____

     Electronic Books   _____

       Skill level accommodations   _____

     Multimedia authoring   _____

     Telecommunicating   _____

   F. Graphics: B/W _____   Color _____   Animation _____

   G. Price: $375.00

   H. Preview Policy: None _____   30-day _____   Other _____

(continued)

II. Educational Objectives
    A. State Purpose: To increase children's ability to hear phonemes within words

    B. Subject Area Focus:

Math	_____	Reading	_____	Art	_____
Foreign Language	_____	Social Studies	_____	Science	_____
Music	_____	Literature	_____	Other	_____

III. Questions to Consider When Evaluating Software

    A. Does the content of the program reflect a sound learning theory? If so, which one? Is the program's subject matter accurate and logically presented?

_____

_____

    B. Does the program promote exploration and critical thinking?

_____

    C. Does the software span a range of skill abilities?

_____

    D. Do students have control of the program? (i.e., Is it self-paced? Can they navigate through the program easily?)

_____

    E. Can the program be adapted to large groups, small groups, and individual instruction?

_____

    F. Does the program accommodate different ability levels?

_____

    G. Does the program provide supportive and positive feedback to students?

_____

    H. Are teaching materials provided to accompany the program? If so, describe them.

_____

    I. Is the program sensitive to multiculturalism? In what ways?

_____

    J. Are the program directions clear enough to be used independently, or does the program require teacher support?

_____

    K. Does the school, classroom, or lab have the technical and educational support necessary to maximize the use of the program?

_____

    L. Does the program have multimedia features? If so, do they enhance learning?

_____

IV. Rating (Rate items on a scale of 1 to 4; 4 is the highest.)
    A. Usability _____
    B. Content _____
    C. Design _____
    D. Difficulty _____

Source: Designed by Jean Camp, Instructional Technology Coordinator, The University of North Carolina at Greensboro, Unpublished. Courtesy of Mary Olson, The University of North Carolina at Greensboro.

FORM 24   Checklist for School Personnel Interviews

NAME OF INTERVIEWER: _____

DATE OF INTERVIEWS: _____

SCHOOL : _____

OBJECTIVE OF OBSERVATION: _____

_____

Instructions to the Interviewer: Schedule a conference with an appropriate person from each administrative division of the school. If a specific service is not identified, discuss with the principal or assistant principal how the school provides such a service or otherwise meets the needs of the students. Use checklists I–VI below to (1) formulate your questions and (2) ensure that you ask appropriate questions. You may add some of your own topics to the list. Check off each item for which you obtain an answer. Take notes in the space provided.

I. Guidance, Testing, Evaluation, and Reporting

NAME OF PERSON INTERVIEWED: _____

TITLE OF PERSON INTERVIEWED: _____

DATE, TIME, AND PLACE OF INTERVIEW: _____

APPROXIMATE LENGTH OF INTERVIEW: _____

_____ 1. Purpose of guidance program

_____ 2. Procedures for obtaining services

_____ 3. Services of guidance program (individual and group)

_____ 4. Referral services

_____ 5. Services for pregnant students and single parents

_____ 6. Teachers' role in guidance

_____ 7. Students' role in guidance

_____ 8. Parents' role in guidance

_____ 9.   Standardized tests and purposes

_____ 10. School's grading/reporting policies

_____ 11. School's promotion/retention policies

_____ 12. Academic advising and placement of students

Notes:

(continued)

II. Library or Media Center/Instructional Materials and Equipment

NAME OF PERSON INTERVIEWED: _____

TITLE OF PERSON INTERVIEWED: _____

DATE, TIME, AND PLACE OF INTERVIEW: _____

APPROXIMATE LENGTH OF INTERVIEW: _____

____ 1. Available library materials related to subject and/or grade level

____ 2. Library or media center hours for students and teachers

____ 3. Procedures for using library or media center (class/students/teachers)

____ 4. Vertical file and appropriate contents

____ 5. Computer indexing of library materials

____ 6. Equipment and media available for teachers' library/media center use

____ 7. Checkout policies for students, teachers, and classes

____ 8. Equipment and media available for classroom use

____ 9. Procedures for instructing students in library/media center use

____ 10. Assistance available for use of equipment and media

____ 11. Availability and procedures for computer use by students and teachers

____ 12. Procedures for selection and review of library materials and media

Notes:

(continued)

III. Health Services

NAME OF PERSON INTERVIEWED: _____

TITLE OF PERSON INTERVIEWED: _____

DATE, TIME, AND PLACE OF INTERVIEW: _____

APPROXIMATE LENGTH OF INTERVIEW: _____

_____   1. Available health services at school

_____   2. Services available through school referral

_____   3. Sex education and condom distribution

_____   4. Services for pregnant students

_____   5. Procedures for teacher with ill/injured child

_____   6. Procedures for dealing with HIV-positive student

_____   7. School safety precautions, policies, and regulations

_____   8. Other county/community services available to students

_____   9. Health and related issues taught in classes

Notes:

(continued)

IV. Curriculum Resource Person or Assistant Principal for Curriculum

NAME OF PERSON INTERVIEWED: _____

TITLE OF PERSON INTERVIEWED: _____

DATE, TIME, AND PLACE OF INTERVIEW: _____

APPROXIMATE LENGTH OF INTERVIEW: _____

_____ 1. School, district, county, or state curriculum guides

_____ 2. Multicultural aspects of the curriculum

_____ 3. School's organization for instruction:

      _____ 3a. grouping

      _____ 3b. departmentalization

      _____ 3c. chain of command

      _____ 3d. curricular offerings

      _____ 3e. extracurricular offerings

      _____ 3f. scheduling for teachers and students

_____ 4. Planning and reflection requirements for teachers

_____ 5. In-service and other opportunities for teachers

_____ 6. Observation and evaluation of teachers (Standards for Teaching, pp. 37–39)

_____ 7. Procedures for selection and review of textbooks and classroom materials

_____ 8. Teachers' role in curriculum development and implementation—May suggest ideas—not always implemented

_____ 9. Community's role in curriculum development and implementation—None

_____ 10. Procedures for dealing with controversial issues and/or materials—None

_____ 11. Special-education teachers

_____ 12. Reading teachers

_____ 13. Speech pathologists—None

_____ 14. Gifted-program teachers

_____ 15. Social-adjustment teachers, including drop-out prevention and in-school suspension—Started 1990–1991 year—seems to be helping

_____ 16. Dean of boys/girls—Yes

_____ 17. Music, art, and drama teachers—Yes—once a week

_____ 18. Other special teachers (bilingual, physical education)

_____ 19. Procedures for mainstreaming students

Notes:

(continued)

V. Person in Charge of Student Discipline

NAME OF PERSON INTERVIEWED: _____

TITLE OF PERSON INTERVIEWED: _____

DATE, TIME, AND PLACE OF INTERVIEW: _____

APPROXIMATE LENGTH OF INTERVIEW: _____

____ 1. School policies/regulations regarding student behavior and appearance

____ 2. Student handbook

____ 3. Procedures for severe discipline referrals

____ 4. Substance-abuse programs

____ 5. Dropout prevention programs

____ 6. School-administered discipline

____ 7. Referrals to other agencies

____ 8. Involvement of law enforcement in the school

Notes:

(continued)

VI. Principal or Assistant Principal

NAME OF PERSON INTERVIEWED: _____

TITLE OF PERSON INTERVIEWED: _____

DATE, TIME, AND PLACE OF INTERVIEW: _____

APPROXIMATE LENGTH OF INTERVIEW: _____

____ 1. School policies/regulations regarding teacher behavior and appearance

____ 2. Faculty handbook. Yes

____ 3. Faculty meetings (time and how used) Weekly, 3:30, Discuss Parent's Day, Routines, Curriculum-Testing

____ 4. Organizational pattern of local schools (i.e., board, central office, and/or school)

____ 5. Specialized type of school, such as magnet

____ 6. Specialized programs, such as before- and after-school programs and preschool or childcare programs

____ 7. Information about the community served by the school

____ 8. Community and parent involvement in the school

____ 9. Business involvement in the school

____ 10. Professional organizations (union and/or academic)

____ 11. Teachers' extra responsibilities

____ 12. Student employment opportunities and procedures to follow

Notes:

FORM 25   Reflective Observation of Classrooms, Schools, and Curriculum

NAME OF OBSERVER: _____

DATE AND TIME OF OBSERVATION: _____

TEACHER/SCHOOL : _____

GRADE LEVEL AND/OR SUBJECT: _____

OBJECTIVE OF OBSERVATION: _____

_____

Instructions to the Observer: Use Form 25 to respond to the following questions/statements when you have completed your observations.

1. Select

    a. What did you observe about the classroom that was different from and/or similar to your past experience?

    b. What did you observe about the school that was different from and/or similar to your past experience?

    c. What did you observe about the curriculum that was different from and/or similar to your past experience?

    d. What principles did you use from the INTASC Standards?

2. Describe

    a. Briefly describe your anecdotal observations of the school.

    b. Briefly describe your structured observation of strategies that challenge students' multiple intelligences.

    c. Did the school have the resources/materials that you expected it to have? Describe.

3. Analyze

    a. How has the curriculum changed since you were in elementary/high school?

    b. How did your observation of multicultural/antibias education compare/contrast to your own school experience?

4. Appraise

    a. What did you learn from these observations?

    b. How effective were you in completing the forms related to curriculum and technology?

    c. What sources of information about schools, classrooms, and curriculum were most helpful to you?

5. Transform

    a. What did you learn about technological resources that can help you in your teaching?

    b. What new knowledge and skills will you incorporate in your teaching?

Source: Adapted from North Carolina State Department of Public Instruction. *Performance Based Licensure.* Raleigh, NC, 1998–1999.

FORM 26   **Anecdotal Record for Observing Students**

NAME OF OBSERVER: _____

DATE AND TIME OF OBSERVATION: _____

LENGTH OF OBSERVATION: _____

PERSON AND/OR EVENT OBSERVED: _____

GRADE LEVEL AND/OR SUBJECT: _____

OBJECTIVE OF OBSERVATION: _____

_____

Instructions to the Observer: Write a detailed account of your subject, noting his or her appearance, background, abilities, interaction with others, habits, class responsiveness, behavior, and so on. Try to be as objective as possible.

FORM 27   Shadowing Form

NAME OF SHADOWED STUDENT: _____

NAME OF OBSERVER: _____

DATE AND TIME OF SHADOW: _____

GRADE LEVEL AND/OR SUBJECT: _____

OBJECTIVE OF SHADOW: _____

GENERAL DESCRIPTION OF LOCATION: _____

Instructions to the Observer: Select a student to shadow for an entire school day. Use a separate page for each class period or segment of the school day you observe. Every five to fifteen minutes, record what the subject of the observation is doing; also indicate what other students and teachers are doing. At the end of the day, summarize the shadowing experience. If possible, interview the student and report the results.

SUBJECT/CLASS: _____

Time (recorded every five to fifteen minutes)	What Subject Was Doing	What Classmates and Teacher Were Doing

(continued)

SUBJECT/CLASS: _____

Time (recorded every five to fifteen minutes)	What Subject Was Doing	What Classmates and Teacher Were Doing

The following should be completed at the end of the shadowing experience:

1. **Overview:** Summarize how the student seemed to be involved, how the student interacted with teachers and peers, what the student seemed to learn, and how the student seems to feel about the class.

2. **Report of interview with student:**

FORM 28   **Profile Card**

NAME OF OBSERVER: _____

STUDENT: _____

DATE AND TIME OF OBSERVATION: _____

GRADE LEVEL AND/OR SUBJECT: _____

LOCATION: _____

OBJECTIVE OF OBSERVATION: _____

_____

Instructions to the Observer: Record your observations in two-minute intervals.

**Time (recorded
every two minutes)**   **Student's Activities/Attitudes**

FORM 29   **Descriptive Profile Chart**

PLOTTED BY: _____

DATE AND TIME OF OBSERVATION: _____

STUDENT: _____

SCHOOL: _____

GRADE LEVEL: _____

INTERVAL: _____

OBJECTIVE OF OBSERVATION: _____

_____

Instructions to the Observer: Record brief phrases to indicate the activities of the student during discussion and work periods. Place student activities under "application" if they show involvement in the lesson; if not, place them under "distraction."

DISCUSSION PERIOD		WORK PERIOD	
Application	**Distraction**	**Application**	**Distraction**

Source: Adapted from John Devor. *The Experience of Student Teaching,* 1964.

FORM 30   Coding System to Observe Student Participation in Lessons

NAME OF OBSERVER: _____

DATE AND TIME OF OBSERVATION: _____

STUDENT: _____

GRADE LEVEL: _____

TOPIC: _____

OBJECTIVE OF OBSERVATION: _____

_____

Instructions to the Observer: Place a slash [/] in the appropriate column to indicate student activities during a single lesson.

Important Contributions	Minor Contributions	Distracting Remarks

FORM 31   **Incomplete Sentence Inventory**

NAME OF OBSERVER: _____

DATE AND TIME OF OBSERVATION: _____

STUDENT: _____

GRADE LEVEL AND/OR SUBJECT: _____

OBJECTIVE OF OBSERVATION: _____

_____

Instructions to the Observer: Determine the purpose of completing an informal inventory. Then design some incomplete sentences related to your objective. A sample answer for the first question should be provided in the instructions to the student. Observer can read incomplete sentences to children who are unable to read.

Instructions to the Student: Complete each sentence as honestly and completely as possible. For example, you might complete the first questions as follows:

_____

_____

_____

1. _____

_____

2. _____

_____

3. _____

_____

4. _____

_____

5. _____

_____

6. _____

_____

7. _____

_____

8. _____

_____

9. _____

_____

FORM 32   Tally Chart of Student-Group Selections

NAME OF OBSERVER: _____

DATE AND TIME OF OBSERVATION: _____

SCHOOL: _____

OBJECTIVE OF OBSERVATION: _____

_____

Instructions to the Observer: List students on left side. Then tally the first, second, and third choices made by each student in the chart below.

Chosen Choosers																								
Chosen 1																								
Chosen 2																								
Chosen 3																								
Totals																								

Source: Frederick J. McDonald. *Educational Psychology,* 2nd ed., Wadsworth Publishing, 1965, 634.

FORM 33   Sociogram Based on Charted Student Preferences

NAME OF OBSERVER: _____

DATE AND TIME OF OBSERVATION: _____

SCHOOL: _____

GRADE LEVEL AND/OR SUBJECT: _____

OBJECTIVE OF OBSERVATION: _____

_____

Instructions to the Observer: Use the tally chart of student-group selections to put the names of the most-selected students in a prominent place on the page. Identify males by placing their names in circles, females by placing their names in boxes. Then, put the names of students selected by those few most-selected students next to them. If they selected each other, connect them with a dotted line. If not, draw an arrow to the student selected. Proceed in this fashion until all names are represented on the form.

FORM 34   Reasonable Public School Expectations for Students

NAME OF OBSERVER: _____

DATE AND TIME OF OBSERVATION: _____

SCHOOL/TEACHER: _____

STUDENT: _____

GRADE LEVEL AND/OR SUBJECT: _____

AREA OF IDENTIFICATION (DISABILITY, IF KNOWN): _____

OBJECTIVE OF OBSERVATION: _____

Instructions to the Observer: What follows is a checklist of reasonable performance and behavior that teachers can expect from non-disabled students. In order to develop an Individual Educational Plan (IEP) for a disabled student, it is necessary to determine which of these expectations he or she is able to meet with no curriculum or classroom modifications. In the right-hand column, indicate the extent to which the student is successful in each of these categories. Note that some of this information may be available only from the student's academic file or teacher; it is important that you make no assumptions and obtain appropriate documentation.

Developmental Areas	Very	Moderate	Limited	None
A. Academic Development 1. Reading 2. Writing 3. Mathematics				
B. Social Development 1. Interaction with other students 2. Interaction with teacher or other staff				
C. Physical Development 1. Uses regular transportation to school; walks or rides school bus 2. Reports to homeroom or other central location by her/himself 3. Obeys school rules with other students 4. Goes to class with regular curriculum a. regular volume of curriculum b. regular rate of presentation of material c. at a reading level that is grade-level appropriate 5. Has homework assignments in every class 6. Changes classes when the bell rings 7. Mingles in hallway before next class				

(continued)

Developmental Areas	Very	Moderate	Limited	None
8. Has lunch with other youngsters				
9. Goes to gym/PE with other youngsters				
10. Dresses for gym/PE				
11. Goes to the restroom as classes change				
12. Has recess/free time with others				
13. Attends regular school assemblies				
14. Takes regular tests without modifications				
15. Participates in extracurricular activities				
16. Goes on school field trips or outings				
17. Does homework each night				
18. Takes homework back to teacher each day				
19. Attends school each day with very few excused absences				
20. Makes up work if absent				

Source: Adapted from a form used by the Asheville, North Carolina Public Schools.

FORM 35　Information-Processing Categories of Instructional Modifications

NAME OF OBSERVER: _____

DATE AND TIME OF OBSERVATION: _____

SCHOOL/TEACHER: _____

STUDENT: _____

GRADE LEVEL AND/OR SUBJECT: _____

AREA OF IDENTIFICATION (DISABILITY, IF KNOWN): _____

OBJECTIVE OF OBSERVATION: _____

Instructions to the Observer: What follows is a checklist of modifications targeted to the disabled student. Any variety of these modifications may be needed in order for a disabled student to be successful in the school or classroom environment and/or to achieve curricular goals. Observe a disabled student who is in the regular classroom and check [✓] those modifications that are currently being employed. If a modification is needed but is not currently employed, place an asterisk [*] to the left of the item.

Note: It may be necessary to interview the classroom teacher to determine whether some of these items are currently employed.

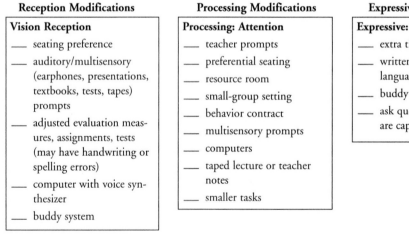

Reception Modifications

Vision Reception
___ seating preference
___ auditory/multisensory (earphones, presentations, textbooks, tests, tapes) prompts
___ adjusted evaluation measures, assignments, tests (may have handwriting or spelling errors)
___ computer with voice synthesizer
___ buddy system

Processing Modifications

Processing: Attention
___ teacher prompts
___ preferential seating
___ resource room
___ small-group setting
___ behavior contract
___ multisensory prompts
___ computers
___ taped lecture or teacher notes
___ smaller tasks

Expressive Modifications

Expressive: Oral
___ extra time for responding
___ written answers or sign language
___ buddy system for reports
___ ask questions that students are capable of answering

(continued)

Reception Modifications

Auditory Reception

___ seating preference

___ student scribes

___ paired oral/written prompts

___ visual presentation

___ computers

___ buddy system

Processing Modifications

Processing: Organization

___ teacher's outline or Xeroxed notes

___ highlighted text

___ prepared study sheets

___ individual behavior contacts

___ modification of assignment format

___ extended time on major assignments or shorter assignments

___ help organizing work

___ interview with parent/caregiver

Processing: Memory

___ shorter time on assignments

___ prepared study sheets

___ paired oral and written work

___ calculators and computers

___ answer list for fill-in-the-blank questions

___ no penalty for poor spelling

Expressive Modifications

Expressive: Writing

___ no penalty for poor handwriting

___ use of word processor (or typewriter)

___ test and report modifications (oral, shorter, more time)

___ student scribe for notes or teacher's notes Xeroxed (tape recording)

Source: Adapted from a form used by the Asheville, North Carolina Public Schools: *Reception Modifications.*

FORM 36   Reflective Observation of Students

NAME OF OBSERVER: _____

DATE AND TIME OF OBSERVATION: _____

TEACHER/SCHOOL : _____

GRADE LEVEL AND/OR SUBJECT: _____

OBJECTIVE OF OBSERVATION: _____

_____

Instructions to the Observer: Use Form 36 to respond to the following questions after you have completed your observations.

1. **Select**
    a. What anecdotal observations of students did you complete?
    b. What structured observation of students did you complete?
    c. What principles from INTASC Standards did you address?
    d. How many of the characteristics of an effective inclusive classroom did you observe?

2. **Describe**
    a. What are the unique characteristics that distinguish these students from others you have observed (e.g., needs, background, learning styles, prior experiences)?
    b. What steps did you take to assess the needs of these students?
    c. From whom and in what ways did you solicit information about the students' experiences, learning behaviors, and needs?

3. **Analyze**
    a. How will your assessment of the characteristics and needs of these students affect your planning, tutoring, and teaching?
    b. How did the cultural, ethnic, and racial characteristics of these students influence you and your interactions with them?
    c. How effective was your participation in the inclusive classroom model?

4. **Appraise**
    a. What sources of information were most helpful to you as you consider planning and teaching these students?
    b. What observation(s) improved your understanding of the diverse needs of students at this age/grade?

5. **Transform**
    a. What did you learn about the diverse nature and needs of students?
    b. What new knowledge and skills will you incorporate in your teaching?

Source: Adapted from North Carolina State Department of Public Instruction. *Performance Based Licensure.* Raleigh, NC, 1998–1999.

FORM 37   Anecdotal Record of Preteaching Activities

STUDENT: _____

TEACHER: _____

GRADE LEVEL: _____

DATE: _____

OBJECTIVE: _____

_____

Instructions to Student Participant: Keep an account of the activities you participated in prior to actual teaching. Indicate how you felt about each day's events.

FORM 38   Checklist of Routines for Helping the Teacher

STUDENT: _____

TEACHER: _____

GRADE LEVEL AND/OR SUBJECT: _____

DATE: _____

OBJECTIVE: _____

_____

Instructions to Student Participant: All of the following duties are important to the management of the instructional environment. You will need to learn to complete these while simultaneously teaching the students and managing the class. To help you learn to do so efficiently, complete all tasks appropriate to your teaching situation and indicate the date each is accomplished. Please have the classroom teacher sign this form when all appropriate activities have been successfully completed.

Activity   **Date Completed**

1. Make a seating chart . . . .   _____
2. Take attendance . . . .   _____
3. Run errands for the classroom teacher . . . .   _____
4. Help with classroom housekeeping. . . . .   _____
5. Organize materials needed for a lesson . . . .   _____
6. Make copies of materials needed for the lesson . . . .   _____
7. Help pass out materials to the students. . . . .   _____
8. Arrange a bulletin board . . . .   _____
9. Check out books from the library to be used by students in the classroom . . . . . .   _____
10. Check out media to be used in a lesson . . . .   _____
11. Make a chart or graph . . . .   _____
12. Make a transparency or stencil. . . . .   _____
13. Run a film, filmstrip, videotape, etc.. . . . .   _____
14. Get supplementary materials needed for a lesson (magazine illustrations,
    pamphlets, maps, etc.) . . . .   _____
15. Develop a bibliography for an upcoming unit. . . . .   _____
16. Correct papers. . . . .   _____
17. Set up or help set up a lab . . . .   _____
18. Write news/assignments on the chalkboard. . . . .   _____
19. Set up a learning center . . . .   _____
20. Set up an experiment or a demonstration . . . .   _____
21. Obtain a speaker to come to class, or help organize a class field trip. . . . .   _____
22. Help gather materials for a class party. . . . .   _____
23. Help make costumes for a class play. . . . .   _____
24. Send out a class newsletter to parents . . . .   _____
25. Other (please list below): . . . .   _____

I certify that the student participant listed above has successfully completed all of the above activities that are appropriate to my classroom.

_____

(Classroom teacher's signature)

FORM 39.1   Checklist of Routines Involving Students

STUDENT: _____

TEACHER: _____

GRADE LEVEL AND/OR SUBJECT: _____

DATES: _____

OBJECTIVE OF OBSERVATION: _____

_____

Instructions to Student Participant: All of the following activities are important to the instruction of the students. You will need to learn to complete these while simultaneously teaching the students and managing the class. To help you learn to do so efficiently, complete all tasks appropriate to your teaching situation and indicate the date each is accomplished. Please have the classroom teacher sign this form when all appropriate activities have been successfully completed.

Activity	Date Completed
1. Orient a new student.	_____
2. Help individual students with seatwork	_____
3. Work with a club or student activity.	_____
4. Assist a small group	_____
5. Work with an individual student in a lab (i.e., computer, language, or science).	_____
6. Assist a disabled student.	_____
7. Assist students with library research	_____
8. Monitor a test.	_____
9. Collect money.	_____
10. Hand out and collect materials.	_____
11. Listen to an individual student read or recite a lesson	_____
12. Give a test or a quiz.	_____
13. Assist young children with clothing	_____
14. Bring books or materials to share with the students.	_____
15. Supervise students outside the classroom	_____
16. Read aloud or tell a story.	_____
17. Help students in a learning center	_____
18. Accompany students to a school office, the bus, or the playground	_____
19. Attend a parent-teacher conference.	_____
20. Work with the teacher in developing an IEP (Individual Education Plan) for a mainstreamed student	_____
21. Accompany students to before- or after-school programs	_____
22. Help monitor the hallway, lunchroom, or playground	_____
23. Other (please list below):	

I certify that the student participant listed above has successfully completed all of the above activities that are appropriate to my classroom.

_____

(Classroom teacher's signature)

FORM 39.2　Checklist for Kidwatching

STUDENT: _____

TEACHER: _____

GRADE LEVEL AND/OR SUBJECT: _____

DATES: _____

TIME: _____

OBJECTIVE: _____

Instructions: Become familiar with the statements below. Check activity observed and record the date(s) you observed the activity, then write a brief statement of what you specifically observed.

Check　　**Date**　　**Activity Observed**

1. ____　____　Participates in group talk (discussions about books, stories/plays, science experiments, math problems).
EXAMPLE:

2. ____　____　Asks teacher questions (for assistance, about language, about content).
EXAMPLE:

3. ____　____　Leads conversations.
EXAMPLE:

4. ____　____　Participates and takes turns appropriately in conversations.
EXAMPLE:

5. ____　____　Builds on what others say.
EXAMPLE:

6. ____　____　Speaks clearly and audibly; used comprehensible speech.
EXAMPLE:

(continued)

7. ____ ____   Listens when others speak.

                    EXAMPLE:

8. ____ ____   Demonstrates understanding of oral directions.

                    EXAMPLE:

9. ____ ____   Explains how to do or make something.

                    EXAMPLE:

10. ____ ____   Writes for a specific purpose on an assigned topic.

                    EXAMPLE:

11. ____ ____   Demonstrates knowledge of punctuation (spacing, commas, period, question marks, and capitalization).

                    EXAMPLE:

12. ____ ____   Writes sentences in appropriate grammatical form.

                    EXAMPLE:

13. ____ ____   Expresses interest in specific book(s), character(s), magazine(s).

                    EXAMPLE:

14. ____ ____   Attempts to read unknown (sounding out, context clues).

                    EXAMPLE:

15. ____ ____   Demonstrates understanding of what has been read.

                    EXAMPLE:

Adapted from Owocki, G. and Goodman, Y. (2002). Kidwatching: Documenting Children's Literacy Development.

FORM 40.1   Lesson Plan Form 1

STUDENT: _____

TEACHER: _____

GRADE LEVEL AND/OR SUBJECT: _____

DATE AND TIME: _____

OBJECTIVE: _____

_____

Instructions to the Student Participant: Whether your plan covers several classroom sessions or only one, each lesson should include an outline of your goal, objectives, materials, and expected lesson duration in addition to the seven steps listed below:

Goal:

OBJECTIVES:

MATERIALS:

Duration:

FIRST CLASS

   1. Anticipatory Set

(continued)

2. Objective

3. Teacher Input

4. Checking for Understanding

5. Guided Practice

(continued)

6. Independent Practice

7. Closure

Source: Lois Sprinthall. *A Strategy Guide for Teachers: Guidebook for Supervisors of Novice Teachers.* Unpublished manuscript. Based on the work of Madeline Hunter.

FORM 40.2 Lesson Plan Form 2

STUDENT: _____

TEACHER: _____

GRADE LEVEL AND/OR SUBJECT: _____

TOPICS: _____

DATE AND TIME: _____

Objectives

Key Concepts

Materials

Procedures

Evaluation

FORM 40.3   Lesson Plan Form 3

DATE/TIME: _____

TIME: _____

STUDENT: _____

TEACHER: _____

GRADE LEVEL AND/OR SUBJECT: _____

Objective:

INTASC STANDARDS

Lesson Objectives

Materials

Warm-up Activity

Lesson

Assessment	Homework Assignment

Esl/Ec Strategies	Lesson Evaluation/Changes (Reflection)

Source: Adapted from Robert Ventura, Nancy Reid and Margaret Lee: (2001) State Department of Public Instruction Raleigh, NC 27602

FORM 41   **Unit Plan Format**

STUDENT: _____

TEACHER: _____

GRADE LEVEL AND/OR SUBJECT: _____

DATE: _____

UNIT: _____

DURATION: _____

Objective:

Overview

Purposes

Competency Goals

(continued)

Specific Objectives for this Unit

Calendar of Activities

Assessment: Complete a Rubric (see pp. 129–130)

FORM 42   Reflective Observation of Preteaching and Planning

NAME OF OBSERVER: _____

DATE AND TIME OF OBSERVATION: _____

TEACHER/SCHOOL: _____

GRADE LEVEL AND/OR SUBJECT: _____

OBJECTIVE OF OBSERVATION: _____

_____

Instructions to the Observer: Respond to the following questions on this form after you have completed participation, preteaching, and planning.

1. Select
   a. What preteaching activities did you complete?
   b. What kind of planning did you do before your teaching?
   c. What principles from INTASC Standards did you address in your plan?
   d. What can a rubric help you do?

2. Describe
   a. List the steps you used in the planning process.
   b. Describe the parts of your lesson plan.
   c. Describe the parts of your unit plan.
   d. Describe Kidwatching.

3. Analyze
   a. How do you relate planning a lesson to teaching a lesson?
   b. How did your preteaching and planning prepare you for your future teaching?
   c. Which preteaching activities were most helpful to you?
   d. Compare/contrast a rubric scoring with the scoring listed at the end of the unit.

4. Appraise
   a. What planning techniques were most helpful to you?
   b. How effective were you in checking classroom routines?
   c. How effective were you in checking students' routines?
   d. How does Kidwatching influence teacher planning?

5. Transform
   a. What lesson and/or unit planning techniques will you use in your future teaching? Why?
   b. What additional planning skills would you like to develop?
   c. What did you learn about planning for using the Internet that you can use in your classroom teaching?
   d. How will you incorporate rubrics in your future teaching?

Source: Adapted from North Carolina State Department of Public Instruction. *Performance Based Licensure,* Raleigh, NC, 1998–1999.

FORM 43   Checklist of Tutoring Activities

STUDENT: _____

NAME OF PUPIL(S) TUTORED (IF APPROPRIATE): _____

TEACHER: _____

GRADE LEVEL AND/OR SUBJECT: _____

DATES: _____

OBJECTIVE: _____

Instructions to Student Participant: Listed below and on the following pages are several types of short-term and long-term tutoring activities in which you can participate. As you complete these activities, indicate the date each is accomplished. At the end of each section there is space for your comments about what you learned from the tutoring activities. Please have the classroom teacher sign this form when your activities have been completed.

Short-Term, Informal Tutoring Activities	**Date Completed**
1. Ask individual students questions about something they are reading or writing, a picture they are drawing, or a project they are working on.	_____
2. Discuss with individual students, stories they have read.	_____
3. Help students with their seatwork.	_____
4. Answer questions students have about their individual work.	_____
5. Assist students with learning computer skills	_____
6. Comment on what you learned from these activities:	_____

(continued)

Long-Term, Planned Tutoring Activities	Date Completed

1. Teaching skills that have not been mastered by individual students (grammar, composition, reading, mathematical computations, times tables, word problems, word processing, using a computer program, using a table of contents, reading a textbook for meaning, cutting out objects, using a microscope, etc.). List the skill(s) you taught: _____

2. Diagnosing a student's strength or weakness (administering a specific individual test, listening to a student read, asking a student questions on a variety of levels,watching a student do a mathematical computation, observing a student using a computer program, watching a student use a piece of equipment, etc.). List the method(s) you employed and what you were attempting to diagnose: _____

3. Remedying a weakness (helping a student learn to cut out a shape with scissors, assisting a student with rules of phonics or grammar, drilling a student on vocabulary, showing a student how to find meaning in a paragraph, demonstrating for a student how to use a piece of equipment safely, etc.).List the method(s) you employed and the weakness you were attempting to remedy: _____

4. Developing a special talent (teaching the student a technique of drawing, reading a piece of student writing and providing support and suggestions, listening to a student read and discussing what has been read, talking to a student about a historical event, working with a student on a science project, helping a student complete a woodworking project, teaching basic computer programming, taking the student to a museum, etc.). List the method(s) you employed and the talent you were attempting to develop: _____

(continued)

Long-Term, Planned Tutoring Activities	Date Completed

5. Other. List specific long-range tutoring activities in which you have participated: _____

6. Comment on what you learned from these activities: _____

I certify that the student participant listed above has successfully completed those tutoring activities indicated above.

_____

(Classroom teacher's signature)

FORM 44   Checklist for Planning a Tutorial

STUDENT: _____

NAME OF PUPIL(S) TUTORED: _____

GRADE LEVEL AND/OR SUBJECT: _____

DATES: _____

OBJECTIVE: _____

_____

Instructions to Tutor: As you complete each of the following in your tutoring plans indicate the date completed.

Planning Activity	Date Completed
1. Discuss the student you will tutor with the classroom teacher.	_____
2. Discuss possible tutoring topics and techniques with the classroom teacher.	_____
3. Carefully plan an initial "getting-to-know-you" session with the student.	_____
4. Diagnose student strengths and weaknesses as necessary.	_____
5. Check INTASC standards and performance-based principles.	_____
6. Check available curriculum guides to determine skills to be taught and their sequence.	_____
7. Review management and discipline procedures with classroom teacher.	_____
8. Set a specific objective for each tutoring session.	_____
9. Develop a plan for each tutoring session (appropriate plan formats can be found in Chapter 5 pp. 121–126).	_____
10. Develop strategies that utilize your knowledge of multiple intelligences.	_____
11. Discuss special needs of mainstreamed or English as Second Language (ESL) student, if appropriate, with teacher.	_____
12. Consult appropriate resources for teaching techniques and materials.	_____
13. Make sure all necessary materials are available and copied prior to each tutoring session.	_____
14. Monitor the pupil's progress by keeping a log of each day's tutoring.	_____
15. Discuss student's progress with the classroom teacher. Ask for additional suggestions for helping the student.	_____

FORM 45   Reflections on Tutoring Activities

NAME OF TUTOR: _____

DATE AND TIME OF RECORD: _____

TEACHER/SCHOOL/GRADE: _____

OBJECTIVE OF OBSERVATION: _____

_____

Instructions: Use this form to respond to the questions after you have completed your tutoring.

1. **Select**
   a. What kind(s) of tutoring activities did you complete?
   b. Why did you decide to do the kind(s) of tutoring you did?
   c. How did the tutoring activities relate to the student(s) age(s)?
   d. What performance-based standard(s) (the ten principles) did you address?

2. **Describe**
   a. Briefly describe the pupil you tutored (age, gender, background, etc.).
   b. What special needs/interests did you consider when you planned the tutoring activity(ies)?
   c. What resources did you use?
   d. How did you monitor student progress?

3. **Analyze**
   a. How did your preplanning with the classroom teacher help you in planning for your tutoring sessions?
   b. How did the characteristics of the student affect your planning and tutoring?
   c. Did your tutoring plan allow for modification due to unanticipated student input? How?
   d. Why did you select the teaching strategies you incorporated in your lesson?
   e. What management and discipline principles did you implement?

4. **Appraise**
   a. How different/similar were your objectives for each tutoring session?
   b. How effective were you in using available resources for your tutoring?

5. **Transform**
   a. What did you learn about planning for tutoring?
   b. How did you adjust your teaching as a result of student assessment?
   c. What did you learn about the synergy of teaching and discipline?

Source: Adapted from North Carolina State Department of Public Instruction. *Performance Based Licensure,* Raleigh, NC, 1998–1999.

FORM 46   Preplanning Small-Group Checklist

STUDENT: _____

TEACHER: _____

GRADE LEVEL AND/OR SUBJECT: _____

DATES: _____

OBJECTIVE: _____

Instructions to Student Participant: As you complete each of the following in planning for your small group, indicate the date completed.

Preplanning Activity	Date Completed
1. Discuss possible types of small-group teaching with the classroom teacher.	_____
2. Discuss the assignment of students to the small group.	_____
3. Discuss the classroom teacher's goal for the small group.	_____
4. Consider the needs, interests, abilities, and intelligences of the students who will participate in the instructional group. Discuss these issues with the classroom teacher.	_____
5. Develop an assessment tool or technique that can measure the progress of several students simultaneously. (e.g., Students complete mathematics problems that begin slightly below their level of achievement and continue beyond their level of achievement. Students answer questions about reading samples that are below their reading level and continue beyond their reading level. Students complete multiple-choice items on a leveled vocabulary list. Students attempt to perform part of a one-act play. Students read parts orally in a short play, etc.) A rubric can be a good tool to measure this type of achievement.	_____
6. Determine a specific objective for each small-group session.	_____
7. Determine which of the INTASC standards can be addressed in the small-group lesson.	_____
8. Review management and discipline procedures	_____
9. Develop a plan for each small-group session. (Appropriate plan formats can be found in Chapter 5, pp. 121–126.)	_____
10. Consult appropriate resources for teaching techniques and materials.	_____
11. Make sure all necessary materials are available and copied prior to each small-group session.	_____
12. Monitor the pupils' progress by having them complete individual practice exercises related to each session's objective.	_____
13. Discuss the students' progress with the classroom teacher. Ask for additional suggestions for helping the students.	_____

FORM 47   Small-Group Teaching Checklist

STUDENT: _____

TEACHER: _____

GRADE LEVEL AND/OR SUBJECT: _____

TOPIC: _____

DATE AND TIME: _____

OBJECTIVE: _____

Instructions to Student Participant: Use this checklist while planning and teaching your small group. To be sure that your lesson includes each of the following, check [✓] each item off as it occurs.

Teaching Activity	Appears in Lesson
1. The students' attention is grabbed.	_____
2. The objective of the lesson is related to the students.	_____
3. Prerequisite knowledge is ascertained through questions and answers, a quiz, completion of an exercise, etc.	_____
4. If appropriate, gaps in needed information are filled in.	_____
5. New information, skills, or materials are presented through explanation, demonstration, discussion, etc.	_____
6. Individual tasks are assigned to each group member.	_____
7. Student performance is elicited and monitored through independent work.	_____
8. Teacher feedback is provided to each student.	_____
9. Student work is related to previous and future learning.	_____
10. Students review what they have learned in the lesson.	_____
11. The objective for the next small-group lesson is determined and communicated to the students.	_____

FORM 48   Reflections on Small-Group Teaching

NAME OF PRESERVICE TEACHER: _____

DATE AND TIME OF RECORD: _____

TEACHER/SCHOOL/GRADE: _____

OBJECTIVE OF LESSON: _____

_____

Instructions: Use this form to respond to the following questions after you have completed your small-group teaching.

1. **Select**
   a. What were the characteristics (age, gender, background) of the pupils in your small group?
   b. What concepts/skills did you address?
   c. What INTASC standards did you address?
   d. What technique(s) did you use to "grab" students' attention?

2. **Describe**
   a. What diverse student needs did you consider in your planning to teach the small groups?
   b. Briefly describe the resources/materials you used.
   c. How did you address multiple intelligences?
   d. What teaching strategies did you incorporate in your lesson?

3. **Analyze**
   a. How did your assessment of prior student learning influence your lesson?
   b. How did the characteristics of the pupils affect your planning and teaching?
   c. What performance modes did you use (e.g., writing, speaking, art)?
   d. How did you modify your plan and teaching to adjust to the unexpected?

4. **Appraise**
   a. How successful was your teaching? What was most effective? What was least effective?
   b. What did the students learn?
   c. How successful was your management and discipline?

5. **Transform**
   a. What did you learn about selecting and using varied teaching strategies?
   b. What did you learn about planning for teaching a small group?
   c. How could you improve your management and discipline?

Source: Adapted from North Carolina State Department of Public Instruction *Performance Based Licensure,* Raleigh, NC, 1998–1999.

FORM 49   Checklist for Working with Large Groups

STUDENT: _____

TEACHER: _____

GRADE LEVEL AND/OR SUBJECT: _____

DATES: _____

OBJECTIVE: _____

Instructions to Student Participant: As you complete each of these activities, place a check [✓] in the right-hand column.

Activity	Completed

Management of the Classroom

1. Discuss management rules with the classroom teacher. _____

2. Ascertain consequences for infractions with the classroom teacher. _____

3. Use only the discipline methods sanctioned by the classroom teacher and the school. _____

4. Communicate the rules and consequences to the students so that they know you will enforce them. _____

5. Enforce rules and apply consequences consistently. _____

6. Do not threaten if you do not intend to carry through on the threat (e.g., "If you aren't quiet, I'll keep you all after school."). _____

7. Make eye contact with as many students as possible. _____

8. Call students by name. (Make a temporary seating chart to help you learn names or have the students make, wear, or display name tags.) _____

Teaching

1. Carefully plan lessons and divide them into clear segments. (Use a planning format such as those in Chapter 5, pp. 121–126) _____

2. Be sure all materials are copied and ready to distribute. _____

3. Preview all materials prior to using or showing them. _____

4. Preread anything you intend to use. _____

5. Maintain instructional momentum (i.e., Keep up the pace; do not spend too long on any one element of the plan; do not overexplain). _____

6. Be certain that students understand what is expected (i.e., Ask them to explain to you what they are to do; place assignments on the chalkboard prior to the lesson; make sure instructions and printing on handouts are clear; provide clear examples). _____

7. Be sure students know how to perform and are capable of accomplishing the task. (Beware of asking students to do tasks for which they do not have prerequisite knowledge or skills; check with the classroom teacher to be sure they will be able to accomplish what you expect.) _____

(continued)

Activity	Completed

8. Review previous lessons and prerequisite knowledge or skills required for this lesson.   _____

9. Actively involve the students in the lesson.   _____

10. Use teaching methodology appropriate to the subject and the maturity of the students (e.g., labs in science classes, oral reading and independent writing in English and language arts, problem solving in mathematics, research in social studies, etc.).   _____

11. Employ a variety of teaching techniques so that all types of learners can achieve (e.g., audiovisuals, hands-on activities, problem solving, student-designed charts and graphs, laboratories, demonstrations, the Internet).   _____

12. Assess students' level of mastery of skills and concepts as often as possible (e.g., classwork that requires demonstration of mastery, observation of students completing classwork, homework that is not merely drill, quizzes, journal entries, writing assignments, use of a rubric).   _____

13. Expect mastery of skills and concepts after a period of teaching, practice, coaching, assessing, reteaching, etc.   _____

14. Do not expect all students to master all concepts and skills in the same way or at the same time. Group students to provide additional assistance to those who have not mastered important concepts and skills. Use different teaching techniques with these students, or allow those who have mastered the skills or concepts to tutor those who have not.

FORM 50   Reflections on Large-Group Teaching

TEACHER: _____

DATE AND TIME OF RECORD: _____

GRADE LEVEL AND/OR SUBJECT: _____

OBJECTIVE: _____

Instructions: You will use this form to respond to the questions.

1. **Select**
   a. What concepts/skills did you address in the lesson?
   b. Why did you address these concepts/skills?
   c. How do these concepts/skills relate to the students' ages and ability levels?
   d. What management techniques did you use?

2. **Describe**
   a. Briefly describe the characteristics of the students (gender, age, race, ability, disability levels).
   b. What resources/materials did you use?
   c. What multiple intelligences did you address?
   d. What role(s) (coach, audience, facilitator) did you play to encourage student learning?
   e. What teaching strategies did you incorporate?
   f. What student assessment technique(s) did you use prior to planning your lesson?
   g. What assessment of students' learning did you apply at the conclusion of your lesson?

3. **Analyze**
   a. How did the characteristics of the students affect your lesson plan?
   b. How did you utilize different performance modes (writing, speaking, reading, doing experiments, solving puzzles)? Why?
   c. Did you modify your plan because of unanticipated events? How?
   d. Why did you select the particular teaching and assessment strategies you incorporated in your lesson?
   e. Evaluate the assessment strategies you used in your lesson.
   f. How did the students respond to your enforcement of rules and application of consequences?
   g. How did you incorporate INTASC, state, and district standards in your lesson?

4. **Appraise**
   a. How successful was your lesson? What was most effective? Least effective?
   b. How did your choice of teaching strategies increase the students' opportunities to engage in critical thinking and problem solving?
   c. What changes will you make in your management and discipline plan?

5. **Transform**
   a. What did you learn from planning your lesson? What did you learn from teaching the lesson?
   b. What did you learn about the teaching strategies you used?
   c. How did you adjust instruction as a result of the assessment of student learning?
   d. What did you learn about homework?

Source: Adapted from North Carolina State Department of Public Instruction. *Performance Based Licensure,* Raleigh, NC, 1998–1999.

FORM 51   Reflections on Keeping a Portfolio

NAME OF PRESERVICE TEACHER: _____

NAME OF CLASSROOM TEACHER: _____

NAME OF SCHOOL: _____

DATE(S) OF PREPARING THE PORTFOLIO: _____

OBJECTIVE: _____

_____

Instructions: Make a list of the ten performance-based standards (Chapter 1, pp. 7–9). Refer to them as you respond to the statements/questions as given below. After you have completed your portfolio, respond to the statements/questions on this form.

1. Select
   a. What was your objective for preparing a portfolio?
   b. How did you organize your portfolio?

2. Describe
   a. List the observation, participation and teaching forms, documents, and artifacts which you selected for inclusion in your portfolio.
   b. Briefly describe assistance you received from classroom teachers, university professors, and peers.
   c. Briefly describe any problems/concerns you experienced.

3. Analyze
   a. How did your reflections on completed observations, participation, and teaching help or hinder you as you prepared your portfolio?
   b. How did you decide which forms, documents, or artifacts related to each performance-based standard?

4. Appraise
   a. How effective were you in relating your work to the ten performance indicators from the INTASC standards?
   b. How successful were you in keeping a portfolio?

5. Transform
   a. What did you learn about teaching from keeping a portfolio?
   b. What did you learn about yourself as a preservice/future classroom teacher?
   c. How is your philosophy of teaching and learning reflected in your portfolio?

Source: Adapted from North Carolina State Department of Public Instruction. *Performance Based Licensure,* Raleigh, NC, 1998–1999.

Glossary

Anectodal observation: A written account of an observed classroom event, a student, or the teaching of a lesson for a specified period of time.

Artifact: Any piece of evidence used for demonstration purposes. Most items will come from everyday materials, plans, student work completed in the classroom. Others will come from observations, evaluations, letters to/from parents, photos, videos.

Degree of precision: Knowing how to manage a variety of instructional events in large-group instruction.

Inclusion: Students with disabilities are included in the regular classroom. The regular classroom teacher and the special education teacher work with the same group of students.

Kidwatching: The observation and assessment of the student's oral and written language development.

Large-group instruction: Using carefully detailed teaching strategies to match the diversity of learners in a large group.

Lesson plan: A carefully planned design for a specific educational event, including objectives, motivation, teaching techniques, materials, practice, feedback, and review.

Multiple intelligences: The eight types of student intelligences as identified by Howard Gardner, indicating the diverse nature of human intelligence rather than just the singular IQ.

Objective observations: Observing the entire event, setting goals, and recording information completely, accurately, and objectively.

Participating: Assisting in a variety of noninstructional duties, then moving to instructional duties, such as tutoring.

Planning: Following a series of specifically designed steps in a particular lesson plan format.

Poetry Circle: A group of five students comparing/contrasting five different poems on the same theme and their authors, usually in preparation for an oral presentation to the class.

Portfolio: A collection of documents that give evidence of growth and development toward becoming a teacher.

Reflections: Looking back on one's observations, participation, and teaching to assess strengths and weaknesses for further growth and development.

Rubric: The criteria for scoring a piece of work which also articulates the gradations of quality for each of the criteria.

Small-group instruction: Teaching a small group using a completed lesson plan.

Standards: A common core of teaching knowledge as expressed in the ten INTASC performance-based principles to be acquired by all teachers.

Structured observations: Objective observations of a predetermined classroom event, student, or teacher in which data are recorded, using a prepared format such as a checklist.

Systematic observations: Planned, objective, goal-oriented observations of different classroom situations over an extended period of time.

Synergetic Discipline: Involves teacher recognition of the seven needs which motivate a student's behavior: security, hope, acceptance, dignity, power, enjoyment, and competence.

Synergetic Teaching: Includes teacher ethics, trust, charisma, communication, interest, cooperation, class agreements, and procedures for problem resolution.

Teaching styles: The unique way in which an individual teacher organizes instruction, based on his/her philosophy of teaching and learning.

Tutoring–Formal: A series of well-planned lessons after first diagnosing the strengths and weaknesses of a student.

Tutoring–Informal: Short-term teaching that usually guides one student in learning specific tasks, such as writing a story.

References

Amidon, E. J., and N. A. Flanders. 1963. *The Role of the Teacher in the Classroom.* Minneapolis: Paul S. Amidon and Associates.

Anderson, L. 1991. *Student Teaching Journal.* University of North Carolina at Asheville. Unpublished manuscript.

Andrade, H. 2002. *Understanding Rubrics.* http:www.middle.web.com/rubrics. HG.html

Asheville City Board of Education. 1996. *Reception Modification.* Asheville, NC: Author.

Bergen, D., and J. Coscia. 2001. "Brain Research and Childhood Education: Implication for Educators." Olney, MD. *Journal of the Association for Childhood Education International.*

Bliss, T., and J. Mazur. "How INTASC Standards Come Alive Through Case Studies." Paper presented at the annual meeting of American Association of Colleges for Teacher Education, Phoenix, AZ, February 1997.

Bloom. B. S., et al. 1956. *Taxonomy of Educational Objectives, Handbook I: Cognitive Domain.* New York: David McKay.

Borich, G. D., and D. B. Martin. 1999. *Observation Skills for Effective Teaching.* 3rd ed. Upper Saddle River, NJ: Merrill.

Boyd, D. 1999. "Teaching Styles: Unit 9 Modulers." Starkville, MS: Mississippi State University. http://www.ais-missstate.edu.ais/ unit9modulers.num.

Brookings Institution's Brown Center. October 22, 2003. "Do Students Have Too Much Home Work?" in *Education Week.* Author.

Brophy, J. 1984. *Looking Into Classrooms.* 3rd ed. New York: Harper and Row.

Brown, T. J. 1968. *Student Teaching in a Secondary School.* 2nd ed. New York: Harper and Row.

Bruner, J. S. 1960. *The Process of Education.* New York: Vintage.

Bushweller, K. (Ed.) "Technology Counts 2004: Global Links: Lessons from the World". *Education Week* 23 (35) 8–9. Marion, OH: Editorial Projects in Education.

Camp, J. 1997. *Technology Usage in the Classroom or Lab.* Greensboro, NC: University of North Carolina at Greensboro.

Carnegie Corporation of New York. 2001. *Teachers for a New Era: A National Initiative to Improve the Quality of Teaching.* New York: Author. www.carnegie.org/sub/program/teachers.html.

Carnegie Corporation of New York. 2002. *Teaching as a Clinical Profession: A New Challenge for Education.* New York: Author.

Center for the Study of Teachers and Policy. 2001. *Teacher Preparation Research: Current Knowledge, Gaps and Recommendations* (documents-01-01). Seattle: University of Washington.

Chance, L., V. G. Morris, and S. Rakes. 1996. "Fostering Sensitivity to Diverse Cultures through an Early Field Experience Collaborative." *Journal of Teacher Education* 47 (5) (November, December): 386–389.

Charles, C.M. 2002. *Building Classroom Discipline.* 7th ed. Boston: Allyn and Bacon.

Cohen, E. G. 1994. *Designing Groupwork.* 2nd ed. New York: Teachers College Press.

Council of Chief State School Officers. 1992. www.ccsso.org/intasc.st.html

Cotton, L. 2002. *Schoolwide and Classroom Discipline.* www.nwrel.org/scpdsirs/5/cu9.html

Darling-Hammond, L. 1999. *Reshaping Teaching Policy, Preparation and Practice: Influences of the National Board for Professional Standards.* Washington, D.C.: American Association of Colleges for Teacher Education.

deGroot, M. June 2002. "Multimedia Projectors: A Key Component in the Classroom of the Future." *The Journal: Technological Horizons in Education* 29 (11): 18-24.

Derman-Sparks, L. 1999. "Markers of Multicultural/Antibias Education." *Young Children* 54 (5): 43.

Devor, J. 1964. *The Experience of Student Teaching.* New York: MacMillan.

Dewey, J. 1921. *How We Think.* Boston: D.C. Heath.

Dewey, J. 1938. *Experience and Education.* New York: Collier.

Duckett, W. R. 1999. *Observation and the Evaluation of Teaching.* National Symposium for Professionals in Evaluation and Research (NSPER: 80). Bloomington, IN: Phi Delta Kappa.

Evertson, C. M., and J. L. Green. 1986. "Observation as Inquiry and Method." In *Handbook on Research on Teaching.* 3rd ed., M. C. Whittrock,, ed. (162–213). New York: Macmillan.

Flanders, N. 1985. *Analyzing Teacher Behavior.* Reading, MA: Addison-Wesley.

Funk, S. S., J. L. Hoffman, A. Keithley, and B. E. Long. *Cognitive Behaviors and Verbs.* Tallahassee, FL: Florida State University.

Gagne, R. M., and L. Briggs. 1979. *Principles of Instructional Design.* New York: Holt, Rinehart, and Winston.

Galley, M. January 8, 2004. "Help Spills Over." in *Education Week* 23 (17): 30-31. Marion, OH: Editorial Projects in Education.

Gardner, H. 1993. *Multiple Intelligences: The Theory in Practice.* New York: Basic Books.

Gardner, J. 2000. *Multiple Intelligences for the 21st Century.* New York: Basic Books.

Gartner, A. and D. K. Lipsky. 1999. "Inclusive Education: Where is it Going? In *Inclusion: Policy and Practice.* Thomas Lombardi, ed. Bloomington, IN: Phi Beta Kappa Educational Foundation.

Garvin, Pl, ed. 2003. *Developing Knowledgeable Teachers: A Standards-Based Teacher Education Project.* Washington, D.C.: American Association of Colleges for Teacher Education.

Gill, H. 2002. "Kid Watching: A Naturalistic Assessment Technique." www.ehhs.cmichieder/ins/kidart.perf.

Goodman, Y. 1996. *Notes from a Kidwatcher.* Portsmouth, NH: Heineman.

Grant, C., and Sleeter, C. 1998. *Turning on Learning: Five Approaches for Multicultural Teaching Plans for Race, Class, Gender, and Disability.* (2nd Edition) Upper Saddle River, NJ. Prentice-Hall.

Hansen, K. (Preservice Student). 2001. "Learning from Doing: A Case Study." University of North Carolina at Ashville: Unpublished.

Hansen, K. (Preservice Student). October 2001. "Observation of a Sixth Grade Language Arts Teacher." University of North Carolina at Ashville: Unpublished.

Harbison, H. (Preservice Student). 2003. "Getting it All Together: A Case Study." University of North Carolina at Ashville: Unpublished.

Harbision, H. (Preservice Student). 2003. "Unit Plan." University of North Carolina at Ashville: Unpublished.

Heumann, J. E. 1999. "Inclusion: The Challenge, the Opportunity." In *Inclusion: Policy and Practice.* Thomas Lombardi, ed. Bloomington, IN: Phi Beta Kappa Educational Foundation.

Holm, L. and Horn, C. 2003. "Priming Schools of Education for Today's Teachers." *Education Digest* 45 (3): 25–31.

Hunt, J. B., Jr. 2003. *No Dream Denied: A Pledge to America's Children.* Washington, D.C.: National Commission on Teaching and American's Future.

Hunter, M. 1984. "Knowing, Teaching, and Supervising." In *Using What We Know about Teaching: 1984 Yearbook of Association for Supervision and Curriculum Development.*

———.1985a. "Building Effective Elementary Schools." In *Education on Trial.* E. W. J. Johnson, ed. (53–57). San Francisco: ICS Press.

Hymes, J. L. 1978. *Behavior and Misbehavior: A Teacher's Guide to Action.* Westport, CT: Greenwood.

Jackson, P. W. 1986. *Life in Classrooms.* New York: Holt, Rinehart and Winston.

Jacobson, L. September 17, 2003. "N.Y.C. Puts 1200 New Parent Liaisons in Schools." In *Education Week* 23 (3): 5.

Jones, J. 2003. *Early Literary Assessment Systems: Essential Elements.* Chap. 5. Princeton, NJ: Educational Testing Service.

Jones, M., and M. Tadlock. 1999. "Shadowing Middle Schoolers to Understand Them Better." *Middle School Journal* 30 (4): 57–61.

Kelly, C. 2003. "The Role of Parents in the Education of Exceptional Students." Aberdeen, MS: Aberdeen High School. Unpublished.

Kounin, J. S. 1970. *Discipline and Group Management in Classrooms.* New York: Holt, Rinehart, and Winston.

La Canada Unified School District. 2001. "K-12 Homework Guidelines." www.lcusd.netDistrict/pdgs

Lackney, J.A. 1998. "12 Design Principles Based on Brain-based Learning Research." www.designshare.com/Research Based Learn 98.html

Lawrence-Lightfoot, S. 2003. *The Essential Conversation: What Parents and Teachers Can Learn from Each Other.* NY: Random House.

Lombardi, T.P., ed. 1999. *Inclusion: Policy and Practice.* Bloomington, IN: Phi Beta Kappa Educational Foundation.

Loughran, J.J. 2002. "Effective Reflective Practices: In Search of Meaning in Learning About Teaching." *Journal of Teacher Education* 53 (3): 33-43.

Mack-Kirschner, A. 2003. *A Teachers Guide to National Board Certification.* Portsmouth, NH: Heineman.

Manning, M. L. 1993. *Developmentally Appropriate Middle-Level Schools.* Wheaton, MD: Association for Childhood Education International.

McDonald, F. J. 1965. *Educational Psychology* 2nd Ed. Belmont, CA. Wadsworth.

McNeeley, S.L. 1997. *Observing Students and Teachers.* Needham Heights, MA: Allyn and Bacon.

Minor, L.C., A.J. Onwuegbuzie, A.E. Witcher, and T.L. James. November/December 2002. "Preservice Teachers" Educational Beliefs and their Perceptions of Characteristics of Effective Teaching." *Journal of Educational Research* 96 (3): 116-127.

Moffett, C. 1993. "Teacher's Corner on Brain Research." www.mcps.K12:US.departmants/eii/howwelearn.html

Morales, C. October 29, 2003. "Homework Problems: As Seen By a Student." In *Education Week.*

Morehead, M., and D. Cropp. 1994. "Enhancing Pre-Service Observation Experience with Structured Clinical Experiences." *The Teacher Educator* 29 (4): 2–8.

Murphy, S. M. 1998. "Reflection in Portfolios and Beyond." *The Clearing House* 72 (1): 7–9.

Napier, M. 2002. *Z is for Zamboni: A Hockey Alphabet.* Chelsea, MI: Sleeping Bear Press.

National Association of State Education Chiefs (NASTEC). 1999. *Field Experiences Required Prior to Student Teaching.* Boston: Author.

National Association of State Education Directors of Teacher Education and Certification. 2002. *The NAS-DTEC 2002 Manual.* Mashpee, MA: NASDTEC.

National Coalition for Parent Involvement. 2001. "Building Family—School Partnerships That Work." www.ncpie.org/

National Commission on Teaching and America's Future. 2003. *No Dream Denied: A Pledge to America's Children.* Washington, D.C.: Author.

National Council for Accreditation of Teacher Education. 1997. *Standards, Procedures, and Policies for the Accreditation of Professional Education Units.* Washington, D.C.: Author.

National Council for Accreditation of Teacher Education. 2002. *Professional Standards for the Accreditation of Schools, Colleges, and Departments of Education.* Washington, D.C.: Author.

National Council for Accreditation of Teacher Education. June 13, 2002. "NCATE: The Standard of Excellence in Teacher Education." (1-4). ncate.org/newsbrfs/hgt

National Educational Technology Standards (NETS). March 2003. "Educational Technology Standards for Teachers." www.iste.org/standards/.

Nettles, D. H., and P. B. Petrick. 1995. *Portfolio Development for Preservice Teachers.* Bloomington, IN: Phi Delta Kappa Educational Foundation.

North Carolina State Department of Public Instruction. 1998–1999. *Performance Based Licensure.* Raleigh, NC: Author.

North Carolina State Department of Public Instruction. 1998. *The Reflective Practitioner.* Raleigh, NC: Author.

North Carolina Department of Public Instruction. 2001. "The INTASC Standards." Raleigh, NC: Authors. www.dpi.nc.us/pbl/pblintasc.html.

North Carolina Teaching Academy. 2001. *Learning Styles:* Raleigh, NC: North Carolina State Department of Public Instruction.

North Carolina State Department of Public Instruction. 2003. *Computer/Technology Skills Curriculum.* Raleigh, NC.

North Carolina Department of Public Instruction. 2003. *North Carolina Social Studies Standard Course of Study.* Raleigh, NC: Authors.

Ornstein, A. C. 1990. *Strategies for Effective Teaching.* New York: HarperCollins.

Owocki, G. and Goodman, Y. 2002. *Kidwatching: Documenting Children's Literacy Development.* Portsmouth, NH: Heinemann.

Parsons, T., and E. Shills, eds. 1951. *Toward a General Theory of Action.* Cambridge, MA: Harvard University Press.

Perkins, H. 1969. *Human Development and Education.* Belmont, CA: Wadsworth.

Perry, N. E. and P. H. Winne. 2001. "Individual Differences and Diversity in Twentieth-Century Classrooms" in *National Society for the Study of Education.* Lyn Corno, ed. 100-139. Chicago, IL: University of Chicago Press.

Philbeck, K. and Price, S. 1997. "Form for Classroom Map." UNC-Asheville. Unpublished.

Phillion, J. 2003. "What is the Professional Portfolio?" Purdue University: Ohio School of Education. www.edci.purdue.edu/phillion EDCT 2-5 partyiew.html.

Pierce, D. R. 1996. "Early Field Experiences and Teacher Preparation: Authentic Learning." *The Teacher Educator* 31, (3) (Winter): 217–225.

PL 94-142. 1975. *Education For All Handicapped Children Act.* Washington, D.C.: U.S. Congress.

PL 101-476. 1997. *Individuals With Disabilities Education Act.* Washington, D.C.: U.S. Congress.

Pohan, C.A. 2003. "Creating Caring and Democratic Communities in Our Classrooms and Schools." in *Childhood Education* (79, 6): 369-37.

Rexroth, K. 1973. "Art of Literature" in *Encyclopaedia Britannica* (Volume 10, p. 1044) Chicago, Ill. The Helen Benton Publisher.

Rieman, P. L. 2000. *Teaching Portfolios: Presenting Your Professional Best.* Boston: McGraw-Hill.

Rodgers, C.R. 2002. "Seeing Student Learning: Teacher Change and the Role of Reflection." *Harvard Educational Review.* 72 (2): 230-251.

Sanders, N. M. 1966. *Classroom Questions: What Kinds?* New York: Harper and Row.

Shalaway, L. 1998 *Learning to Teach: Not Just For Beginners.* Danbury, CT: Scholastic.

Sherman, L. W. 2000. Sociometry in the Classroom: How to Do It. www.users.muohio.edu/shermalw/sociometryfiles/socio are.html.

Shulman, L. "Portfolios in Historical Perspective." Paper presented at the Portfolio Conference, Radcliffe College, Cambridge, MA, January 1994.

Simcoe Board of Education. 1996. "Examination of Curricular Strategies That Challenge Multiple Intelligences." Midhurst, Ontario, Canada: Author. http://wwwscoe.onca/mm/mmst.num.

Sluss, D., and S. Minner. 1999. "The Changing Roles of Early Childhood Educators in Preparing New Teachers." *Childhood Education* 75 (5): 280–284.

Spinelli, J. 2002 *Loser.* New York: Scholastic.

Sprinthall, L. 1986. "An Adapted Madeline Hunter Lesson Plan." In *A Strategy Guide for Teachers: Guidebook for Supervisors of Novice Teachers.* Department of Curriculum and Instruction, College of Education and Psychology, North Carolina State University. Raleigh, NC: Unpublished manuscript.

Stone, J. R., and M. Castellano. 2002. "New Roles for Career and Technical Preparation Programs in Educating At-Risk Students: Promises and Possibilities." in *Educating At-Risk Students, Part II.* National Society for the Study of Education (NSSE) 248-268. Chicago, IL: University of Chicago Press.

Ternes, E. October 1, 2003. *Do Students Have Too Much Homework?* College Park: University of Maryland Electric Pub.

Ur, P. 1981. *Discussions That Work: Task-Centered Fluency Practice.* Cambridge, U.K.: Cambridge University Press.

U.S. Department of Education. 2002. "The No Child Left Behind Act of 2001." (P.L. 107-110). Washington, D.C.: Author. www.ed.gov/offices/OESE/esea/exec-summ.html.

U.S. Department of Education. 1999. *Teacher Quality: A Report on the Preparation and Qualifications of Public School Teachers.* National Center for Education Statistics (NCES). Washington, D.C.

Ventura, R, N. Reid, and M. Lee. 2001. "Lesson Plan Form 3" (From the Coach to Coach Project). Raleigh, NC: State Department of Public Instruction.

Walberg, H. and Anderson, G. 1968. "Classroom Climate and Individual Learning". *Journal of Educational Psychology 59* (6): 414–419.

Wasserman, S. 1999. "Shazam! You're a Teacher." *Phi Delta Kappan* 6 (6): 464–467.

Willis, S. 1995. When Parents Object to Classroom Practice: Resolving Conflicts over Techniques, Materials. www.ascd.org/readingroom/eduplate.

Wilson, S. M., R. E. Floden, and J. Ferrini—Munday. 2001. *Teacher Preparation Research: Current Knowledge, Gaps and Recommendations.* University of Washington: Center for the Study of Teaching and Policy.

Wise A. E. and J. A. Leibbrand. May/June 2001. "Standards in the New Millennium: Where We Are, Where We're Headed." *Journal of Teacher Education* 244-55.

Wiseman, D. L., S. L. Knight, and D. D. Cooner. 2002. *Becoming a Teacher in a Field-based Setting: An Introduction to Education and Classrooms.* Belmont, CA: Wadsworth/Thomson Learning.

Yapp, R. H., and B. Young. 1999. "A Model For Beginning Teacher Support and Assessment." *Action in Teacher Education* 21 (1):27–31.

Zemelman, S., Daniels, H. and Hyde, A. 1998. *Best Practice: New Standards for Teaching and Learning in America's Schools.* Portsmouth, NH: Heinemann.